1993

SO-BIV-644

3 0301 00089389 7

Christopher Marlowe's
EDWARD II
Text and Major Criticism

Also edited by Irving Ribner:

THE COMPLETE PLAYS OF
CHRISTOPHER MARLOWE

CHRISTOPHER MARLOWE'S
DR. FAUSTUS: TEXT AND MAJOR CRITICISM

CHRISTOPHER MARLOWE'S
THE JEW OF MALTA: TEXT AND MAJOR CRITICISM

Christopher Marlowe's
EDWARD II

Text and Major Criticism

Edited by Irving Ribner

STATE UNIVERSITY OF NEW YORK *at Stony Brook*

THE ODYSSEY PRESS *New York*

LIBRARY
College of St. Francis
JOLIET, ILL.

Copyright © 1970 by Western Publishing Company, Inc.
Published by The Odyssey Press,
a Division of Western Publishing Company, Inc.

All rights reserved.

Library of Congress Catalog Card Number: 70–101696

PRINTED IN THE UNITED STATES OF AMERICA

ACKNOWLEDGMENTS

Acknowledgment is gratefully made for permission to reprint the following material:

Barnes and Noble, Inc. For passage from *Shakespeare's Dramatic Heritage* by Glynne Wickham. Published by Routledge and Kegan Paul, 1969. Reprinted by permission of the publisher and Barnes and Noble, Inc.

Cambridge University Press. For "History Without Morality: 'Edward II' " from *The Dramatist and the Received Idea* by Wilbur Sanders. Published by Cambridge University Press, 1968. Reprinted by permission of the publisher.

Chatto and Windus, Ltd. For passage from *Christopher Marlowe* by Michel Poirier, published 1951. Reprinted by permission of Chatto and Windus, Ltd.

English Studies. For "The Dramatic Structure of Edward II" by Robert Fricker. Published by *English Studies*, 1953. Reprinted by permission of the author and *English Studies*.

Harvard University Press. For passage from *From Mankind to Marlowe* by David Bevington. Cambridge, Mass.: Harvard University Press, Copyright 1962, by the President and Fellows of Harvard College. Reprinted by permission of the publishers.

Clifford Leech. For "Marlowe's Edward II: Power and Suffering," *Critical Quarterly*, I. Reprinted by permission of the author.

Methuen and Company, Ltd. For passage from *English Tragedy before Shakespeare* by Wolfgang Clemen and *The English History Play in the Age of Shakespeare* by Irving Ribner. Published by Methuen and Company, Ltd., 1965. Reprinted by permission of the publisher.

Tulane Drama Review. For "Edward II: The Shadow of Action" by Eugene M. Waith from the *Tulane Drama Review*, Volume 8, Number 4, Summer 1964. Copyright © 1964, Tulane Drama Review. Reprinted by permission. All rights reserved.

822.3
R 485

Contents

147, 456

Preface

Edward II is one of the very few plays by Christopher Marlowe (1564–1593) which have come down to us in a text which is at all reliable. Written probably in late 1591 or 1592, it may have been printed for the first time in 1593, for there is some reason to suspect an edition of that year, no copy of which has survived. Our earliest extant text is an octavo printed in 1594, two copies of which today survive, one in the Landesbibliothek in Cassel, Germany, and the other in the Zentralbibliothek in Zurich, Switzerland. Later quartos printed in 1598, 1612 and 1622 have no independent authority, since they all stem from the octavo of 1594, upon which the present edition is based. A good text of a play written at a time when Marlowe had reached the height of his poetic and dramatic powers—only *Doctor Faustus* could have been written later, and the date of that play is extremely uncertain—may provide a surer insight into his special genius than can be gleaned from any other of his surviving plays. If there is a distinctively Marlovian vision of tragedy, we are likely to find it in this play. And if Marlowe had any distinctive conception of history, it is to be found here also, for *Edward II* is not only a work of great tragic power, but also one of the greatest of the English history plays, a special kind of drama which came into prominence in the final decade of the sixteenth century and was virtually dead by the end of the first decade of the seventeenth. In composition *Edward II* followed closely after Shakespeare's *Henry VI* plays, upon whose example Marlowe built, and it in turn prepared the way for the great series of plays from *Richard II* through *Henry V* which Shakespeare was to write after Marlowe's untimely death in 1593.

As tragedy and as history the play presents special problems, and
it has been the special relation of these two modes of expression to
one another which has most absorbed the attention of critics. The
hero of the play is both a suffering individual human being and a
king who brings his country close to disaster by his inability to exercise political power. Some critics have seen Marlowe as concerned
only with the first of these aspects of his hero and others have seen
him as primarily occupied with the second. It is obvious that neither
of these dimensions of the play can be ignored, for each is undeniably
present, and only a kind of criticism which does justice to both can
have real validity. The present volume is designed to accompany a
text of the play with a sampling of critical essays which approach
the play from as many points of view as possible. Since the major
task of criticism of *Edward II* has been to delineate Marlowe's manner of encompassing the private and the public spheres of action
within a single unified dramatic experience, to this particular problem some of the essays are directed. Other essays attempt to place
the play within its special literary and historical context, to explore
its dramatic structure, its language, the degree to which it embodies
an inherited dramatic tradition, and its special relation to Shakespeare's *Richard II*, a play with which it must inevitably be associated.

For his principal source Marlowe went to the 1587 edition of
Raphael Holinshed's *Chronicles of England, Scotland, and Ireland*, the
great compilation upon which Shakespeare drew also for his historical plays. Marlowe probably also consulted the chronicles of
Robert Fabyan and John Stow, and he appears to have read Thomas
Churchyard's poem "The Two Mortimers" in the 1578 edition of
A Mirror for Magistrates. Upon the raw events of history Marlowe
imposed his own tragic pattern, and in order to do so he was forced,
sometimes drastically, to modify the facts as he found them. The play
deals with a fairly complicated period of English history whose major
feature was a struggle for power between the king and his barons.
It ranges from the accession of King Edward II in 1307 to the execution of Roger Mortimer in 1330. Not only did Marlowe translate the
larger political issues into closely personal terms, but he condensed
the events of some twenty-three years into what seems to be a relatively brief period of time.

The text of *Edward II* and the Textual Notes are reprinted from
The Complete Plays of Christopher Marlowe, published by the Odyssey

Press in 1963. Old spelling quotations from Marlowe's plays have been modernized in line with the present text.

IRVING RIBNER

State University of New York, Stony Brook

The troublesome

raigne and lamentable death of
Edward *the second, King of*
England: with the tragicall
fall of proud Mortimer:

As it was sundrie times publiquely acted
in the honourable citie of London, by the
right honourable the Earle of Pem-
brooke his seruants.

Written by Chri. Marlow *Gent.*

Imprinted at London for *William Iones*
dwelling neere Holbourne conduit, at the
signe of the Gunne. 1594.

THE TROUBLESOME REIGN AND LAMENTABLE DEATH OF EDWARD THE SECOND

THE PLAYERS

King Edward the Second
Prince Edward, his Son, afterwards King Edward the Third
Earl of Kent, Brother of King Edward the Second
Gaveston
Warwick
Lancaster
Pembroke
Arundel
Leicester
Berkeley
Mortimer senior
Mortimer junior, his Nephew
Spencer senior
Spencer junior, his Son
Archbishop of Canterbury
Bishop of Coventry
Bishop of Winchester

Baldock
Beaumont
Trussel
Gurney
Matrevis
Lightborn
Sir John of Hainault
Levune
Rice ap Howell
Abbot, Monks, Herald, Lords, Poor Men, James, Mower, Champion, Messengers, Soldiers, and Attendants
Queen Isabella, Wife of King Edward the Second
Niece to King Edward the Second, daughter of the Duke of Gloucester
Ladies

THE SCENE
England, France.

I,i.

Enter Gaveston, reading on a letter that was brought him from the king.

Gaveston. 'My father is deceased. Come, Gaveston,
And share the kingdom with thy dearest friend.'
Ah, words that make me surfeit with delight!
What greater bliss can hap to Gaveston
Than live and be the favorite of a king?   5
Sweet prince, I come; these, these thy amorous lines
Might have enforced me to have swum from France,
And, like Leander, gasped upon the sand,

I,i.

1 *Gaveston* Son of a Gascon knight in the service of King Edward I, he had been brought up as a childhood friend of Edward II.

7 *France* Gaveston had been banished to his native Gascony by King Edward I.

The young Edward II's first act upon becoming king was to call his friend home in 1307.

8 *Leander* hero of the Greek love story who nightly swam the Hellespont to be with his beloved Hero; he finally

So thou wouldst smile and take me in thy arms.
The sight of London to my exiled eyes   10
Is as Elysium to a new-come soul;
Not that I love the city or the men,
But that it harbors him I hold so dear,
The king, upon whose bosom let me die,
And with the world be still at enmity.   15
What need the arctic people love starlight,
To whom the sun shines both by day and night?
Farewell base stooping to the lordly peers.
My knee shall bow to none but to the king.
As for the multitude that are but sparks,   20
Raked up in embers of their poverty—
Tanti; I'll fawn first on the wind
That glanceth at my lips and flieth away.
But how now, what are these?
                 Enter three Poor Men.
Poor Men.   Such as desire your worship's service.   25
Gaveston.   What canst thou do?
First Poor Man.   I can ride.
Gaveston.   But I have no horses. What art thou?
Second Poor Man.   A traveler.
Gaveston.   Let me see—thou wouldst do well   30
To wait at my trencher and tell me lies at dinner time,
And as I like your discoursing, I'll have you.
And what art thou?
Third Poor Man.   A soldier, that hath served against the Scot.
Gaveston.   Why, there are hospitals for such as you.   35
I have no war, and therefore, sir, be gone.
Third Poor Man.   Farewell, and perish by a soldier's hand,
That wouldst reward them with an hospital.
Gaveston.   Ay, ay, these words of his move me as much
As if a goose should play the porpentine   40
And dart her plumes, thinking to pierce my breast.
But yet it is no pain to speak men fair.
I'll flatter these and make them live in hope.   *[Aside.]*
You know that I came lately out of France,
And yet I have not viewed my lord the king.   45
If I speed well, I'll entertain you all.

drowned. Marlowe retold the story in his poem *Hero and Leander.*
14 *die* swoon with joy. There is little justification for the emendation, 'lie' adopted by some modern editors.
20–21 *sparks . . . poverty* Fires were kept alive overnight by raking ashes over the live embers.
22 *Tanti* So much for that (an expression of contempt).
31 *trencher* a flat wooden dish on which food was served.
35 *hospitals* homes for disabled soldiers.
40 *porpentine* porcupine (supposed in popular superstition to be able to dart its quills).

Poor Men. We thank your worship.
Gaveston. I have some business; leave me to myself.
Poor Men. We will wait here about the court.

Exeunt [Poor Men].

Gaveston. Do. These are not men for me.   50
I must have wanton poets, pleasant wits,
Musicians, that with touching of a string
May draw the pliant king which way I please.
Music and poetry is his delight;
Therefore I'll have Italian masks by night,   55
Sweet speeches, comedies, and pleasing shows;
And in the day, when he shall walk abroad,
Like sylvan nymphs my pages shall be clad.
My men, like satyrs grazing on the lawns,
Shall with their goat-feet dance an antic hay.   60
Sometime a lovely boy in Dian's shape,
With hair that gilds the water as it glides,
Crownets of pearl about his naked arms,
And in his sportful hands an olive tree,
To hide those parts which men delight to see,   65
Shall bathe him in a spring; and there, hard by,
One like Actæon peeping through the grove,
Shall by the angry goddess be transformed,
And running in the likeness of an hart,
By yelping hounds pulled down, and seem to die—   70
Such things as these best please his majesty.
My lord! Here comes the king and the nobles
From the parliament. I'll stand aside.

[He retires.]

*Enter King [Edward], Lancaster, Mortimer Senior, Mortimer
Junior, Edmund, Earl of Kent, Guy, Earl of Warwick, [and
others].*

King Edward. Lancaster!

51 *wanton* amorous.

55 *Italian masks* elaborate Elizabethan entertainments involving disguises,
thought in the sixteenth century to have
come from Italy, but actually of obscure
origins, although certainly influenced by
Italian customs. Marlowe here is anach-
ronistic, since there were no masks in
Edward's time.

59 *grazing* strolling.

60 *antic hay* an old-fashioned dance.

61 *Dian* the Greek goddess of chastity
and the hunt (to be portrayed by a boy,
as were all women's parts in Elizabethan
entertainments).

63 *Crownets* bracelets.

67 *Actæon* a hunter, in Greek mythology, transformed by Diana into a stag
after having seen her bathing, and then
killed by his own hounds. The story is
in Ovid's *Metamorphoses*.

73 SD *Edmund* an anachronism, since
Edmund of Woodstock, Earl of Kent,
Edward's half-brother, was not born un-
til 1301, and thus was only six years old
at the time of Gaveston's recall in 1307.
The Mortimers, similarly, had no actual
part in the opposition to Gaveston.
Thomas, Earl of Lancaster, grandson of
Henry III, was a powerful opponent of
Gaveston, the Spencers, and Edward II.

Lancaster. My lord.   75
Gaveston. That Earl of Lancaster do I abhor. [*Aside.*]
King Edward. Will you not grant me this? In spite of them
   I'll have my will, and these two Mortimers,
   That cross me thus, shall know I am displeased. [*Aside.*]
Mortimer Senior. If you love us, my lord, hate Gaveston.   80
Gaveston. That villain Mortimer! I'll be his death. [*Aside.*]
Mortimer Junior. Mine uncle here, this earl, and I myself
   Were sworn to your father at his death,
   That he should ne'er return into the realm.
   And know, my lord, ere I will break my oath,   85
   This sword of mine, that should offend your foes,
   Shall sleep within the scabbard at thy need,
   And underneath thy banners march who will,
   For Mortimer will hang his armor up.
Gaveston. *Mort Dieu!* [*Aside.*]   90
King Edward. Well, Mortimer, I'll make thee rue these words.
   Beseems it thee to contradict thy king?
   Frown'st thou thereat, aspiring Lancaster?
   The sword shall plane the furrows of thy brows,
   And hew these knees that now are grown so stiff.   95
   I will have Gaveston, and you shall know
   What danger 'tis to stand against your king.
Gaveston. Well done, Ned! [*Aside.*]
Lancaster. My lord, why do you thus incense your peers,
   That naturally would love and honor you   100
   But for that base and obscure Gaveston?
   Four earldoms have I besides Lancaster—
   Derby, Salisbury, Lincoln, Leicester;
   These will I sell to give my soldiers pay,
   Ere Gaveston shall stay within the realm;   105
   Therefore, if he be come, expel him straight.
Kent. Barons and earls, your pride hath made me mute,
   But now I'll speak, and to the proof, I hope.
   I do remember in my father's days,
   Lord Percy of the north, being highly moved,   110
   Braved Mowbery in presence of the king;
   For which, had not his highness loved him well,   ⌐
   He should have lost his head; but with his look
   The undaunted spirit of Percy was appeased,
   And Mowbery and he were reconciled.   115
   Yet dare you brave the king unto his face?
   Brother, revenge it, and let these their heads
   Preach upon poles for trespass of their tongues.
Warwick. O, our heads!
King Edward. Ay, yours; and therefore I would wish you grant— 120

   108 *to the proof* irrefutably.   111 *Braved* challenged.

Warwick. Bridle thy anger, gentle Mortimer.
Mortimer Junior. I cannot, nor I will not; I must speak.
Cousin, our hands I hope shall fence our heads
And strike off his that makes you threaten us.
Come, uncle, let us leave the brainsick king   125
And henceforth parley with our naked swords.
Mortimer Senior. Wiltshire hath men enough to save our heads.
Warwick. All Warwickshire will love him for my sake.
Lancaster. And northward Gaveston hath many friends.
Adieu, my lord, and either change your mind,   130
Or look to see the throne, where you should sit,
To float in blood, and at thy wanton head
The glozing head of thy base minion thrown.
                    Exeunt [all but King Edward, Kent,
                              Gaveston and Attendants].
King Edward. I cannot brook these haughty menaces.
Am I a king, and must be overruled?   135
Brother, display my ensigns in the field;
I'll bandy with the barons and the earls,
And either die or live with Gaveston.
Gaveston. I can no longer keep me from my lord.
                              [He comes forward.]
King Edward. What, Gaveston! Welcome! Kiss not my hand;   140
Embrace me, Gaveston, as I do thee.
Why shouldst thou kneel? Knowest thou not who I am?
Thy friend, thyself, another Gaveston!
Not Hylas was more mourned of Hercules
Than thou hast been of me since thy exile.   145
Gaveston. And since I went from hence, no soul in hell
Hath felt more torment than poor Gaveston.
King Edward. I know it. Brother, welcome home my friend.
Now let the treacherous Mortimers conspire,
And that high minded Earl of Lancaster!   150
I have my wish in that I joy thy sight,
And sooner shall the sea o'erwhelm my land,
Than bear the ship that shall transport thee hence.
I here create thee Lord High Chamberlain,
Chief Secretary to the state and me,   155
Earl of Cornwall, King and Lord of Man.

123 *Cousin* any relative outside the immediate family. Mortimer was very distantly related to the king.
132 *wanton* irresponsible.
133 *glozing* flattering. *minion* favorite.
137 *bandy* exchange blows.
144 *Hylas . . . Hercules* Hylas was a youth who accompanied Hercules with Jason on the quest for the golden fleece and was carried off by Nymphs when he went ashore at Nysia to draw water. Hercules mourned and searched for him but could find only an echo.
156 *King and Lord of Man* Rulers of the Isle of Man, between England and Ireland, had certain sovereign rights and were called kings.

Gaveston. My lord, these titles far exceed my worth.
Kent. Brother, the least of these may well suffice
For one of greater birth than Gaveston.
King Edward. Cease, brother, for I cannot brook these words.   160
Thy worth, sweet friend, is far above my gifts;
Therefore, to equal it, receive my heart.
If for these dignities thou be envied,
I'll give thee more; for but to honor thee,
Is Edward pleased with kingly regiment.   165
Fearst thou thy person? Thou shalt have a guard.
Wantest thou gold? Go to my treasury.
Wouldst thou be loved and feared? Receive my seal;
Save or condemn, and in our name command
Whatso thy mind affects or fancy likes.   170
Gaveston. It shall suffice me to enjoy your love,
Which whiles I have, I think myself as great
As Caesar riding in the Roman street,
With captive kings at his triumphant car.
        Enter the Bishop of Coventry.
King Edward. Whither goes my lord of Coventry so fast?   175
Coventry. To celebrate your father's exequies.
But is that wicked Gaveston returned?
King Edward. Ay, priest, and lives to be revenged on thee,
That wert the only cause of his exile.
Gaveston. 'Tis true, and but for reverence of these robes,   180
Thou shouldst not plod one foot beyond this place.
Coventry. I did no more than I was bound to do;
And, Gaveston, unless thou be reclaimed,
As then I did incense the parliament,
So will I now, and thou shalt back to France.   185
Gaveston. Saving your reverence, you must pardon me.
King Edward. Throw off his golden mitre, rend his stole,
And in the channel christen him anew.
Kent. Ah, brother, lay not violent hands on him,
For he'll complain unto the see of Rome.   190
Gaveston. Let him complain unto the see of hell;
I'll be revenged on him for my exile.
King Edward. No, spare his life, but seize upon his goods.
Be thou lord bishop and receive his rents,
And make him serve thee as thy chaplain.   195
I give him thee—here, use him as thou wilt.
Gaveston. He shall to prison and there die in bolts.
King Edward. Ay, to the Tower, the Fleet, or where thou wilt.
Coventry. For this offence, be thou accursed of God!
King Edward. Who's there? Convey this priest to the Tower.   200

188 *channel* open gutter through which   198 *Fleet* a London prison.
sewage flowed.

Coventry. True, true.
King Edward. But in the meantime, Gaveston, away,
  And take possession of his house and goods.
  Come, follow me, and thou shalt have my guard
  To see it done and bring thee safe again.   205
Gaveston. What should a priest do with so fair a house?
  A prison may beseem his holiness.

                                              [*Exeunt.*]

✱

              Enter both the Mortimers, Warwick and Lancaster.   I,ii.
Warwick. 'Tis true, the bishop is in the Tower,
  And goods and body given to Gaveston.
Lancaster. What! Will they tyrannise upon the church?
  Ah, wicked king! Accursèd Gaveston!
  This ground, which is corrupted with their steps,   5
  Shall be their timeless sepulcher or mine.
Mortimer Junior. Well, let that peevish Frenchman guard him sure;
  Unless his breast be sword-proof he shall die.
Mortimer Senior. How now! Why droops the Earl of Lancaster?
Mortimer Junior. Wherefore is Guy of Warwick discontent?   10
Lancaster. That villain Gaveston is made an earl.
Mortimer Senior. An earl!
Warwick. Ay, and besides Lord Chamberlain of the realm,
  And Secretary too, and Lord of Man.
Mortimer Senior. We may not, nor we will not suffer this.   15
Mortimer Junior. Why post we not from hence to levy men?
Lancaster. 'My Lord of Cornwall,' now at every word!
  And happy is the man whom he vouchsafes,
  For vailing of his bonnet, one good look.
  Thus, arm in arm, the king and he doth march.   20
  Nay more, the guard upon his lordship waits,
  And all the court begins to flatter him.
Warwick. Thus leaning on the shoulder of the king,
  He nods, and scorns, and smiles at those that pass.
Mortimer Senior. Doth no man take exceptions at the slave?   25
Lancaster. All stomach him, but none dare speak a word.
Mortimer Junior. Ah, that bewrays their baseness, Lancaster!
  Were all the earls and barons of my mind,

I,ii.

1 *Warwick* Guy, Earl of Warwick,
historically was the most persistent foe
of Gaveston and Edward II.
  6 *timeless* premature.
  19 *vailing of his bonnet* lifting his hat.

25 *take exceptions at* object to.
  26 *stomach* are angry at (the stomach
was regarded as the producer of choler,
and therefore the seat of anger).
  27 *bewrays* reveals.

We'll hale him from the bosom of the king,
And at the court gate hang the peasant up,   30
Who, swoll'n with venom of ambitious pride,
Will be the ruin of the realm and us.
            Enter the [Arch]bishop of Canterbury [and an Attendant].
Warwick.   Here comes my lord of Canterbury's grace.
Lancaster.   His countenance bewrays he is displeased.
Canterbury.   First were his sacred garments rent and torn,   35
Then laid they violent hands upon him; next
Himself imprisoned, and his goods asseized.
This certify the Pope; away, take horse.
                                    [Exit Attendant.]
Lancaster.   My lord, will you take arms against the king?
Canterbury.   What need I? God himself is up in arms,   40
When violence is offered to the church.
Mortimer Junior.   Then will you join with us that be his peers,
To banish or behead that Gaveston?
Canterbury.   What else, my lords? For it concerns me near;
The bishopric of Coventry is his.   45
                    Enter Queen [Isabella].
Mortimer Junior.   Madam, whither walks your majesty so fast?
Queen Isabella.   Unto the forest, gentle Mortimer,
To live in grief and baleful discontent,
For now my lord the king regards me not,
But dotes upon the love of Gaveston.   50
He claps his cheeks and hangs about his neck,
Smiles in his face and whispers in his ears,
And when I come, he frowns, as who should say,
'Go whither thou wilt, seeing I have Gaveston.'
Mortimer Senior.   Is it not strange that he is thus bewitched?   55
Mortimer Junior.   Madam, return unto the court again.
That sly inveigling Frenchman we'll exile
Or lose our lives; and yet, ere that day come,
The king shall lose his crown, for we have power,
And courage too, to be revenged at full.   60
Canterbury.   But yet lift not your swords against the king.
Lancaster.   No, but we'll lift Gaveston from hence.
Warwick.   And war must be the means, or he'll stay still.
Queen Isabella.   Then let him stay; for rather than my lord
Shall be oppressed by civil mutinies,   65
I will endure a melancholy life,
And let him frolic with his minion.
Canterbury.   My lords, to ease all this, but hear me speak:

---

37 *asseized* taken possession of.
45, SD *Queen Isabella* Daughter of King Philip the Fair of France, she was born in 1292 and married king Edward in 1308. Her affair with Mortimer occurred much later.
47 *forest* wilderness (the queen is speaking figuratively).

We and the rest that are his counselors
Will meet and with a general consent   70
Confirm his banishment with our hands and seals.
Lancaster. What we confirm the king will frustrate.
Mortimer Junior. Then may we lawfully revolt from him.
Warwick. But say, my lord, where shall this meeting be?
Canterbury. At the New Temple.   75
Mortimer Junior. Content.
Canterbury. And, in the meantime, I'll entreat you all
To cross to Lambeth and there stay with me.
Lancaster. Come then, let's away.
Mortimer Junior. Madam, farewell.   80
Queen Isabella. Farewell, sweet Mortimer, and for my sake
Forbear to levy arms against the king.
Mortimer Junior. Ay, if words will serve; if not, I must.

[*Exeunt.*]

Enter Gaveston and the Earl of Kent.   I,iii.
Gaveston. Edmund, the mighty prince of Lancaster,
That hath more earldoms than an ass can bear,
And both the Mortimers, two goodly men,
With Guy of Warwick, that redoubted knight,
Are gone towards Lambeth. There let them remain.   5

[*Exeunt.*]

I,iv.

Enter [Lancaster, Warwick, Pembroke, Mortimer Senior, Mortimer Junior, the Archbishop of Canterbury and Attendants].
Lancaster. Here is the form of Gaveston's exile;
May it please your lordship to subscribe your name.
Canterbury. Give me the paper.

[*He subscribes, as do the others after him.*]
Lancaster. Quick, quick, my lord; I long to write my name.
Warwick. But I long more to see him banished hence.   5
Mortimer Junior. The name of Mortimer shall fright the king,
Unless he be declined from that base peasant.

Enter King [Edward, Kent,] and Gaveston.
King Edward. What? Are you moved that Gaveston sits here?
It is our pleasure; we will have it so.

75 *New Temple* **house founded by the**
Knights Templar.

78 *Lambeth* **a palace held by the**
Archbishops of Canterbury since 1179.

Lancaster.   Your grace doth well to place him by your side,   10
For nowhere else the new earl is so safe.
Mortimer Senior.   What man of noble birth can brook this sight?
Quam male conveniunt!
See what a scornful look the peasant casts.
Pembroke.   Can kingly lions fawn on creeping ants?   15
Warwick.   Ignoble vassal, that like Phaeton
Aspir'st unto the guidance of the sun.
Mortimer Junior.   Their downfall is at hand, their forces down.
We will not thus be faced and over-peered.
King Edward.   Lay hands on that traitor Mortimer!   20
Mortimer Senior.   Lay hands on that traitor Gaveston!
Kent.   Is this the duty that you owe your king?
Warwick.   We know our duties; let him know his peers.
King Edward.   Whither will ye bear him? Stay, or ye shall die.
Mortimer Senior.   We are no traitors; therefore threaten not.   25
Gaveston.   No, threaten not, my lord, but pay them home!
Were I a king—
Mortimer Junior.   Thou villain, wherefore talks thou of a king,
That hardly art a gentleman by birth?
King Edward.   Were he a peasant, being my minion,   30
I'll make the proudest of you stoop to him.
Lancaster.   My lord, you may not thus disparage us.
Away, I say, with hateful Gaveston!
Mortimer Senior.   And with the Earl of Kent that favors him.
                    [*Attendants remove Kent and Gaveston.*]
King Edward.   Nay, then lay violent hands upon your king.   35
Here, Mortimer, sit thou in Edward's throne.
Warwick and Lancaster, wear you my crown.
Was ever king thus over-ruled as I?
Lancaster.   Learn then to rule us better and the realm.
Mortimer Junior.   What we have done, our heart-blood shall main-
    tain.   40
Warwick.   Think you that we can brook this upstart pride?
King Edward.   Anger and wrathful fury stops my speech.
Canterbury.   Why are you moved? Be patient, my lord,
And see what we your counselors have done.
Mortimer Junior.   My lords, now let us all be resolute,   45
And either have our wills or lose our lives.
King Edward.   Meet you for this, proud overdaring peers?
Ere my sweet Gaveston shall part from me,

I,iv.

13 *Quam male conveniunt.* How badly
they suit one another.
16 *Phaeton* See note *I Tamb.* IV,ii,49.
19 *faced and over-peered* bullied and

looked down upon (with a probable pun
on 'peer').
28 *villain* (1) scoundrel (2) peasant
bound to the land.
32 *disparage* vilify.

This isle shall fleet upon the ocean
And wander to the unfrequented Inde.   50
Canterbury.   You know that I am legate to the Pope;
On your allegiance to the see of Rome,
Subscribe as we have done to his exile.
Mortimer Junior.   Curse him if he refuse, and then may we
Depose him and elect another king.   55
King Edward.   Ay, there it goes! But yet I will not yield;
Curse me, depose me, do the worst you can.
Lancaster.   Then linger not, my lord, but do it straight.
Canterbury.   Remember how the bishop was abused.
Either banish him that was the cause thereof,   60
Or I will presently discharge these lords
Of duty and allegiance due to thee.
King Edward.   It boots me not to threat; I must speak fair.
The legate of the Pope will be obeyed. [*Aside.*]
My lord, you shall be Chancellor of the realm,   65
Thou, Lancaster, High Admiral of our fleet;
Young Mortimer and his uncle shall be earls,
And you, Lord Warwick, President of the North,
And thou of Wales. If this content you not,
Make several kingdoms of this monarchy   70
And share it equally amongst you all,
So I may have some nook or corner left
To frolic with my dearest Gaveston.
Canterbury.   Nothing shall alter us; we are resolved.
Lancaster.   Come, come, subscribe.   75
Mortimer Junior.   Why should you love him whom the world hates so?
King Edward.   Because he loves me more than all the world.
Ah, none but rude and savage-minded men
Would seek the ruin of my Gaveston;
You that be noble-born should pity him.   80
Warwick.   You that are princely-born should shake him off.
For shame subscribe, and let the lown depart.
Mortimer Senior.   Urge him, my lord.
Canterbury.   Are you content to banish him the realm?
King Edward.   I see I must, and therefore am content. 85
Instead of ink I'll write it with my tears.
                              [*He subscribes*].
Mortimer Junior.   The king is love-sick for his minion.
King Edward.   'Tis done, and now, accursèd hand, fall off!
Lancaster.   Give it me; I'll have it published in the streets.
Mortimer Junior.   I'll see him presently dispatched away.   90
Canterbury.   Now is my heart at ease.
Warwick.   And so is mine.

49 *fleet* float.   63 *boots* avails.
50 *Inde* India.   82 *lown* peasant.

Pembroke   This will be good news to the common sort.
Mortimer Senior.   Be it or no, he shall not linger here.
                    Exeunt [all except King Edward].
King Edward.   How fast they run to banish him I love.
They would not stir, were it to do me good.   95
Why should a king be subject to a priest?
Proud Rome, that hatchest such imperial grooms,
For these thy superstitious taper-lights,
Wherewith thy antichristian churches blaze,
I'll fire thy crazèd buildings and enforce   100
The papal towers to kiss the lowly ground.
With slaughtered priests may Tiber's channel swell,
And banks raised higher with their sepulchers.
As for the peers that back the clergy thus,
If I be king, not one of them shall live.   105
                    Enter Gaveston.
Gaveston.   My lord, I hear it whispered everywhere
That I am banished and must fly the land.
King Edward.   'Tis true, sweet Gaveston—O, were it false!
The legate of the Pope will have it so,
And thou must hence, or I shall be deposed.   110
But I will reign to be revenged of them,
And therefore, sweet friend, take it patiently.
Live where thou wilt, I'll send thee gold enough;
And long thou shalt not stay, or if thou dost,
I'll come to thee; my love shall ne'er decline.   115
Gaveston.   Is all my hope turned to this hell of grief?
King Edward.   Rend not my heart with thy too-piercing words.
Thou from this land, I from myself am banished.
Gaveston.   To go from hence grieves not poor Gaveston,
But to forsake you, in whose gracious looks   120
The blessedness of Gaveston remains;
For nowhere else seeks he felicity.
King Edward.   And only this torments my wretched soul,
That, whether I will or no, thou must depart.
Be governor of Ireland in my stead,   125
And there abide till fortune call thee home.
Here take my picture, and let me wear thine;
                    [They exchange pictures.]
O, might I keep thee here as I do this,
Happy were I, but now most miserable.
Gaveston.   'Tis something to be pitied of a king.   130
King Edward.   Thou shalt not hence; I'll hide thee, Gaveston.
Gaveston.   I shall be found, and then 'twill grieve me more.
King Edward.   Kind words and mutual talk makes our grief greater;
Therefore, with dumb embracement, let us part—

100 *crazèd* ruined.

Stay, Gaveston, I cannot leave thee thus. 135
Gaveston. For every look my lord drops down a tear;
Seeing I must go, do not renew my sorrow.
King Edward. The time is little that thou hast to stay,
And therefore give me leave to look my fill.
But come, sweet friend, I'll bear thee on thy way. 140
Gaveston. The peers will frown.
King Edward. I pass not for their anger. Come, let's go.
O that we might as well return as go.
                    Enter Queen Isabella.
Queen Isabella. Whither goes my lord?
King Edward. Fawn not on me, French strumpet; get thee gone. 145
Queen Isabella. On whom but on my husband should I fawn?
Gaveston. On Mortimer, with whom, ungentle queen—
I say no more; judge you the rest, my lord.
Queen Isabella. In saying this, thou wrong'st me, Gaveston.
Is't not enough that thou corrupts my lord 150
And art a bawd to his affections,
But thou must call mine honor thus in question?
Gaveston. I mean not so; your grace must pardon me.
King Edward. Thou art too familiar with that Mortimer,
And by thy means is Gaveston exiled. 155
But I would wish thee reconcile the lords,
Or thou shalt ne'er be reconciled to me.
Queen Isabella. Your highness knows it lies not in my power.
King Edward. Away then; touch me not. Come, Gaveston.
Queen Isabella. Villain, 'tis thou that robb'st me of my lord. 160
Gaveston. Madam, 'tis you that rob me of my lord.
King Edward. Speak not unto her; let her droop and pine.
Queen Isabella. Wherein, my lord, have I deserved these words?
Witness the tears that Isabella sheds,
Witness this heart, that sighing for thee breaks, 165
How dear my lord is to poor Isabel.
King Edward. And witness heaven how dear thou art to me.
There weep; for till my Gaveston be repealed,
Assure thyself thou com'st not in my sight.
                    Exeunt [King] Edward and Gaveston.
Queen Isabella. O miserable and distressèd queen! 170
Would, when I left sweet France and was embarked,
That charming Circes, walking on the waves,
Had changed my shape, or at the marriage-day
The cup of Hymen had been full of poison,
Or with those arms that twined about my neck 175

---

140 *bear* accompany.
142 *pass* care.
151 *affections* idle inclinations.

172 *charming* having power to en-
chant. *Circes* variant of Circe, the en-
chantress of Homer's *Odyssey*.
174 *Hymen* Greek god of marriage.

I had been stifled, and not lived to see
The king my lord thus to abandon me.
Like frantic Juno will I fill the earth
With ghastly murmur of my sighs and cries,
For never doted Jove on Ganymede   180
So much as he on cursèd Gaveston.
But that will more exasperate his wrath;
I must entreat him, I must speak him fair,
And be a means to call home Gaveston.
And yet he'll ever dote on Gaveston,   185
And so am I for ever miserable.

      Enter [Lancaster, Warwick, Pembroke, Mortimer Senior, and
                      Mortimer Junior].

Lancaster.   Look where the sister of the king of France
Sits wringing of her hands and beats her breast.
Warwick.   The king, I fear, hath ill entreated her.
Pembroke.   Hard is the heart that injures such a saint.   190
Mortimer Junior.   I know 'tis 'long of Gaveston she weeps.
Mortimer Senior.   Why? He is gone.
Mortimer Junior.   Madam, how fares your grace?
Queen Isabella.   Ah, Mortimer! Now breaks the king's hate forth,
And he confesseth that he loves me not.
Mortimer Junior.   Cry quittance, madam, then, and love not him.   195
Queen Isabella.   No, rather will I die a thousand deaths,
And yet I love in vain; he'll ne'er love me.
Lancaster.   Fear ye not, madam; now his minion's gone,
His wanton humor will be quickly left.
Queen Isabella.   O never, Lancaster! I am enjoined   200
To sue unto you all for his repeal.
This wills my lord, and this must I perform,
Or else be banished from his highness' presence.
Lancaster.   For his repeal, madam? He comes not back,
Unless the sea cast up his shipwreck body.   205
Warwick.   And to behold so sweet a sight as that,
There's none here but would run his horse to death.
Mortimer Junior.   But, madam, would you have us call him home?
Queen Isabella.   Ay, Mortimer, for till he be restored,
The angry king hath banished me the court;   210
And therefore, as thou lovest and tender'st me,
Be thou my advocate unto these peers.
Mortimer Junior.   What, would ye have me plead for Gaveston?

178–180 *Juno . . . Ganymede* Juno,
queen of the gods, was enraged when
her husband, Jove, carried off the hand-
some boy, Ganymede to be his cup-
bearer and favorite. The story is told in
Ovid's *Metamorphoses*.

186, SD *Pembroke* Aymer de Valence,

at first opposed Edward and Gaveston,
but joined the king's party after a
quarrel with Lancaster and Warwick.
He died in 1324, while serving as the
king's envoy in France.

189 *entreated* treated.
191 *'long of* because of.

Mortimer Senior. Plead for him he that will; I am resolved.
Lancaster. And so am I, my lord. Dissuade the queen.   215
Queen Isabella. O Lancaster, let him dissuade the king,
  For 'tis against my will he should return.
Warwick. Then speak not for him; let the peasant go.
Queen Isabella. 'Tis for myself I speak, and not for him.
Pembroke. No speaking will prevail, and therefore cease.   220
Mortimer Junior. Fair queen, forbear to angle for the fish
  Which, being caught, strikes him that takes it dead.
  I mean that vile torpedo, Gaveston,
  That now, I hope, floats on the Irish seas.
Queen Isabella. Sweet Mortimer, sit down by me awhile,   225
  And I will tell thee reasons of such weight
  As thou wilt soon subscribe to his repeal.
Mortimer Junior. It is impossible, but speak your mind.
Queen Isabella. Then thus, but none shall hear it but ourselves.
                        [She talks to Mortimer Junior apart.]
Lancaster. My lords, albeit the queen win Mortimer,   230
  Will you be resolute and hold with me?
Mortimer Senior. Not I, against my nephew.
Pembroke. Fear not, the queen's words cannot alter him.
Warwick. No? Do but mark how earnestly she pleads.
Lancaster. And see how coldly his looks make denial.   235
Warwick. She smiles; now for my life his mind is changed.
Lancaster. I'll rather lose his friendship, I, than grant.
Mortimer Junior. Well, of necessity it must be so.
  My lords, that I abhor base Gaveston,
  I hope your honors make no question,   240
  And therefore, though I plead for his repeal,
  'Tis not for his sake, but for our avail;
  Nay for the realm's behoof, and for the king's.
Lancaster. Fie, Mortimer, dishonor not thyself!
  Can this be true, 'twas good to banish him?   245
  And is this true, to call him home again?
  Such reasons make white black and dark night day.
Mortimer Junior. My lord of Lancaster, mark the respect.
Lancaster. In no respect can contraries be true.
Queen Isabella. Yet, good my lord, hear what he can allege.   250
Warwick. All that he speaks is nothing; we are resolved.
Mortimer Junior. Do you not wish that Gaveston were dead?
Pembroke. I would he were.
Mortimer Junior. Why then, my lord, give me but leave to speak.
Mortimer Senior. But, nephew, do not play the sophister.   255
Mortimer Junior. This which I urge is of a burning zeal

---

223 *torpedo* cramp-fish or electric ray.   255 *play the sophister* use false argu-
248 *respect* consideration of a special   ments.
situation.

To mend the king and do our country good.
Know you not Gaveston hath store of gold,
Which may in Ireland purchase him such friends
As he will front the mightiest of us all?   260
And whereas he shall live and be beloved,
'Tis hard for us to work his overthrow.
Warwick.   Mark you but that, my lord of Lancaster.
Mortimer Junior.   But were he here, detested as he is,
How easily might some base slave be suborned   265
To greet his lordship with a poniard,
And none so much as blame the murderer,
But rather praise him for that brave attempt
And in the chronicle enrol his name
For purging of the realm of such a plague.   270
Pembroke.   He saith true.
Lancaster.   Ay, but how chance this was not done before?
Mortimer Junior.   Because, my lords, it was not thought upon.
Nay, more, when he shall know it lies in us
To banish him and then to call him home,   275
'Twill make him vail the top-flag of his pride,
And fear to offend the meanest nobleman.
Mortimer Senior.   But how if he do not, nephew?
Mortimer Junior.   Then may we with some color rise in arms;
For howsoever we have borne it out,   280
'Tis treason to be up against the king;
So shall we have the people of our side,
Which for his father's sake lean to the king,
But cannot brook a night-grown mushrump,
Such a one as my lord of Cornwall is,   285
Should bear us down of the nobility.
And when the commons and the nobles join,
'Tis not the king can buckler Gaveston.
We'll pull him from the strongest hold he hath.
My lords, if to perform this I be slack,   290
Think me as base a groom as Gaveston.
Lancaster.   On that condition, Lancaster will grant.
Warwick.   And so will Pembroke and I.
Mortimer Senior.   And I.
Mortimer Junior.   In this I count me highly gratified,
And Mortimer will rest at your command.   295
Queen Isabella.   And when this favor Isabel forgets,
Then let her live abandoned and forlorn.
But see, in happy time, my lord the king,
Having brought the Earl of Cornwall on his way,

---

279 *color* pretext, excuse.   288 *buckler* protect (literally with a
284 *mushrump* mushroom (one of many   shield).
variant forms).

Is new returned. This news will glad him much,   300
Yet not so much as me. I love him more
Than he can Gaveston; would he loved me
But half so much, then were I treble-blessed!
Enter King Edward, mourning.
King Edward. He's gone, and for his absence thus I mourn.
Did never sorrow go so near my heart   305
As doth the want of my sweet Gaveston;
And could my crown's revenue bring him back,
I would freely give it to his enemies
And think I gained, having bought so dear a friend.
Queen Isabella. Hark, how he harps upon his minion.   310
King Edward. My heart is as an anvil unto sorrow,
Which beats upon it like the Cyclops' hammers
And with the noise turns up my giddy brain
And makes me frantic for my Gaveston.
Ah, had some bloodless Fury rose from hell   315
And with my kingly scepter struck me dead,
When I was forced to leave my Gaveston.
Lancaster. *Diablo!* What passions call you these?
Queen Isabella. My gracious lord, I come to bring you news.
King Edward. That you have parlèd with your Mortimer.   320
Queen Isabella. That Gaveston, my lord, shall be repealed.
King Edward. Repealed? The news is too sweet to be true.
Queen Isabella. But will you love me, if you find it so?
King Edward. If it be so, what will not Edward do?
Queen Isabella. For Gaveston, but not for Isabel.   325
King Edward. For thee, fair queen, if thou lovest Gaveston;
I'll hang a golden tongue about thy neck,
Seeing thou hast pleaded with so good success.
Queen Isabella. No other jewels hang about my neck
Than these, my lord; nor let me have more wealth   330
Than I may fetch from this rich treasury.
O how a kiss revives poor Isabel!
King Edward. Once more receive my hand, and let this be
A second marriage twixt thyself and me.
Queen Isabella. And may it prove more happy than the first.   335
My gentle lord, bespeak these nobles fair,
That wait attendance for a gracious look
And on their knees salute your majesty.
King Edward. Courageous Lancaster, embrace thy king.
And, as gross vapors perish by the sun,   340
Even so let hatred with thy sovereign's smile.
Live thou with me as my companion.
Lancaster. This salutation overjoys my heart.
King Edward. Warwick shall be my chiefest counselor.

312 *Cyclops* See note to *Dido* I,i,147.   330 *these* i.e., Edward's **arms.**

These silver hairs will more adorn my court   345
  Than gaudy silks or rich embroidery.
  Chide me, sweet Warwick, if I go astray.
Warwick.   Slay me, my lord, when I offend your grace.
King Edward.   In solemn triumphs and in public shows,
  Pembroke shall bear the sword before the king.   350
Pembroke.   And with this sword Pembroke will fight for you.
King Edward.   But wherefore walks young Mortimer aside?
  Be thou commander of our royal fleet;
  Or, if that lofty office like thee not,
  I make thee here Lord Marshal of the realm.   355
Mortimer Junior.   My lord, I'll marshal so your enemies,
  As England shall be quiet and you safe.
King Edward.   And as for you, Lord Mortimer of Chirke,
  Whose great achievements in our foreign war
  Deserves no common place, nor mean reward,   360
  Be you the general of the levied troops
  That now are ready to assail the Scots.
Mortimer Senior.   In this your grace hath highly honored me,
  For with my nature war doth best agree.
Queen Isabella.   Now is the king of England rich and strong,   365
  Having the love of his renownèd peers.
King Edward.   Ay, Isabel, ne'er was my heart so light.
  Clerk of the crown, direct our warrant forth
  For Gaveston to Ireland.
                    [Enter Beaumont.]
                  Beaumont, fly
  As fast as Iris or Jove's Mercury.   370
Beaumont.   It shall be done, my gracious lord.
                                            [Exit.]
King Edward.   Lord Mortimer, we leave you to your charge.
  Now let us in and feast it royally.
  Against our friend the Earl of Cornwall comes,
  We'll have a general tilt and tournament,   375
  And then his marriage shall be solemnized;
  For wot you not that I have made him sure
  Unto our cousin, the Earl of Gloucester's heir?
Lancaster.   Such news we hear, my lord.
King Edward.   That day, if not for him, yet for my sake,   380
  Who in the triumph will be challenger,
  Spare for no cost; we will requite your love.

358 *Chirke* border city between Shrop-
shire and Wales, of which the elder
Mortimer was lord.
  370 *Iris . . . Mercury* Iris was the
messenger of Juno, as Mercury was that
of Jove.
  374 *Against* in preparation for the

time when. *Earl of Cornwall* i.e., Gaveston.
  378 *Earl . . . heir* Gilbert de Clare,
eighth Earl of Gloucester, was married
to King Edward's sister. Their daughter,
Margaret, became the wife of Gaveston.

Warwick. In this or ought your highness shall command us.
King Edward. Thanks, gentle Warwick. Come, let's in and revel.
                Exeunt all except the Mortimers.
Mortimer Senior. Nephew, I must to Scotland; thou stayest here.   385
  Leave now to oppose thyself against the king.
  Thou seest by nature he is mild and calm,
  And, seeing his mind so dotes on Gaveston,
  Let him without controlment have his will.
  The mightiest kings have had their minions.   390
  Great Alexander loved Hephaestion;
  The conquering Hercules for Hylas wept,
  And for Patroclus stern Achilles drooped.
  And not kings only, but the wisest men:
  The Roman Tully loved Octavius,   395
  Grave Socrates, wild Alcibiades.
  Then let his grace, whose youth is flexible
  And promiseth as much as we can wish,
  Freely enjoy that vain, light-headed earl,
  For riper years will wean him from such toys.   400
Mortimer Junior. Uncle, his wanton humor grieves not me;
  But this I scorn, that one so basely born
  Should by his sovereign's favor grow so pert
  And riot it with the treasure of the realm.
  While soldiers mutiny for want of pay,   405
  He wears a lord's revenue on his back,
  And, Midas-like, he jets it in the court
  With base outlandish cullions at his heels,
  Whose proud fantastic liveries make such show,
  As if that Proteus, god of shapes, appeared.   410
  I have not seen a dapper Jack so brisk.
  He wears a short Italian hooded cloak,
  Larded with pearl, and in his Tuscan cap
  A jewel of more value than the crown.
  While others walk below, the king and he   415
  From out a window laugh at such as we,
  And flout our train, and jest at our attire.

391 *Hephaestion* the close friend and companion of Alexander the Great.

392 *Hylas* See note at I,i,144.

393 *Patroclus* the friend of Achilles, whose slaying by Hector finally aroused Achilles to action and brought an end to the Trojan war.

395 *Tully* Marcus Tullius Cicero, the great Roman orator and statesman. He had no relation to the Emperor Augustus Caesar (Octavius) comparable to that of Gaveston to Edward.

396 *Alcibiades* a somewhat rakish young man of noble birth and good looks befriended by the Greek philosopher, Socrates.

400 *toys* foolish pastimes.

407 *Midas-like* like Midas, the mythical king endowed by Dionysius with the power to turn all he touched to gold. *jets it* struts.

408 *outlandish cullions* foreign scoundrels.

410 *Proteus* a sea deity who changed his shape whenever men tried to restrain him.

Uncle, 'tis this that makes me impatient.
Mortimer Senior. But, nephew, now you see the king is changed.
Mortimer Junior. Then so am I, and live to do him service.   420
But whiles I have a sword, a hand, a heart,
I will not yield to any such upstart.
You know my mind; come, uncle, let's away.

Exeunt.

Enter Spencer [Junior] and Baldock.   II,i.
Baldock. Spencer,
Seeing that our lord th' Earl of Gloucester's dead,
Which of the nobles dost thou mean to serve?
Spencer Junior. Not Mortimer, nor any of his side,
Because the king and he are enemies.   5
Baldock, learn this of me: a factious lord
Shall hardly do himself good, much less us,
But he that hath the favor of a king
May with one word advance us while we live.
The liberal Earl of Cornwall is the man   10
On whose good fortune Spencer's hope depends.
Baldock. What, mean you then to be his follower?
Spencer Junior. No, his companion, for he loves me well
And would have once preferred me to the king.
Baldock. But he is banished; there's small hope of him.   15
Spencer Junior. Ay, for a while; but, Baldock, mark the end.
A friend of mine told me in secrecy
That he's repealed and sent for back again,
And even now a post came from the court
With letters to our lady from the king,   20
And as she read she smiled, which makes me think
It is about her lover Gaveston.
Baldock. 'Tis like enough, for since he was exiled
She neither walks abroad nor comes in sight.
But I had thought the match had been broke off   25
And that his banishment had changed her mind.
Spencer Junior. Our lady's first love is not wavering;
My life for thine she will have Gaveston.

II,i.
SD *Spencer Junior* Hugh le Despenser, who married the elder sister of Gaveston s wife, daughter of the Earl of Gloucester. Always a strong partisan of King Edward, he was executed at Hereford in November, 1326, one month after the execution of his father. *Baldock* Robert of Baldock, keeper of the king's privy seal, fled with King Edward, was captured in November, 1326, and died the following year.

Baldock.   Then hope I by her means to be preferred,
   Having read unto her since she was a child.   30
Spencer Junior.   Then, Baldock, you must cast the scholar off
   And learn to court it like a gentleman.
   'Tis not a black coat and a little band,
   A velvet-caped cloak, faced before with serge,
   And smelling to a nosegay all the day,   35
   Or holding of a napkin in your hand,
   Or saying a long grace at a table's end,
   Or making low legs to a nobleman,
   Or looking downward with your eyelids close,
   And saying, 'Truly, an't may please your honor,'   40
   Can get you any favor with great men;
   You must be proud, bold, pleasant, resolute,
   And now and then stab, as occasion serves.
Baldock.   Spencer, thou knowest I hate such formal toys
   And use them but of mere hypocrisy.   45
   Mine old lord whiles he lived was so precise
   That he would take exceptions at my buttons,
   And being like pin's heads, blame me for the bigness;
   Which made me curate-like in mine attire,
   Though inwardly licentious enough   50
   And apt for any kind of villainy.
   I am none of these common pedants, I,
   That cannot speak without *propterea quod.*
Spencer Junior.   But one of those that saith *quandoquidem*
   And hath a special gift to form a verb.   55
Baldock.   Leave off this jesting, here my lady comes.
Enter the King's Niece.
Niece.   The grief for his exile was not so much
   As is the joy of his returning home.
   This letter came from my sweet Gaveston.
   What needst thou, love, thus to excuse thyself?   60
   I know thou couldst not come and visit me.
   'I will not long be from thee, though I die.'   [*She reads.*]
   This argues the entire love of my lord.
   'When I forsake thee, death seize on my heart.'   [*She reads.*]
   But rest thee here where Gaveston shall sleep.   65
[*She places the letter in her bosom.*]
   Now to the letter of my lord the king.
   He wills me to repair unto the court
   And meet my Gaveston. Why do I stay,
   Seeing that he talks thus of my marriage day?
   Who's there? Baldock!   70

---

33 *black coat* the traditional garb of
the scholar.
53–54 *propterea quod . . . quandoqui-*
dem Both are terms meaning 'because'
and used in formal rhetoric.
55 *form a verb* use language eloquently.

See that my coach be ready; I must hence.
Baldock. It shall be done, madam.
Niece. And meet me at the park-pale presently.
                                                        Exit [Baldock].
Spencer, stay you and bear me company,
For I have joyful news to tell thee of.   75
My lord of Cornwall is a-coming over
And will be at the court as soon as we.
Spencer Junior. I knew the king would have him home again.
Niece. If all things sort out as I hope they will,
Thy service, Spencer, shall be thought upon.   80
Spencer Junior. I humbly thank your ladyship.
Niece. Come, lead the way; I long till I am there.
                                                        [Exeunt.]

✳

II,ii.

*Enter [King] Edward, Queen [Isabella], Lancaster, Mortimer
    [Junior], Warwick, Pembroke, Kent [and] Attendants.*
King Edward. The wind is good; I wonder why he stays;
I fear me he is wracked upon the sea.
Queen Isabella. Look, Lancaster, how passionate he is,
And still his mind runs on his minion.
Lancaster. My lord—   5
King Edward. How now! What news? Is Gaveston arrived?
Mortimer Junior. Nothing but Gaveston! What means your grace?
You have matters of more weight to think upon;
The king of France sets foot in Normandy.
King Edward. A trifle! We'll expel him when we please.   10
But tell me, Mortimer, what's thy device
Against the stately triumph we decreed?
Mortimer Junior. A homely one, my lord, not worth the telling.
King Edward. Prithee let me know it.
Mortimer Junior. But seeing you are so desirous, thus it is: 15
A lofty cedar tree, fair flourishing,
On whose top-branches kingly eagles perch,
And by the bark a canker creeps me up
And gets unto the highest bough of all;
The motto, *Æque tandem.*   20
King Edward. And what is yours, my lord of Lancaster?

<hr>

71 *coach* an anachronism, since coaches
were not introduced into England until
the middle of the sixteenth century.

II,ii.

2 *wracked* shipwrecked.

11 *device* a painting on a shield, accompanied by a motto.
18 *canker* canker-worm, a striped green
caterpillar which destroys plants.
20 *Æque tandem* equally at last (the
sense being that Gaveston, the canker,

Lancaster. My lord, mine's more obscure than Mortimer's.
Pliny reports there is a flying fish
Which all the other fishes deadly hate,
And therefore, being pursued, it takes the air.   25
No sooner is it up, but there's a fowl
That seizeth it; this fish, my lord, I bear;
The motto this: *Undique mors est.*
King Edward. Proud Mortimer! Ungentle Lancaster!
Is this the love you bear your sovereign?   30
Is this the fruit your reconcilement bears?
Can you in words make show of amity,
And in your shields display your rancorous minds?
What call you this but private libelling
Against the Earl of Cornwall and my brother?   35
Queen Isabella. Sweet husband, be content; they all love you.
King Edward. They love me not that hate my Gaveston.
I am that cedar, shake me not too much;
And you the eagles; soar ye ne'er so high,
I have the jesses that will pull you down;   40
And *Æque tandem* shall that canker cry
Unto the proudest peer of Britainy.
Though thou compar'st him to a flying fish,
And threatenest death whether he rise or fall,
'Tis not the hugest monster of the sea,   45
Nor foulest harpy, that shall swallow him.
Mortimer Junior. If in his absence thus he favors him,
What will he do whenas he shall be present?
Lancaster. That shall we see; look where his lordship comes.
                    Enter Gaveston.
King Edward. My Gaveston!   50
Welcome to Tynemouth! Welcome to thy friend!
Thy absence made me droop and pine away;
For, as the lovers of fair Danaë,
When she was locked up in a brazen tower,
Desired her more and waxed outrageous,   55
So did it sure with me. And now thy sight
Is sweeter far than was thy parting hence

will finally reach the top of the tree
and be equal with the eagle, Edward).

23 *Pliny* Gaius Plinius Secundus, or
Pliny the Elder, Roman author of the
Naturalis Historia. Actually there is no
such account in Pliny, although there
is a description similar to Marlowe's in
Sir John Hawkins' account of his second
voyage to Guiana, published in 1565.

28 *Undique mors est* Death is on all
sides.

40 *jesses* short straps, usually of leather,
tied to the legs of trained hawks and
used to control them.

46 *harpy* legendary bird with the head
of a woman.

53 *Danaë* legendary Greek heroine who,
although locked up in a tower by her
father, was wooed by Zeus in the form
of a shower of gold. Greek mythology
does not record that she had other lovers.

College of St. Francis Library
Joliet, Illinois

Bitter and irksome to my sobbing heart.
Gaveston. Sweet lord and king, your speech preventeth mine,
  Yet have I words left to express my joy.   60
  The shepherd nipped with biting winter's rage
  Frolics not more to see the painted spring,
  Than I do to behold your majesty.
King Edward. Will none of you salute my Gaveston?
Lancaster. Salute him? Yes. Welcome Lord Chamberlain.   65
Mortimer Junior. Welcome is the good Earl of Cornwall.
Warwick. Welcome, Lord Governor of the Isle of Man.
Pembroke. Welcome, Master Secretary.
Kent. Brother, do you hear them?
King Edward. Still will these earls and barons use me thus?   70
Gaveston. My lord, I cannot brook these injuries.
Queen Isabella. Ay me, poor soul, when these begin to jar.
                                               [Aside.]
King Edward. Return it to their throats; I'll be thy warrant.
Gaveston. Base, leaden earls, that glory in your birth,
  Go sit at home and eat your tenants' beef,   75
  And come not here to scoff at Gaveston,
  Whose mounting thoughts did never creep so low
  As to bestow a look on such as you.
Lancaster. Yet I disdain not to do this for you.
                               [He draws his sword.]
King Edward. Treason, treason! Where's the traitor?   80
Pembroke. Here! Here!
King Edward. Convey hence Gaveston; they'll murder him.
Gaveston. The life of thee shall salve this foul disgrace.
Mortimer Junior. Villain, thy life unless I miss mine aim.
                         [He wounds Gaveston.]
Queen Isabella. Ah, furious Mortimer, what hast thou done?   85
Mortimer Junior. No more than I would answer, were he slain.
                   [Exit Gaveston with Attendants.]
King Edward. Yes, more than thou canst answer, though he live.
  Dear shall you both aby this riotous deed.
  Out of my presence; come not near the court.
Mortimer Junior. I'll not be barred the court for Gaveston.   90
Lancaster. We'll hale him by the ears unto the block.
King Edward. Look to your own heads; his is sure enough.
Warwick. Look to your own crown, if you back him thus.
Kent. Warwick, these words do ill beseem thy years.
King Edward. Nay, all of them conspire to cross me thus,   95
  But if I live, I'll tread upon their heads
  That think with high looks thus to tread me down.
  Come, Edmund, let's away and levy men;
  'Tis war that must abate these barons' pride.
          Exit King [Edward with Queen Isabella and Kent].

62 *painted* adorned with flowers.   88 *aby* pay for.

Warwick.   Let's to our castles, for the king is moved.   100
Mortimer Junior.   Moved may he be, and perish in his wrath!
Lancaster.   Cousin, it is no dealing with him now.
   He means to make us stoop by force of arms,
   And therefore let us jointly here protest
   To prosecute that Gaveston to the death.   105
Mortimer Junior.   By heaven, the abject villain shall not live.
Warwick.   I'll have his blood or die in seeking it.
Pembroke.   The like oath Pembroke takes.
Lancaster.   And so doth Lancaster.
   Now send our heralds to defy the king,
   And make the people swear to put him down.   110
                    Enter a Messenger.
Mortimer Junior.   Letters? From whence?
Messenger.   From Scotland, my lord.
         [*He gives letters to Mortimer, who reads.*]
Lancaster.   Why, how now, cousin, how fares all our friends?
Mortimer Junior.   My uncle's taken prisoner by the Scots.
Lancaster.   We'll have him ransomed, man; be of good cheer.
Mortimer Junior.   They rate his ransom at five thousand pound.   115
   Who should defray the money but the king,
   Seeing he is taken prisoner in his wars?
   I'll to the king.
Lancaster.   Do, cousin, and I'll bear thee company.
Warwick.   Meantime, my lord of Pembroke and myself   120
   Will to Newcastle here and gather head.
Mortimer Junior.   About it then, and we will follow you.
Lancaster.   Be resolute and full of secrecy.
Warwick.   I warrant you.
         [*Exeunt all but Mortimer Junior and Lancaster.*]
Mortimer Junior.   Cousin, and if he will not ransom him,   125
   I'll thunder such a peal into his ears
   As never subject did unto his king.
Lancaster.   Content, I'll bear my part. Holla! Who's there?
               [*Enter a Guard.*]
Mortimer Junior.   Ay, marry, such a guard as this doth well.
Lancaster.   Lead on the way.   130
Guard.   Whither will your lordships?
Mortimer Junior.   Whither else but to the king?
Guard.   His highness is disposed to be alone.
Lancaster.   Why, so he may, but we will speak to him.
Guard.   You may not in, my lord.   135
Mortimer Junior.   May we not?
               [*Enter King Edward and Kent.*]
King Edward.   How now! What noise is this?

104 *protest* vow.   113 *uncle's . . . Scots* There is **no** his-
109 *defy* renounce allegiance to.   torical basis for this episode.
                                      121 *gather head* raise an army.

Who have we there? Is't you?

                                         [Going.]

Mortimer Junior. Nay, stay, my lord, I come to bring you news;
  Mine uncle's taken prisoner by the Scots.   140
King Edward. Then ransom him.
Lancaster. 'Twas in your wars; you should ransom him.
Mortimer Junior. And you shall ransom him, or else—
Kent. What, Mortimer! You will not threaten him?
King Edward. Quiet yourself; you shall have the broad seal   145
  To gather for him thoroughout the realm.
Lancaster. Your minion Gaveston hath taught you this.
Mortimer Junior. My lord, the family of the Mortimers
  Are not so poor, but, would they sell their land,
  Would levy men enough to anger you.   150
  We never beg, but use such prayers as these.
                            [He grasps his sword.]
King Edward. Shall I still be haunted thus?
Mortimer Junior. Nay, now you are here alone, I'll speak my mind.
Lancaster. And so will I, and then, my lord, farewell.
Mortimer Junior. The idle triumphs, masks, lascivious shows, 155
  And prodigal gifts bestowed on Gaveston,
  Have drawn thy treasure dry and made thee weak,
  The murmuring commons overstretchèd hath.
Lancaster. Look for rebellion; look to be deposed.
  Thy garrisons are beaten out of France,   160
  And, lame and poor, lie groaning at the gates.
  The wild O'Neil, with swarms of Irish kerns,
  Lives uncontrolled within the English pale.
  Unto the walls of York the Scots made road
  And unresisted drave away rich spoils.   165
Mortimer Junior. The haughty Dane commands the narrow seas,
  While in the harbor ride thy ships unrigged.
Lancaster. What foreign prince sends thee ambassadors?
Mortimer Junior. Who loves thee, but a sort of flatterers?
Lancaster. Thy gentle queen, sole sister to Valois,   170
  Complains that thou hast left her all forlorn.
Mortimer Junior. Thy court is naked, being bereft of those
  That makes a king seem glorious to the world;
  I mean the peers, whom thou shouldst dearly love.
  Libels are cast again thee in the street,   175
  Ballads and rhymes made of thy overthrow.

145–146 *broad seal . . . realm* royal
license to collect alms (as a beggar) for
him. The king is being contemptuous
and insulting.

152 *haunted* pursued.

162 *O'Neil* Shane O'Neil was an Irish
leader of Marlowe's own day. *kerns* foot-
soldiers.

170 *Valois* See note to *Massacre at
Paris*, xviii,46. Queen Isabella's brothers
actually were not of the house of Valois,
although her cousin, Philip of Valois, did
eventually become king of France.

Lancaster. The Northern borderers, seeing their houses burnt,
 Their wives and children slain, run up and down,
 Cursing the name of thee and Gaveston.
Mortimer Junior. When wert thou in the field with banner spread? 180
 But once, and then thy soldiers marched like players,
 With garish robes, not armor, and thyself,
 Bedaubed with gold, rode laughing at the rest,
 Nodding and shaking of thy spangled crest,
 Where women's favors hung like labels down. 185
Lancaster. And thereof came it that the fleering Scots,
 To England's high disgrace, have made this jig:

> *Maids of England, sore may you mourn,*
> *For your lemans you have lost at Bannocksbourn,*
> *With a heave and a ho!* 190
> *What weeneth the King of England,*
> *So soon to have won Scotland?*
> *With a rombelow!*

Mortimer Junior. Wigmore shall fly to set my uncle free.
Lancaster. And when 'tis gone, our swords shall purchase more. 195
 If ye be moved, revenge it as you can.
 Look next to see us with our ensigns spread.
       [Exit with Mortimer Junior.]
King Edward. My swelling heart for very anger breaks.
 How oft have I been baited by these peers,
 And dare not be revenged, for their power is great! 200
 Yet, shall the crowing of these cockerels
 Affright a lion? Edward, unfold thy paws,
 And let their lives' blood slake thy fury's hunger.
 If I be cruel and grow tyrannous,
 Now let them thank themselves and rue too late. 205
Kent. My lord, I see your love to Gaveston
 Will be the ruin of the realm and you,
 For now the wrathful nobles threaten wars,
 And therefore, brother, banish him for ever.
King Edward. Art thou an enemy to my Gaveston? 210
Kent. Ay, and it grieves me that I favored him.
King Edward. Traitor, begone! Whine thou with Mortimer.
Kent. So will I, rather than with Gaveston.
King Edward. Out of my sight, and trouble me no more.
Kent. No marvel though thou scorn thy noble peers, 215

185 *labels* pieces of parchment used to affix seals to documents.
186 *fleering* jeering.
187 *jig* mocking song.
189 *lemans* sweethearts. *Bannocksbourn* battle against the Scots, fought on June

21, 1314, in which the English suffered a crushing defeat.
193 *rombelow* a meaningless term used in refrains.
194 *Wigmore* Mortimer Junior's estate. *shall fly* i.e., will be sold.
201 *cockerels* young roosters.

When I thy brother am rejected thus.
King Edward.   Away!

                                        Exit [Kent].

Poor Gaveston, that hast no friend but me,
Do what they can, we'll live in Tynemouth here,
And so I walk with him about the walls,   220
What care I though the earls begirt us round?
Here comes she that's cause of all these jars.
  Enter Queen [Isabella, with the King's Niece, two] Ladies,
      [Gaveston,] Baldock, and Spencer [Junior].
Queen Isabella.   My lord, 'tis thought the earls are up in arms.
King Edward.   Ay, and 'tis likewise thought you favor 'em.
Queen Isabella.   Thus do you still suspect me without cause?   225
Niece.   Sweet uncle, speak more kindly to the queen.
Gaveston.   My lord, dissemble with her; speak her fair.
                              [Aside to King Edward.]
King Edward.   Pardon me, sweet, I forgot myself.
Queen Isabella.   Your pardon is quickly got of Isabel.
King Edward.   The younger Mortimer is grown so brave   230
That to my face he threatens civil wars.
Gaveston.   Why do you not commit him to the Tower?
King Edward.   I dare not, for the people love him well.
Gaveston.   Why, then we'll have him privily made away.
King Edward.   Would Lancaster and he had both caroused   235
A bowl of poison to each other's health.
But let them go, and tell me what are these.
Niece.   Two of my father's servants whilst he lived.
May't please your grace to entertain them now?
King Edward.   Tell me, where wast thou born? What is thine
      arms?   240
Baldock.   My name is Baldock, and my gentry
I fetched from Oxford, not from heraldry.
King Edward.   The fitter art thou, Baldock, for my turn.
Wait on me, and I'll see thou shalt not want.
Baldock.   I humbly thank your majesty.   245
King Edward.   Knowest thou him, Gaveston?
Gaveston.   Ay, my lord;
His name is Spencer; he is well allied.
For my sake, let him wait upon your grace.
Scarce shall you find a man of more desert.
King Edward.   Then, Spencer, wait upon me; for his sake   250
I'll grace thee with a higher style ere long.
Spencer Junior.   No greater titles happen unto me
Than to be favored of your majesty.
King Edward.   Cousin, this day shall be your marriage feast.
And, Gaveston, think that I love thee well,   255
To wed thee to our niece, the only heir

Unto the Earl of Gloucester late deceased.
Gaveston. I know, my lord, many will stomach me,
But I respect neither their love nor hate.
King Edward. The headstrong barons shall not limit me;   260
He that I list to favor shall be great.
Come, let's away; and when the marriage ends,
Have at the rebels and their 'complices.

                                                Exeunt.

                         *

                                                        II,iii.
Enter Lancaster, Mortimer [Junior,] Warwick, Pembroke, Kent
                    [and others].
Kent. My lords, of love to this our native land
I come to join with you and leave the king,
And in your quarrel and the realm's behoof
Will be the first that shall adventure life.
Lancaster. I fear me you are sent of policy,   5
To undermine us with a show of love.
Warwick. He is your brother; therefore have we cause
To cast the worst and doubt of your revolt.
Kent. Mine honor shall be hostage of my truth;
If that will not suffice, farewell, my lords.   10
Mortimer Junior. Stay, Edmund; never was Plantagenet
False of his word, and therefore trust we thee.
Pembroke. But what's the reason you should leave him now?
Kent. I have informed the Earl of Lancaster.
Lancaster. And it sufficeth. Now, my lords, know this,   15
That Gaveston is secretly arrived
And here in Tynemouth frolics with the king.
Let us with these our followers scale the walls
And suddenly surprise them unawares.
Mortimer Junior. I'll give the onset.
Warwick.   And I'll follow thee.   20
Mortimer Junior. This tottered ensign of my ancestors,
Which swept the desert shore of that Dead Sea
Whereof we got the name of Mortimer,
Will I advance upon these castle walls.
Drums, strike alarum, raise them from their sport,   25
And ring aloud the knell of Gaveston.
Lancaster. None be so hardy as to touch the king,

258 *stomach* take offense at.

II,iii.   8 *cast* anticipate.
  5 *policy* political deception.   21 *tottered* tattered.

But neither spare you Gaveston nor his friends.

Exeunt.

Enter *King [Edward] and Spencer [Junior].* II,iv.

King Edward.   O tell me, Spencer, where is Gaveston?
Spencer Junior.   I fear me he is slain, my gracious lord.
King Edward.   No, here he comes. Now let them spoil and kill.
    [Enter] to them [Queen Isabella, the King's Niece,] Gaveston,
                    [and Others].
Fly, fly, my lords, the earls have got the hold;
Take shipping and away to Scarborough;   5
Spencer and I will post away by land.
Gaveston.   O stay, my lord, they will not injure you.
King Edward.   I will not trust them. Gaveston, away.
Gaveston.   Farewell, my lord.
King Edward.   Lady, farewell.   10
Niece.   Farewell, sweet uncle, till we meet again.
King Edward.   Farewell, sweet Gaveston, and farewell, niece.
Queen Isabella.   No farewell to poor Isabel thy queen?
King Edward.   Yes, yes, for Mortimer, your lover's sake.
Queen Isabella.   Heavens can witness I love none but you. 15
            Exeunt [all but Queen] Isabella.
From my embracements thus he breaks away.
O that mine arms could close this isle about,
That I might pull him to me where I would,
Or that these tears that drizzle from mine eyes
Had power to mollify his stony heart,   20
That when I had him we might never part.
        Enter [Lancaster, Warwick, Mortimer Junior, and Others].
                Alarums [within].
Lancaster.   I wonder how he 'scaped?
Mortimer Junior.   Who's this? The queen!
Queen Isabella.   Ay, Mortimer, the miserable queen,
    Whose pining heart her inward sighs have blasted,
    And body with continual mourning wasted.   25
    These hands are tired with haling of my lord
    From Gaveston, from wicked Gaveston,
    And all in vain, for when I speak him fair,
    He turns away and smiles upon his minion.
Mortimer Junior.   Cease to lament, and tell us where's the king? 30
Queen Isabella.   What would you with the king? Is't him you seek?
Lancaster.   No madam, but that cursèd Gaveston.
    Far be it from the thought of Lancaster
    To offer violence to his sovereign.

We would but rid the realm of Gaveston.   35
Tell us where he remains, and he shall die.
Queen Isabella.   He's gone by water unto Scarborough;
   Pursue him quickly, and he cannot 'scape;
   The king hath left him, and his train is small.
Warwick.   Forslow no time. Sweet Lancaster, let's march.   40
Mortimer Junior.   How comes it that the king and he is parted?
Queen Isabella.   That this your army, going several ways,
   Might be of lesser force, and with the power
   That he intendeth presently to raise,
   Be easily suppressed; and therefore be gone.   45
Mortimer Junior.   Here in the river rides a Flemish hoy;
   Let's all aboard and follow him amain.
Lancaster.   The wind that bears him hence will fill our sails.
   Come, come aboard; 'tis but an hour's sailing.
Mortimer Junior.   Madam, stay you within this castle here.   50
Queen Isabella.   No, Mortimer, I'll to my lord the king.
Mortimer Junior.   Nay, rather sail with us to Scarborough.
Queen Isabella.   You know the king is so suspicious,
   As if he hear I have but talked with you,
   Mine honor will be called in question;   55
   And therefore, gentle Mortimer, be gone.
Mortimer Junior.   Madam, I cannot stay to answer you,
   But think of Mortimer as he deserves.
                    [*Exeunt all but Queen Isabella.*]
Queen Isabella.   So well hast thou deserved, sweet Mortimer,
   As Isabel could live with thee forever.   60
   In vain I look for love at Edward's hand,
   Whose eyes are fixed on none but Gaveston;
   Yet once more I'll importune him with prayers.
   If he be strange and not regard my words,
   My son and I will over into France   65
   And to the king my brother there complain
   How Gaveston hath robbed me of his love.
   But yet I hope my sorrows will have end,
   And Gaveston this blessèd day be slain.

                                        Exit.

                Enter Gaveston, pursued.   II,v.
Gaveston.   Yet, lusty lords, I have escaped your hands,
   Your threats, your 'larums, and your hot pursuits;

II,iv.   **II,v.**
40 *Forslow* waste.   2 *'larums* alarms.
46 *Flemish hoy* a small fishing vessel
used in the North Sea.

And though divorcèd from King Edward's eyes,
Yet liveth Pierce of Gaveston unsurprised,
Breathing, in hope—*malgrado* all your beards,   5
That muster rebels thus against your king—
To see his royal sovereign once again.

> *Enter* [*Warwick, Lancaster, Pembroke, Mortimer Junior, Sol-
> diers, James, and other Attendants of Pembroke*].

Warwick.   Upon him, soldiers; take away his weapons.
Mortimer Junior.   Thou proud disturber of thy country's peace,
Corrupter of thy king, cause of these broils,   10
Base flatterer, yield! And were it not for shame,
Shame and dishonor to a soldier's name,
Upon my weapon's point here shouldst thou fall
And welter in thy gore.
Lancaster.   Monster of men,
That, like the Greekish strumpet, trained to arms   15
And bloody wars so many valiant knights,
Look for no other fortune, wretch, than death.
King Edward is not here to buckler thee.
Warwick.   Lancaster, why talk'st thou to the slave?
Go, soldiers, take him hence, for, by my sword,   20
His head shall off. Gaveston, short warning
Shall serve thy turn. It is our country's cause
That here severely we will execute
Upon thy person. Hang him at a bough.
Gaveston.   My lord—   25
Warwick.   Soldiers, have him away.
But for thou wert the favorite of a king,
Thou shalt have so much honor at our hands.
Gaveston.   I thank you all, my lords. Then I perceive
That heading is one, and hanging is the other,   30
And death is all.

> *Enter Earl of Arundel.*

Lancaster.   How now, my lord of Arundel?
Arundel.   My lords, King Edward greets you all by me.
Warwick.   Arundel, say your message.
Arundel.   His majesty,
Hearing that you had taken Gaveston,   35
Entreateth you by me, yet but he may
See him before he dies; for why, he says,

---

5 *malgrado* in spite of.
15 *Greekish strumpet* Helen of Troy.
trained enticed.
18 *buckler* See note at I,iv,288.
28 *so much honor* Gentlemen were
beheaded, hanging being reserved for
common thieves.

31, SD *Arundel* Edmund Fitzalan, Earl
of Arundel, at first opposed King Edward, but later joined the king's part
and was executed by Mortimer in November, 1326.
37 *for why* because.

And sends you word, he knows that die he shall;
And if you gratify his grace so far,
He will be mindful of the courtesy.   40
Warwick.   How now?
Gaveston.   Renownèd Edward, how thy name
  Revives poor Gaveston.
Warwick.   No, it needeth not.
  Arundel, we will gratify the king
  In other matters; he must pardon us in this.
  Soldiers, away with him.   45
Gaveston.   Why, my lord of Warwick,
  Will not these delays beget my hopes?
  I know it, lords, it is this life you aim at;
  Yet grant King Edward this.
Mortimer Junior.   Shalt thou appoint
  What we shall grant? Soldiers, away with him.   50
  Thus we'll gratify the king;
  We'll send his head by thee; let him bestow
  His tears on that, for that is all he gets
  Of Gaveston, or else his senseless trunk.
Lancaster.   Not so, my lord, lest he bestow more cost   55
  In burying him than he hath ever earned.
Arundel.   My lords, it is his majesty's request,
  And in the honor of a king he swears,
  He will but talk with him and send him back.
Warwick.   When, can you tell? Arundel, no; we wot   60
  He that the care of realm remits
  And drives his nobles to these exigents
  For Gaveston, will, if he sees him once,
  Violate any promise to possess him.
Arundel.   Then if you will not trust his grace in keep,   65
  My lords, I will be pledge for his return.
Mortimer Junior.   It is honorable in thee to offer this,
  But for we know thou art a noble gentleman,
  We will not wrong thee so, to make away
  A true man for a thief.   70
Gaveston.   How mean'st thou, Mortimer? That is over-base.
Mortimer Junior.   Away, base groom, robber of king's renown.
  Question with thy companions and thy mates.
Pembroke.   My lord Mortimer, and you, my lords, each one,
  To gratify the king's request therein,   75
  Touching the sending of this Gaveston,
  Because his majesty so earnestly
  Desires to see the man before his death,
  I will upon mine honor undertake
  To carry him and bring him back again;   80

61 *remits* abandons.

Provided this, that you my lord of Arundel
Will join with me.
Warwick.   Pembroke, what wilt thou do?
Cause yet more bloodshed? Is it not enough
That we have taken him, but must we now
Leave him on 'had I wist,' and let him go?   85
Pembroke.   My lords, I will not over-woo your honors,
But if you dare trust Pembroke with the prisoner,
Upon mine oath, I will return him back.
Arundel.   My lord of Lancaster, what say you in this?
Lancaster.   Why, I say, let him go on Pembroke's word.   90
Pembroke.   And you, Lord Mortimer?
Mortimer Junior.   How say you, my lord of Warwick?
Warwick.   Nay, do your pleasures; I know how 'twill prove.
Pembroke.   Then give him me.
Gaveston.   Sweet sovereign, yet I come
To see thee ere I die.
Warwick.   Yet not perhaps,   95
If Warwick's wit and policy prevail.   [*Aside.*]
Mortimer Junior.   My lord of Pembroke, we deliver him you;
Return him on your honor. Sound, away!
            Exeunt [all except] Pembroke, [Arundel,] Gaveston,
                 [James, and other Attendants of Pembroke].
Pembroke.   My lord, you shall go with me.
My house is not far hence, out of the way   100
A little, but our men shall go along.
We that have pretty wenches to our wives,
Sir, must not come so near and balk their lips.
Arundel.   'Tis very kindly spoke, my lord of Pembroke.
Your honor hath an adamant of power   105
To draw a prince.
Pembroke.   So, my lord. Come hither, James.
I do commit this Gaveston to thee.
Be thou this night his keeper; in the morning
We will discharge thee of thy charge. Be gone.
Gaveston.   Unhappy Gaveston, whither goest thou now?   110
                  Exit [Pembroke with Attendants].
Horse-boy.   My lord, we'll quickly be at Cobham.
                                    Exeunt.

                                                    III,i.
    Enter Gaveston mourning, [James, and others of] the Earl of
                    Pembroke's Men.

105 *adamant* magnet.

Gaveston.   O treacherous Warwick, thus to wrong thy friend.
James.   I see it is your life these arms pursue.
Gaveston.   Weaponless must I fall, and die in bands?
 O, must this day be period of my life?
 Center of all my bliss! And ye be men,   5
 Speed to the king.
    Enter Warwick and his company [of Soldiers].
Warwick.   My lord of Pembroke's men,
 Strive you no longer; I will have that Gaveston.
James.   Your lordship doth dishonor to yourself,
 And wrong our lord, your honorable friend.
Warwick.   No, James, it is my country's cause I follow.   10
 Go, take the villain; soldiers, come away.
 We'll make quick work. Commend me to your master,
 My friend, and tell him that I watched it well.
 Come, let thy shadow parley with King Edward.
Gaveston.   Treacherous earl, shall I not see the king?   15
Warwick.   The king of heaven perhaps, no other king.
 Away!
    Exeunt Warwick and his Men with Gaveston.
James.   Come, fellows, it booted not for us to strive;
 We will in haste go certify our lord.
            Exeunt.

                 III,ii.
 Enter King Edward and Spencer [Junior, Baldock, and Nobles
  of the King's side, and Soldiers] with drums and fifes.
King Edward.   I long to hear an answer from the barons
 Touching my friend, my dearest Gaveston.
 Ah, Spencer, not the riches of my realm
 Can ransom him; ah, he is marked to die.
 I know the malice of the younger Mortimer.   5
 Warwick I know is rough, and Lancaster
 Inexorable, and I shall never see
 My lovely Pierce, my Gaveston again.
 The barons overbear me with their pride.
Spencer Junior.   Were I King Edward, England's sovereign,   10
 Son to the lovely Eleanor of Spain,

III,i.

3 *bands* bondage.
5 *Center . . . bliss* i.e., the day of his reunion with the king, which was to be the firm center of his happiness, as the middle of the earth was considered to be the center of the universe.
14 *shadow* ghost.
18 *booted not* was of no avail.

Great Edward Longshanks' issue, would I bear
These braves, this rage, and suffer uncontrolled
These barons thus to beard me in my land,
In mine own realm? My lord, pardon my speech.   15
Did you retain your father's magnanimity,
Did you regard the honor of your name,
You would not suffer thus your majesty
Be counterbuffed of your nobility.
Strike off their heads, and let them preach on poles.   20
No doubt, such lessons they will teach the rest,
As by their preachments they will profit much
And learn obedience to their lawful king.
King Edward.   Yea, gentle Spencer, we have been too mild,
Too kind to them; but now have drawn our sword,   25
And if they send me not my Gaveston,
We'll steel it on their crest and poll their tops.
Baldock.   This haught resolve becomes your majesty,
Not to be tied to their affection,
As though your highness were a schoolboy still,   30
And must be awed and governed like a child.
      Enter Spencer Senior with his truncheon and Soldiers.
Spencer Senior.   Long live my sovereign, the noble Edward,
In peace triumphant, fortunate in wars!
King Edward.   Welcome, old man. Com'st thou in Edward's aid?
Then tell thy prince of whence and what thou art.   35
Spencer Senior.   Lo, with a band of bowmen and of pikes,
Brown bills and targeteers, four hundred strong,
Sworn to defend King Edward's royal right,
I come in person to your majesty,
Spencer, the father of Hugh Spencer there,   40
Bound to your highness everlastingly,
For favors done, in him, unto us all.
King Edward.   Thy father, Spencer?
Spencer Junior.   True, and it like **your grace,**
That pours, in lieu of all your goodness shown,
His life, my lord, before your princely feet.   45
King Edward.   Welcome ten thousand times, old man, again.
Spencer, this love, this kindness to thy king,

III,ii.

12 *Edward Longshanks* King Edward I.
13 *braves* insults.
20 *poles* The heads of traitors were placed on poles and exhibited on London bridge.
22 *preachments* sermons.
27 *poll their tops* behead them (as the tops of trees are trimmed).

29 *their affection* what they affect, or desire.
31 *Spencer Senior* Hugh le Despenser, a strong supporter of Edward II, executed at Bristol in 1326.
37 *Brown bills* bronzed halberds.

Argues thy noble mind and disposition.
Spencer, I here create thee Earl of Wiltshire,
And daily will enrich thee with our favor,   50
That as the sunshine shall reflect o'er thee.
Beside, the more to manifest our love,
Because we hear Lord Bruce doth sell his land
And that the Mortimers are in hand withal,
Thou shalt have crowns of us t'outbid the barons.   55
And, Spencer, spare them not, but lay it on.
Soldiers, a largess, and thrice welcome all.
Spencer Junior.   My lord, here comes the queen.
    Enter Queen [Isabella] and her son, [Prince Edward,] and
            Levune, a Frenchman.
King Edward.   Madam, what news?
Queen Isabella.   News of dishonor, lord, and discontent.
Our friend Levune, faithful and full of trust,   60
Informeth us by letters and by words
That Lord Valois our brother, king of France,
Because your highness hath been slack in homage,
Hath seizèd Normandy into his hands.
These be the letters, this the messenger.   65
King Edward.   Welcome, Levune. Tush, Sib, if this be all,
Valois and I will soon be friends again.
But to my Gaveston; shall I never see,
Never behold thee now? Madam, in this matter
We will employ you and your little son;   70
You shall go parley with the king of France.
Boy, see you bear you bravely to the king,
And do your message with a majesty.
Prince Edward.   Commit not to my youth things of more weight
Than fits a prince so young as I to bear,   75
And fear not, lord and father, heaven's great beams
On Atlas' shoulder shall not lie more safe
Than shall your charge committed to my trust.
Queen Isabella.   Ah, boy, this towardness makes thy mother fear
Thou art not marked to many days on earth.   80
King Edward.   Madam, we will that you with speed be shipped,
And this our son; Levune shall follow you
With all the haste we can dispatch him hence.
Choose of our lords to bear you company,
And go in peace; leave us in wars at home.   85
Queen Isabella.   Unnatural wars, where subjects brave their king;

---

49 *Spencer . . . Wiltshire* Young Spencer historically was never Earl of Wiltshire. This is Marlowe's invention.
66 *Sib* wife.

77 *Atlas* the Titan of Greek mythology
condemned by Zeus to bear the heavens
upon his shoulders.

God end them once! My lord, I take my leave
To make my preparation for France.

                    [*Exit with Prince Edward.*]

                Enter Arundel.

King Edward.   What, Lord Arundel, dost thou come alone?
Arundel.   Yea, my good lord, for Gaveston is dead.   90
King Edward.   Ah, traitors! Have they put my friend to death?
   Tell me, Arundel, died he ere thou cam'st,
   Or didst thou see my friend to take his death?
Arundel.   Neither, my lord, for as he was surprised,
   Begirt with weapons and with enemies round,   95
   I did your highness' message to them all,
   Demanding him of them, entreating rather,
   And said, upon the honor of my name,
   That I would undertake to carry him
   Unto your highness and to bring him back.   100
King Edward.   And tell me, would the rebels deny me that?
Spencer Junior.   Proud recreants.
King Edward.   Yea, Spencer, traitors all.
Arundel.   I found them at the first inexorable.
   The Earl of Warwick would not bide the hearing,
   Mortimer hardly; Pembroke and Lancaster   105
   Spake least. And when they flatly had denied,
   Refusing to receive me pledge for him,
   The Earl of Pembroke mildly thus bespake:
   'My lords, because our sovereign sends for him
   And promiseth he shall be safe returned,   110
   I will this undertake, to have him hence
   And see him re-delivered to your hands.'
King Edward.   Well, and how fortunes that he came not?
Spencer Junior.   Some treason or some villainy was cause.
Arundel.   The Earl of Warwick seized him on his way;   115
   For being delivered unto Pembroke's men,
   Their lord rode home thinking his prisoner safe;
   But ere he came, Warwick in ambush lay,
   And bare him to his death, and in a trench
   Strake off his head, and marched unto the camp.   120
Spencer Junior.   A bloody part, flatly against law of arms.
King Edward.   O shall I speak, or shall I sigh and die!
Spencer Junior.   My lord, refer your vengeance to the sword
   Upon these barons; hearten up your men;
   Let them not unrevenged murder your friends.   125
   Advance your standard, Edward, in the field,
   And march to fire them from their starting holes.

120 *Strake* struck.   animals might take refuge from hunters,
127 *starting holes* holes in which wild   usually to be driven out by fire.

King Edward. By earth, the common mother of us all, *He kneels.*
  By heaven, and all the moving orbs thereof,
  By this right hand, and by my father's sword,   130
  And all the honors 'longing to my crown,
  I will have heads and lives for him as many
  As I have manors, castles, towns, and towers.
                                                        [*He rises.*]
  Treacherous Warwick! Traitorous Mortimer!
  If I be England's king, in lakes of gore   135
  Your headless trunks, your bodies will I trail,
  That you may drink your fill, and quaff in blood,
  And stain my royal standard with the same,
  That so my bloody colors may suggest
  Remembrance of revenge immortally   140
  On your accursèd traitorous progeny,
  You villains that have slain my Gaveston!
  And in this place of honor and of trust,
  Spencer, sweet Spencer, I adopt thee here,
  And merely of our love we do create thee   145
  Earl of Gloucester and Lord Chamberlain,
  Despite of times, despite of enemies.
Spencer Junior. My lord, here's a messenger from the barons
  Desires access unto your majesty.
King Edward. Admit him near.   150
        Enter the Herald from the Barons, with his coat of arms.
Herald. Long live King Edward, England's lawful lord.
King Edward. So wish not they, I wis, that sent thee hither.
  Thou com'st from Mortimer and his 'complices;
  A ranker rout of rebels never was.
  Well, say thy message.   155
Herald. The barons up in arms by me salute
  Your highness with long life and happiness,
  And bid me say, as plainer to your grace,
  That if without effusion of blood
  You will this grief have ease and remedy,   160
  That from your princely person you remove
  This Spencer, as a putrifying branch
  That deads the royal vine, whose golden leaves
  Empale your princely head, your diadem,
  Whose brightness such pernicious upstarts dim,   165
  Say they; and lovingly advise your grace
  To cherish virtue and nobility,
  And have old servitors in high esteem,
  And shake off smooth dissembling flatterers.

131 *'longing* belonging.   Spencer did in fact succeed to the title
146 *Earl of Gloucester* Being married to   following the death of his wife's brother.
the Earl of Gloucester's daughter, young   158 *plainer* complainant.

This granted, they, their honors, and their lives,   170
Are to your highness vowed and consecrate.
Spencer Junior.   Ah, traitors, will they still display their pride?
King Edward.   Away, tarry no answer, but be gone.
  Rebels, will they appoint their sovereign
  His sports, his pleasures, and his company?   175
  Yet, ere thou go, see how I do divorce
                              [*He*] *embrace*[*s*] *Spencer.*
  Spencer from me. Now get thee to thy lords,
  And tell them I will come to chastise them
  For murdering Gaveston. Hie thee, get thee gone.
  Edward with fire and sword follows at thy heels.   180
                              [*Exit Herald.*]
  My lord, perceive you how these rebels swell?
  Soldiers, good hearts, defend your sovereign's right,
  For now, even now, we march to make them stoop.
  Away!
                              Exeunt. Alarums, excursions, a great
                              fight, and a retreat [*sounded within*].

III,iii.
      Enter King [*Edward*], *Spencer Senior, Spencer Junior, and the*
                Noblemen of the King's side.
King Edward.   Why do we sound retreat? Upon them, lords!
  This day I shall pour vengeance with my sword
  On those proud rebels that are up in arms
  And do confront and countermand their king.
Spencer Junior.   I doubt it not, my lord, right will prevail.   5
Spencer Senior.   'Tis not amiss, my liege, for either part
  To breathe awhile; our men, with sweat and dust
  All choked well near, begin to faint for heat,
  And this retire refresheth horse and man.
Spencer Junior.   Here come the rebels.   10
        Enter the Barons, Mortimer [*Junior,*] *Lancaster, Warwick,*
                Pembroke and others.
Mortimer Junior.   Look, Lancaster, yonder is Edward
  Among his flatterers.
Lancaster.   And there let him be
  Till he pay dearly for their company.
Warwick.   And shall, or Warwick's sword shall smite in vain.
King Edward.   What, rebels, do you shrink and sound retreat?   15
Mortimer Junior.   No, Edward, no; thy flatterers faint and fly.
Lancaster.   Thou'd best betimes forsake them, and their trains,
  For they'll betray thee, traitors as they are.

Spencer Junior.   Traitor on thy face, rebellious Lancaster!
Pembroke.   Away, base upstart, brav'st thou nobles thus?   20
Spencer Senior.   A noble attempt and honorable deed,
  Is it not, trow ye, to assemble aid
  And levy arms against your lawful king?
King Edward.   For which ere long their heads shall satisfy,
  T'appease the wrath of their offended king.   25
Mortimer Junior.   Then, Edward, thou wilt fight it to the last
  And rather bathe thy sword in subjects' blood
  Than banish that pernicious company.
King Edward.   Ay, traitors all, rather than thus be braved,
  Make England's civil towns huge heaps of stones   30
  And ploughs to go about our palace gates.
Warwick.   A desperate and unnatural resolution.
  Alarum to the fight! St. George for England,
  And the barons' right.
King Edward.   Saint George for England, and King Edward's right.   35
                   [*Alarums. Exeunt the two parties severally.*]

    Enter [King] Edward [and his followers,] with the Barons [and
                   Kent,] captives.

King Edward.   Now, lusty lords, now, not by chance of war,
  But justice of the quarrel and the cause,
  Vailed is your pride. Methinks you hang the heads,
  But we'll advance them, traitors. Now 'tis time
  To be avenged on you for all your braves   40
  And for the murder of my dearest friend,
  To whom right well you knew our soul was knit,
  Good Pierce of Gaveston, my sweet favorite.
  Ah, rebels, recreants, you made him away!
Kent.   Brother, in regard of thee and of thy land,   45
  Did they remove that flatterer from thy throne.
King Edward.   So, sir, you have spoke; away, avoid our presence.
                                                        [*Exit Kent.*]
  Accursèd wretches, was't in regard of us,
  When we had sent our messenger to request
  He might be spared to come to speak with us,   50
  And Pembroke undertook for his return,
  That thou, proud Warwick, watched the prisoner,
  Poor Pierce, and headed him against law of arms?
  For which thy head shall overlook the rest,
  As much as thou in rage outwent'st the rest.   55
Warwick.   Tyrant, I scorn thy threats and menaces;

III,iii.

33 *St. George* an anachronism, since St.
George was not adopted as the patron
saint of England until the reign of
Edward III.
53 *headed* beheaded.

'Tis but temporal that thou canst inflict.
Lancaster.   The worst is death, and better die to live
Than live in infamy under such a king.
King Edward.   Away with them, my lord of Winchester!   60
These lusty leaders, Warwick and Lancaster,
I charge you roundly, off with both their heads!
Away!
Warwick.   Farewell, vain world.
Lancaster.   Sweet Mortimer, farewell.   65
Mortimer Junior.   England, unkind to thy nobility,
Groan for this grief. Behold how thou art maimed.
King Edward.   Go, take that haughty Mortimer to the Tower;
There see him safe bestowed; and for the rest,
Do speedy execution on them all.   70
Be gone!
Mortimer Junior.   What, Mortimer, can raggèd stony walls
Immure thy virtue that aspires to heaven?
No, Edward, England's scourge, it may not be;
Mortimer's hope surmounts his fortune far.   75
                    [*Exit under guard with the other
                                    captive Barons.*]
King Edward.   Sound, drums and trumpets! March with me, my friends.
Edward this day hath crowned him king anew.
                    Exit [*with all except*] *Spencer Junior,
                                    Levune and Baldock.*
Spencer Junior.   Levune, the trust that we repose in thee
Begets the quiet of King Edward's land.
Therefore be gone in haste, and with advice   80
Bestow that treasure on the lords of France,
That, therewith all enchanted, like the guard
That suffered Jove to pass in showers of gold
To Danaë, all aid may be denied
To Isabel the queen, that now in France   85
Makes friends, to cross the seas with her young son
And step into his father's regiment.
Levune.   That's it these barons and the subtle queen
Long leveled at.
Baldock.   Yea, but, Levune, thou seest
These barons lay their heads on blocks together;
What they intend, the hangman frustrates clean.   90
Levune.   Have you no doubts, my lords, I'll clap so close
Among the lords of France with England's gold,
That Isabel shall make her plaints in vain,

---

57 *temporal . . . inflict* i.e., you can
only harm my body (not my soul).
83–84 *Jove . . . Danaë* See note at II,
ii,53.

87 *regiment* royal authority.
89 *levelled* aimed.
92 *clap so close* work so secretly.

And France shall be obdurate with her tears.   95
Spencer Junior.   Then make for France amain. Levune, away.
  Proclaim King Edward's wars and victories.

                                            Exeunt.

Kent.   Fair blows the wind for France. Blow, gentle gale,
  Till Edmund be arrived for England's good.
  Nature, yield to my country's cause in this.
  A brother, no, a butcher of thy friends,
  Proud Edward, dost thou banish me thy presence?   5
  But I'll to France and cheer the wrongèd queen,
  And certify what Edward's looseness is.
  Unnatural king, to slaughter noblemen
  And cherish flatterers. Mortimer, I stay
  Thy sweet escape. Stand gracious, gloomy night,   10
  To his device.
          Enter Mortimer [Junior,] disguised.
Mortimer Junior.   Holla! Who walketh there?
  Is't you, my lord?
Kent.   Mortimer, 'tis I;
  But hath thy potion wrought so happily?
Mortimer Junior.   It hath, my lord; the warders all asleep,
  I thank them, gave me leave to pass in peace.   15
  But hath your grace got shipping unto France?
Kent.   Fear it not.

                                            Exeunt.

        Enter Queen [Isabella] and her son, [Prince Edward].   IV,ii.
Queen Isabella.   Ah, boy, our friends do fail us all in France.
  The lords are cruel and the king unkind.
  What shall we do?
Prince Edward.   Madam, return to England
  And please my father well, and then a fig
  For all my uncle's friendship here in France.   5
  I warrant you, I'll win his highness quickly;
  'A loves me better than a thousand Spencers.
Queen Isabella.   Ah, boy, thou art deceived, at least in this,
  To think that we can yet be tuned together.
  No, no, we jar too far. Unkind Valois,   10
  Unhappy Isabel, when France rejects,

Whither, oh, whither dost thou bend thy steps?
                    Enter Sir John of Hainault.
Sir John.   Madam, what cheer?
Queen Isabella.   Ah, good Sir John of Hainault,
    Never so cheerless, nor so far distressed.
Sir John.   I hear, sweet lady, of the king's unkindness,   15
    But droop not, madam; noble minds contemn
    Despair. Will your grace with me to Hainault,
    And there stay time's advantage with your son?
    How say you, my lord, will you go with your friends,
    And share of all our fortunes equally?   20
Prince Edward.   So pleaseth the queen, my mother, me it likes.
    The king of England, nor the court of France,
    Shall have me from my gracious mother's side,
    Till I be strong enough to break a staff;
    And then have at the proudest Spencer's head.   25
Sir John.   Well said, my lord.
Queen Isabella.   O, my sweet heart, how do I moan thy wrongs,
    Yet triumph in the hope of thee, my joy.
    Ah, sweet Sir John, even to the utmost verge
    Of Europe or the shore of Tanais,   30
    Will we with thee to Hainault, so we will.
    The marquis is a noble gentleman;
    His grace, I dare presume, will welcome me.
    But who are these?
                    Enter Kent and Mortimer [Junior].
Kent.   Madam, long may you live,
    Much happier than your friends in England do.   35
Queen Isabella.   Lord Edmund and Lord Mortimer alive!
    Welcome to France. The news was here, my lord,
    That you were dead or very near your death.
Mortimer Junior.   Lady, the last was truest of the twain,
    But Mortimer, reserved for better hap,   40
    Hath shaken off the thraldom of the Tower
    And lives t'advance your standard, good my lord.
Prince Edward.   How mean you, and the king, my father, lives?
    No, my Lord Mortimer, I, I trow.
Queen Isabella.   Not, son! Why not? I would it were no worse.   45
    But, gentle lords, friendless we are in France.
Mortimer Junior.   Monsieur le Grand, a noble friend of yours,
    Told us, at our arrival, all the news—
    How hard the nobles, how unkind the king

IV,ii.

12, SD *Sir John of Hainault* uncle of the Princess Philippa, who was to be the wife of King Edward III.

16 *contemn* hold in contempt.

30 *Tanais* the river Don, regarded by Elizabethans as dividing Europe from Asia.

43 *and* if.

Hath showed himself. But, madam, right makes room   50
Where weapons want; and though a many friends
Are made away, as Warwick, Lancaster,
And others of our party and faction,
Yet have we friends, assure your grace, in England
Would cast up caps and clap their hands for joy,   55
To see us there appointed for our foes.
Kent. Would all were well and Edward well reclaimed,
For England's honor, peace, and quietness.
Mortimer Junior. But by the sword, my lord, it must be deserved;
The king will ne'er forsake his flatterers.   60
Sir John. My lords of England, sith the ungentle king
Of France refuseth to give aid of arms
To this distressèd queen his sister here,
Go you with her to Hainault. Doubt ye not
We will find comfort, money, men and friends   65
Ere long, to bid the English king a base.
How say, young prince, what think you of the match?
Prince Edward. I think King Edward will outrun us all.
Queen Isabella. Nay, son, not so; and you must not discourage
Your friends that are so forward in your aid.   70
Kent. Sir John of Hainault, pardon us, I pray;
These comforts that you give our woeful queen
Bind us in kindness all at your command.
Queen Isabella. Yea, gentle brother, and the God of heaven
Prosper your happy motion, good Sir John.   75
Mortimer Junior. This noble gentleman, forward in arms,
Was born, I see, to be our anchor-hold.
Sir John of Hainault, be it thy renown,
That England's queen and nobles in distress
Have been by thee restored and comforted.   80
Sir John. Madam, along, and you, my lord, with me,
That England's peers may Hainault's welcome see.

                                             [*Exeunt.*]

IV,iii.

Enter King [Edward], Arundel, the two Spencers, with Others.
King Edward. Thus after many threats of wrathful war,
Triumpheth England's Edward with his friends;

51 *a many* many (a common Elizabethan usage).
56 *appointed for* ready for battle with.
66 *bid . . . base* i.e., challenge the English king. Prisoner's base was a boys'
game in which a runner was chased from
base to base by another player. To 'bid
a base' is to challenge a player to a run.
67 *match* i.e., the game of prisoner's
base.

And triumph, Edward, with his friends uncontrolled.
My lord of Gloucester, do you hear the news?
Spencer Junior. What news, my lord? 5
King Edward. Why, man, they say there is great execution
Done through the realm. My lord of Arundel,
You have the note, have you not?
Arundel. From the lieutenant of the Tower, my lord.
King Edward. I pray let us see it. [*He takes the note.*] What have we
there? 10
Read it, Spencer. [*He hands it to*] Spencer [*Junior, who*]
reads their names.
Why so; they barked apace a month ago.
Now, on my life, they'll neither bark nor bite.
Now, sirs the news from France? Gloucester, I trow
The lords of France love England's gold so well 15
As Isabel gets no aid from thence.
What now remains? Have you proclaimed, my lord,
Reward for them can bring in Mortimer?
Spencer Junior. My lord, we have; and if he be in England,
'A will be had ere long, I doubt it not. 20
King Edward. If, dost thou say? Spencer, as true as death,
He is in England's ground; our portmasters
Are not so careless of their king's command.
Enter a Messenger.
How now, what news with thee? From whence come these?
Messenger. Letters, my lord, and tidings forth of France; 25
To you, my lord of Gloucester, from Levune.
[*He gives letters to Spencer Junior.*]
King Edward. Read.
Spencer Junior. [*reads*] My duty to your honor premised, &c. I have,
according to instructions in that behalf, dealt with the king of France
his lords, and effected that the queen, all discontented and dis- [30
comforted, is gone; whither, if you ask, with Sir John of Hainault,
brother to the marquis, into Flanders. With them are gone Lord Ed-
mund and the Lord Mortimer, having in their company divers of
your nation, and others; and as constant report goeth, they intend to
give King Edward battle in England sooner than he can look for [35
them. This is all the news of import.
Your honor's in all service, Levune.
King Edward. Ah, villains, hath that Mortimer escaped?
With him is Edmund gone associate?
And will Sir John of Hainault lead the round? 40
Welcome, a God's name, madam, and your son;

IV,iii.
12 *barked* embarked. 40 *round* dance.

England shall welcome you and all your rout.
Gallop apace, bright Phœbus, through the sky,
And dusky night, in rusty iron car,
Between you both shorten the time, I pray,   45
That I may see that most desirèd day
When we may meet these traitors in the field.
Ah, nothing grieves me but my little boy
Is thus misled to countenance their ills.
Come, friends, to Bristow, there to make us strong;   50
And, winds, as equal be to bring them in,
As you injurious were to bear them forth.

                                        [*Exeunt.*]

                                                        IV,iv.
Enter Queen [Isabella,] her son, [Prince Edward,] Kent, Morti-
mer Junior, and Sir John [of Hainault].
Queen Isabella.   Now, lords, our loving friends and countrymen,
Welcome to England all, with prosperous winds.
Our kindest friends in Belgia have we left,
To cope with friends at home; a heavy case
When force to force is knit, and sword and glaive   5
In civil broils makes kin and countrymen
Slaughter themselves in others, and their sides
With their own weapons gored. But what's the help?
Misgoverned kings are cause of all this wrack;
And, Edward, thou art one among them all   10
Whose looseness hath betrayed thy land to spoil
And made the channels overflow with blood.
Of thine own people patron shouldst thou be,
But thou—
Mortimer Junior.   Nay, madam, if you be a warrior,   15
You must not grow so passionate in speeches.
Lords, sith that we are by sufferance of heaven
Arrived and armèd in this prince's right,
Here for our country's cause swear we to him
All homage, fealty, and forwardness;   20
And for the open wrongs and injuries
Edward hath done to us, his queen and land,

43 *Phœbus* the sun god (Apollo) who
drove the chariot of the sun across the
sky.

IV,iv.
3 *Belgia* the Netherlands.

4 *cope* fight.
5 *glaive* lance.
9 *wrack* disaster.
12 *channels* street gutters through
which sewage flowed.

We come in arms to wreck it with the swords,
That England's queen in peace may repossess
Her dignities and honors; and withal   25
We may remove these flatterers from the king,
That havocs England's wealth and treasury.
Sir John.   Sound trumpets, my lord, and forward let us march.
Edward will think we come to flatter him.
Kent.   I would he never had been flattered more.   30

[*Exeunt.*]

IV,v.

*Enter King [Edward,] Baldock, and Spencer Junior, flying
about the stage.*
Spencer Junior.   Fly, fly, my lord, the queen is over-strong;
Her friends do multiply, and yours do fail.
Shape we our course to Ireland, there to breathe.
King Edward.   What, was I born to fly and run away,
And leave the Mortimers conquerors behind?   5
Give me my horse, and let's r'enforce our troops,
And in this bed of honor die with fame.
Baldock.   O no, my lord, this princely resolution
Fits not the time; away, we are pursued.

[*Exeunt.*]

[*Enter*] *Kent alone, with a sword and target.*
Kent.   This way he fled, but I am come too late.   10
Edward, alas, my heart relents for thee.
Proud traitor, Mortimer, why dost thou chase
Thy lawful king, thy sovereign, with thy sword?
Vile wretch, and why hast thou, of all unkind,
Borne arms against thy brother and thy king?   15
Rain showers of vengeance on my cursèd head,
Thou God, to whom in justice it belongs
To punish this unnatural revolt.
Edward, this Mortimer aims at thy life.
O fly him, then! But, Edmund, calm this rage;   20
Dissemble, or thou diest, for Mortimer
And Isabel do kiss while they conspire;
And yet she bears a face of love forsooth.
Fie on that love that hatcheth death and hate.
Edmund, away. Bristow to Longshanks' blood   25
Is false; be not found single for suspect.

IV,v.
23 *wreck it* cause destruction.   14 *unkind* contrary to nature.
27 *havocs* causes havoc with.   25 *Longshanks* See note at III,ii,12.

Proud Mortimer pries near into thy walks.
> *Enter Queen [Isabella], Mortimer [Junior], the young Prince*
> *[Edward], and Sir John of Hainault.*

Queen Isabella.   Successful battles gives the God of kings
  To them that fight in right and fear His wrath.
  Since then successfully we have prevailed,   30
  Thanks be heaven's great architect, and you.
  Ere farther we proceed, my noble lords,
  We here create our well-belovèd son,
  Of love and care unto his royal person,
  Lord Warden of the realm, and sith the fates   35
  Have made his father so unfortunate,
  Deal you, my lords, in this, my loving lords,
  As to your wisdoms fittest seems in all.
Kent.   Madam, without offence, if I may ask,
  How will you deal with Edward in his fall?   40
Prince Edward.   Tell me, good uncle, what Edward do you mean?
Kent.   Nephew, your father; I dare not call him king.
Mortimer Junior.   My lord of Kent, what needs these questions?
  'Tis not in her controlment, nor in ours,
  But as the realm and parliament shall please,   45
  So shall your brother be disposèd of.
  I like not this relenting mood in Edmund.
  Madam, 'tis good to look to him betimes.
>   *[Aside to Queen Isabella.]*
Queen Isabella.   My lord, the Mayor of Bristow knows our mind.
Mortimer Junior.   Yea, madam, and they scape not easily   50
  That fled the field.
Queen Isabella.   Baldock is with the king.
  A goodly chancellor, is he not my lord?
Sir John.   So are the Spencers, the father and the son.
Kent.   This, Edward, is the ruin of the realm.
> *Enter Rice ap Howell and the Mayor of Bristow, with Spencer*
> *Senior, [prisoner, and Attendants].*

Rice.   God save Queen Isabel and her princely son.   55
  Madam, the mayor and citizens of Bristow,
  In sign of love and duty to this presence,
  Present by me this traitor to the state,
  Spencer, the father to that wanton Spencer,
  That, like the lawless Catiline of Rome,   60
  Revelled in England's wealth and treasury.
Queen Isabella.   We thank you all.

---

44 *controlment* power.

54 SD *Rice ap Howell* a partisan of the barons, commissioned by Queen Isabella to stir up opposition to King Edward in Wales and to capture him if possible.

60 *Catiline* Lucius Sergius Catilina, a Roman noble whose famous conspiracy was defeated largely through the efforts of Cicero.

Mortimer Junior.   Your loving care in this
    Deserveth princely favors and rewards.
    But where's the king and the other Spencer fled?
Rice.   Spencer the son, created Earl of Gloucester,   65
    Is with that smooth-tongued scholar Baldock gone
    And shipped but late for Ireland with the king.
Mortimer Junior.   Some whirlwind fetch them back or sink them all.
                                          [Aside.]
    They shall be started thence, I doubt it not.
Prince Edward.   Shall I not see the king my father yet?   70
Kent.   Unhappy is Edward, chased from England's bounds.
                                          [Aside.]
Sir John.   Madam, what resteth? Why stand ye in a muse?
Queen Isabella.   I rue my lord's ill-fortune; but alas,
    Care of my country called me to this war.
Mortimer Junior.   Madam, have done with care and sad complaint;   75
    Your king hath wronged your country and himself,
    And we must seek to right it as we may.
    Meanwhile, have hence this rebel to the block.
    Your lordship cannot privilege your head.
Spencer Senior.   Rebel is he that fights against his prince;   80
    So fought not they that fought in Edward's right.
Mortimer Junior.   Take him away; he prates.
                  [Exeunt Attendants with Spencer Senior.]
                          You, Rice ap Howell,
    Shall do good service to her majesty,
    Being of countenance in your country here,
    To follow these rebellious runagates.   85
    We in meanwhile, madam, must take advice,
    How Baldock, Spencer, and their 'complices,
    May in their fall be followed to their end.
                                Exeunt.

IV,vi.

   Enter the Abbot, Monks, [King] Edward, Spencer [Junior,]
       and Baldock, [the three latter disguised].
Abbot.   Have you no doubt, my lord; have you no fear;
    As silent and as careful will we be
    To keep your royal person safe with us,
    Free from suspect, and fell invasion
    Of such as have your majesty in chase,   5
    Yourself, and those your chosen company,

69 *started* driven from hiding (a   84 *countenance* authority.
hunting term).   85 *runagates* runaways.

As danger of this stormy time requires.
King Edward.   Father, thy face should harbor no deceit.
O, hadst thou ever been a king, thy heart,
Piercèd deeply with sense of my distress,   10
Could not but take compassion of my state.
Stately and proud, in riches and in train,
Whilom I was powerful and full of pomp;
But what is he whom rule and empery
Have not in life or death made miserable?   15
Come, Spencer; come, Baldock, come, sit down by me;
Make trial now of that philosophy
That in our famous nurseries of arts
Thou sucked'st from Plato and from Aristotle.
Father, this life contemplative is heaven.   20
O that I might this life in quiet lead.
But we, alas, are chased, and you, my friends,
Your lives and my dishonor they pursue.
Yet, gentle monks, for treasure, gold nor fee,
Do you betray us and our company.   25
Monks.   Your grace may sit secure, if none but we
Do wot of your abode.
Spencer Junior.   Not one alive, but shrewdly I suspect
A gloomy fellow in a mead below.
'A gave a long look after us, my lord,   30
And all the land I know is up in arms,
Arms that pursue our lives with deadly hate.
Baldock.   We were embarked for Ireland, wretched we,
With awkward winds and sore tempests driven
To fall on shore, and here to pine in fear   35
Of Mortimer and his confederates.
King Edward.   Mortimer! Who talks of Mortimer?
Who wounds me with the name of Mortimer,
That bloody man? Good father. on thy lap
Lay I this head, laden with mickle care.   40
O might I never open these eyes again,
Never again lift up this drooping head,
O never more lift up this dying heart!
Spencer Junior.   Look up, my lord. Baldock, this drowsiness
Betides no good; here even we are betrayed.   45
     *Enter, with Welsh hooks, Rice ap Howell, a Mower, and the
                    Earl of Leicester.*
Mower.   Upon my life, those be the men ye seek.

IV,vi.

40 *mickle* much.
45, SD *Leicester* Henry, Earl of Leicester, younger brother to Thomas, Earl of Lancaster and, like his brother,

a foe of Edward and the Spencers. *Welsh hooks* partisans, with cross pieces below their blades.

Rice.   Fellow, enough. My lord, I pray be short;
   A fair commission warrants what we do.
Leicester.   The queen's commission, urged by Mortimer.
   What cannot gallant Mortimer with the queen?   50
   Alas, see where he sits, and hopes unseen
   T'escape their hands that seek to reave his life.
   Too true it is, *Quem dies vidit veniens superbum,*
   Hunc dies vidit fugiens jacentem.
   But, Leicester, leave to grow so passionate.   55
   Spencer and Baldock, by no other names,
   I arrest you of high treason here.
   Stand not on titles, but obey th'arrest;
   'Tis in the name of Isabel the queen.
   My lord, why droop you thus?   60
King Edward.   O day! The last of all my bliss on earth,
   Center of all misfortune! O my stars,
   Why do you lour unkindly on a king?
   Comes Leicester, then, in Isabella's name
   To take my life, my company from me?   65
   Here, man, rip up this panting breast of mine,
   And take my heart in rescue of my friends.
Rice.   Away with them.
Spencer Junior.   It may become thee yet
   To let us take our farewell of his grace.
Abbot.   My heart with pity earns to see this sight,   70
·   A king to bear these words and proud commands.
King Edward.   Spencer, ah, sweet Spencer, thus then must we part.
Spencer Junior.   We must, my lord, so will the angry heavens.
King Edward.   Nay, so will hell and cruel Mortimer;
   The gentle heavens have not to do in this.   75
Baldock.   My lord, it is in vain to grieve or storm.
   Here humbly of your grace we take our leaves.
   Our lots are cast; I fear me, so is thine.
King Edward.   In heaven we may, in earth never shall we meet.
   And, Leicester, say, what shall become of us?   80
Leicester.   Your majesty must go to Killingworth.
King Edward.   Must! 'Tis somewhat hard, when kings must go.
Leicester.   Here is a litter ready for your grace,
   That waits your pleasure, and the day grows old.
Rice.   As good be gone as stay and be benighted.   85
King Edward.   A litter hast thou? Lay me in a hearse,
   And to the gates of hell convey me hence.
   Let Pluto's bells ring out my fatal knell

53–54 *Quem . . . jacentem* Whom the coming day (dawn) saw in his pride, the departing day (evening) saw cast down. (The lines are from Seneca's *Thyestes.*)

70 *earns* grieves.
81 *Killingworth* Kenilworth castle.
88 *Pluto* Greek god of the underworld.

And hags howl for my death at Charon's shore,
For friends hath Edward none but these and these,   90
And these must die under a tyrant's sword.
Rice. My lord, be going; care not for these,
For we shall see them shorter by the heads.
King Edward. Well, that shall be, shall be. Part we must.
Sweet Spencer, gentle Baldock, part we must.   95
Hence feignèd weeds! Unfeignèd are my woes.
                              [*He throws off his disguise.*]
Father, farewell. Leicester, thou stay'st for me,
And go I must. Life, farewell, with my friends.
                              Exeunt King Edward and Leicester.
Spencer Junior. O, is he gone? Is noble Edward gone,
Parted from hence, never to see us more?   100
Rent, sphere of heaven, and, fire, forsake thy orb!
Earth, melt to air! Gone is my sovereign,
Gone, gone, alas, never to make return.
Baldock. Spencer, I see our souls are fleeted hence;
We are deprived the sunshine of our life.   105
Make for a new life, man; throw up thy eyes
And heart and hand to heaven's immortal throne;
Pay nature's debt with cheerful countenance.
Reduce we all our lessons unto this,
To die, sweet Spencer, therefore live we all;   110
Spencer, all live to die, and rise to fall.
Rice. Come, come, keep these preachments till you come to the place
appointed. You, and such as you are, have made wise work in Eng-
land. Will your lordships away?
Mower. Your worship, I trust, will remember me?   115
Rice. Remember thee, fellow? What else? Follow me to the town.
                              [*Exeunt.*]

✳

                                                                 V,i.
*Enter King [Edward], Leicester, [the] Bishop [of Winchester,
                        and Trussel].*
Leicester. Be patient, good my lord, cease to lament.
Imagine Killingworth Castle were your court
And that you lay for pleasure here a space,
Not of compulsion or necessity.
King Edward. Leicester, if gentle words might comfort me,   5
Thy speeches long ago had eased my sorrows,
For kind and loving hast thou always been.

89 *Charon* boatman who conveyed de-   96 *weeds* clothes.
parted spirits across the river Styx.   101 *Rent* rend.

The griefs of private men are soon allayed,
But not of kings. The forest deer, being struck,
Runs to an herb that closeth up the wounds,   10
But when the imperial lion's flesh is gored,
He rends and tears it with his wrathful paw,
And highly scorning that the lowly earth
Should drink his blood, mounts up into the air.
And so it fares with me, whose dauntless mind   15
The ambitious Mortimer would seek to curb,
And that unnatural queen, false Isabel,
That thus hath pent and mewed me in a prison;
For such outrageous passions cloy my soul,
As with the wings of rancor and disdain   20
Full often am I soaring up to heaven,
To plain me to the gods against them both.
But when I call to mind I am a king,
Methinks I should revenge me of the wrongs
That Mortimer and Isabel have done.   25
But what are kings when regiment is gone,
But perfect shadows in a sunshine day?
My nobles rule, I bear the name of king;
I wear the crown, but am controlled by them,
By Mortimer and my unconstant queen,   30
Who spots my nuptial bed with infamy,
Whilst I am lodged within this cave of care,
Where sorrow at my elbow still attends,
To company my heart with sad laments,
That bleeds within me for this strange exchange.   35
But tell me, must I now resign my crown,
To make usurping Mortimer a king?
Winchester.   Your grace mistakes; it is for England's good
And princely Edward's right we crave the crown.
King Edward.   No, 'tis for Mortimer, not Edward's head;   40
For he's a lamb, encompassèd by wolves,
Which in a moment will abridge his life.
But if proud Mortimer do wear this crown,
Heavens turn it to a blaze of quenchless fire;
Or like the snaky wreath of Tisiphon,   45
Engirt the temples of his hateful head;

V,i.

10 *herb* dittany, or Dictanum, supposed according to legend to possess heal-
ing powers known to wild animals by
instinct.

14 *mounts . . . air* i.e., the lion.

22 *plain me* complain.

26 *regiment* rule, authority.

44 *blaze . . . fire* i.e., like the crown
which Medea gave to Creusa, for whom
Jason had deserted her. When Creusa
placed it upon her head, it burst into
flames, and although the metal melted
it could not be removed.

45 *Tisiphon* See note to *Dido,* II,i,230.

So shall not England's vine be perishèd,
But Edward's name survives, though Edward dies.
Leicester.   My lord, why waste you thus the time away?
They stay your answer; will you yield your crown?   50
King Edward.   Ah, Leicester, weigh how hardly I can brook
To lose my crown and kingdom without cause,
To give ambitious Mortimer my right,
That like a mountain overwhelms my bliss,
In which extreme my mind here murdered is.   55
But what the heavens appoint, I must obey.
Here, take my crown; the life of Edward too:
                           [*He takes off the crown.*]
Two kings in England cannot reign at once.
But stay awhile; let me be king till night,
That I may gaze upon this glittering crown;   60
So shall my eyes receive their last content,
My head, the latest honor due to it,
And jointly both yield up their wishèd right.
Continue ever thou celestial sun;·
Let never silent night possess this clime.   65
Stand still you watches of the element;
All times and seasons, rest you at a stay,
That Edward may be still fair England's king.
But day's bright beams doth vanish fast away,
And needs I must resign my wishèd crown.   70
Inhuman creatures, nursed with tiger's milk,
Why gape you for your sovereign's overthrow?
My diadem I mean, and guiltless life.
See, monsters, see, I'll wear my crown again.
                           [*He puts on the crown.*]
What, fear you not the fury of your king?   75
But, hapless Edward, thou art fondly led;
They pass not for thy frowns as late they did,
But seeks to make a new-elected king;
Which fills my mind with strange despairing thoughts,
Which thoughts are martyrèd with endless torments,   80
And in this torment comfort find I none,
But that I feel the crown upon my head,
And therefore let me wear it yet awhile.
Trussel.   My lord, the parliament must have present news,
And therefore say, will you resign or no?   85
                           The King rageth.
King Edward.   I'll not resign, but whilst I live—
Traitors, be gone, and join you with Mortimer!
Elect, conspire, install, do what you will;

47 *England's vine* the symbolic vine   66 *element* sky.
on the English crown.   77 *pass* care.

Their blood and yours shall seal these treacheries.
Winchester.   This answer we'll return, and so farewell.   90
Leicester.   Call them again, my lord, and speak them fair,
  For if they go, the prince shall lose his right.
King Edward. . . Call thou them back; I have no power to speak.
Leicester.   My lord, the king is willing to resign.
Winchester.   If he be not, let him choose.   95
King Edward.   O would I might, but heavens and earth conspire
  To make me miserable. Here receive my crown.
  Receive it? No, these innocent hands of mine
  Shall not be guilty of so foul a crime.
  He of you all that most desires my blood   100
  And will be called the murderer of a king,
  Take it. What, are you moved? Pity you me?
  Then send for unrelenting Mortimer
  And Isabel, whose eyes, being turned to steel,
  Will sooner sparkle fire than shed a tear.   105
  Yet stay, for rather than I will look on them,
  Here, here!   [*He gives the crown.*]
               Now, sweet God of heaven,
  Make me despise this transitory pomp
  And sit for aye enthronizèd in heaven.
  Come, death, and with thy fingers close my eyes,   110
  Or if I live, let me forget myself.
Winchester.   My lord—
King Edward.   Call me not lord! Away—out of my sight!
  Ah, pardon me; grief makes me lunatic.
  Let not that Mortimer protect my son;   115
  More safety is there in a tiger's jaws
  Than his embracements. Bear this to the queen,
  Wet with my tears, and dried again with sighs.
                              [*He gives a handkerchief.*]
  If with the sight thereof she be not moved,
  Return it back and dip it in my blood.   120
  Commend me to my son, and bid him rule
  Better than I. Yet how have I transgressed,
  Unless it be with too much clemency?
Trussel.   And thus most humbly do we take our leave.
                         [*Exeunt the Bishop of Winchester and Trussel
                                             with the crown.*]
King Edward.   Farewell; I know the next news that they bring   125
  Will be my death, and welcome shall it be.
  To wretched men death is felicity.
                    [*Enter Berkeley, who gives a paper to Leicester.*]

127, SD *Berkeley* Sir Thomas Berkeley,   support of Lancaster. Berkeley castle
who had been deprived of his inheritance   was restored to him by Queen Isabella
by Spencer Junior because of his father's   after she had captured it.

Leicester.   Another post. What news brings he?
King Edward.   Such news as I expect. Come, Berkeley, come,
    And tell thy message to my naked breast.   130
Berkeley.   My lord, think not a thought so villainous
    Can harbor in a man of noble birth.
    To do your highness service and devoir
    And save you from your foes, Berkeley would die.
Leicester.   My lord, the council of the queen commands   135
    That I resign my charge.
King Edward.   And who must keep me now? Must you, my lord?
Berkeley.   Ay, my most gracious lord, so 'tis decreed.
King Edward. [*taking the paper*]   By Mortimer, whose name is written
        here.
    Well may I rent his name that rends my heart!   140
                                      [*He tears the paper.*]
    This poor revenge hath something eased my mind.
    So may his limbs be torn as is this paper.
    Hear me, immortal Jove, and grant it too.
Berkeley.   Your grace must hence with me to Berkeley straight.
King Edward.   Whither you will; all places are alike,   145
    And every earth is fit for burial.
Leicester.   Favor him, my lord, as much as lieth in you.
Berkeley.   Even so betide my soul as I use him.
King Edward.   Mine enemy hath pitied my estate,
    And that's the cause that I am now removed.   150
Berkeley.   And thinks your grace that Berkeley will be cruel?
King Edward.   I know not; but of this am I assured,
    That death ends all, and I can die but once.
    Leicester, farewell.
Leicester.   Not yet, my lord; I'll bear you on your way.   155
                                      Exeunt.

                Enter Mortimer [*Junior*] *and Queen Isabella.*   V,ii.
Mortimer Junior.   Fair Isabel, now have we our desire;
    The proud corrupters of the light-brained king
    Have done their homage to the lofty gallows,
    And he himself lies in captivity.
    Be ruled by me, and we will rule the realm.   5
    In any case take heed of childish fear,
    For now we hold an old wolf by the ears,

V,ii.

140 *rent* rend.   7 *an old wolf by the ears* a popular
144 *Berkeley* Berkeley castle in Glouces-   proverb.
tershire.

That, if he slip, will seize upon us both,
And gripe the sorer, being griped himself.
Think therefore, madam, that imports us much   10
To erect your son with all the speed we may,
And that I be protector over him,
For our behoof will bear the greater sway
Whenas a king's name shall be under writ.
Queen Isabella.   Sweet Mortimer, the life of Isabel,   15
   Be thou persuaded that I love thee well,
   And therefore, so the prince my son be safe,
   Whom I esteem as dear as these mine eyes,
   Conclude against his father what thou wilt,
   And I myself will willingly subscribe.   20
Mortimer Junior.   First would I hear news that he were deposed,
   And then let me alone to handle him.
                         Enter Messenger.
   Letters! From whence?
Messenger.   From Killingworth, my lord.
Queen Isabella.   How fares my lord the king?
Messenger.   In health, madam, but full of pensiveness.   25
Queen Isabella.   Alas, poor soul, would I could ease his grief.
         [*Enter the Bishop of Winchester with the crown.*]
   Thanks, gentle Winchester. Sirrah, be gone.
                                        [*Exit Messenger.*]
Winchester.   The king hath willingly resigned his crown.
Queen Isabella.   O happy news! Send for the prince, my son.
Winchester.   Further, ere this letter was sealed, Lord Berkeley came,   30
   So that he now is gone from Killingworth;
   And we have heard that Edmund laid a plot
   To set his brother free; no more but so.
   The lord of Berkeley is so pitiful
   As Leicester that had charge of him before.   35
Queen Isabella.   Then let some other be his guardian.
Mortimer Junior.   Let me alone, here is the privy seal.
                         [*Exit the Bishop of Winchester.*]
   Who's there? Call hither Gurney and Matrevis.
                              [*To Attendants within.*]
   To dash the heavy-headed Edmund's drift,
   Berkeley shall be discharged, the king removed,   40
   And none but we shall know where he lieth.
Queen Isabella.   But, Mortimer, as long as he survives,
   What safety rest for us or for my son?

11 *erect* establish on the throne.
34 *pitiful* full of pity, easily moved.
38 *Gurney and Matrevis* Thomas Gour-
nay fled the country after King Edward's
murder, was captured at Marseilles, and
died mysteriously on his way back to
England; he was probably murdered to
prevent his revealing his accomplices. Sir
John Maltravers was Edward's jailor.
39 *dash* ruin. *drift* design or plot.

Mortimer Junior.   Speak, shall he presently be dispatched and die?
Queen Isabella.   I would he were, so it were not by my means.   45
                              Enter Matrevis and Gurney.
Mortimer Junior.   Enough.
     Matrevis, write a letter presently
     Unto the lord of Berkeley from ourself
     That he resign the king to thee and Gurney,
     And when 'tis done we will subscribe our name.   50
Matrevis.   It shall be done, my lord.   [*He writes.*]
Mortimer Junior.   Gurney.
Gurney.   My lord.
Mortimer Junior.   As thou intendest to rise by Mortimer,
     Who now makes Fortune's wheel turn as he please,
     Seek all the means thou canst to make him droop,
     And neither give him kind word nor good look.   55
Gurney.   I warrant you, my lord.
Mortimer Junior.   And this above the rest: because we hear
     That Edmund casts to work his liberty,
     Remove him still from place to place by night,
     Till at the last he come to Killingworth,   60
     And then from thence to Berkeley back again.
     And by the way, to make him fret the more,
     Speak curstly to him; and in any case
     Let no man comfort him if he chance to weep,
     But amplify his grief with bitter words.   65
Matrevis.   Fear not, my lord, we'll do as you command.
Mortimer Junior.   So now away; post thitherwards amain.
Queen Isabella.   Whither goes this letter? To my lord the king?
     Commend me humbly to his majesty,
     And tell him that I labor all in vain   70
     To ease his grief and work his liberty,
     And bear him this as witness of my love.
                                        [*She gives a ring.*]
Matrevis.   I will, madam.
                              Exeunt Matrevis and Gurney.
Mortimer Junior.   Finely dissembled. Do so still, sweet queen.
     Here comes the young prince with the Earl of Kent.   75
Queen Isabella.   Something he whispers in his childish ears.
Mortimer Junior.   If he have such access unto the prince,
     Our plots and stratagems will soon be dashed.
Queen Isabella.   Use Edmund friendly as if all were well.
         Enter the young Prince [Edward] and the Earl of Kent talking
                                   with him.
Mortimer Junior.   How fares my honorable lord of Kent?   80
Kent.   In health, sweet Mortimer. How fares your grace?

44 *presently* immediately.   63 *curstly* harshly.
58 *casts* plots.

Queen Isabella.   Well, if my lord your brother were enlarged.
Kent.   I hear of late he hath deposed himself.
Queen Isabella.   The more my grief.
Mortimer Junior.   And mine.   85
Kent.   Ah, they do dissemble.   [*Aside.*]
Queen Isabella.   Sweet son, come hither; I must talk with thee.
Mortimer Junior.   Thou being his uncle and the next of blood,
   Do look to be protector over the prince?
Kent.   Not I, my lord. Who should protect the son,   90
   But she that gave him life? I mean the queen.
Prince Edward.   Mother, persuade me not to wear the crown.
   Let him be king. I am too young to reign.
Queen Isabella.   But be content, seeing it is his highness' pleasure.
Prince Edward.   Let me but see him first, and then I will.   95
Kent.   Ay, do, sweet nephew.
Queen Isabella.   Brother, you know it is impossible.
Prince Edward.   Why, is he dead?
Queen Isabella.   No, God forbid.
Kent.   I would those words proceeded from your heart.   100
Mortimer Junior.   Inconstant Edmund, dost thou favor him,
   That wast a cause of his imprisonment?
Kent.   The more cause have I now to make amends.
Mortimer Junior.   I tell thee, 'tis not meet that one so false
   Should come about the person of a prince.   105
   My lord, he hath betrayed the king his brother,
   And therefore trust him not.
Prince Edward.   But he repents and sorrows for it now.
Queen Isabella.   Come, son, and go with this gentle lord and me.
Prince Edward.   With you I will, but not with Mortimer.   110
Mortimer Junior.   Why, youngling, 'sdain'st thou so of Mortimer?
   Then I will carry thee by force away.
Prince Edward.   Help, uncle Kent; Mortimer will wrong me.
Queen Isabella.   Brother Edmund, strive not; we are his friends.
   Isabel is nearer than the Earl of Kent.   115
Kent.   Sister, Edward is my charge; redeem him.
Queen Isabella.   Edward is my son, and I will keep him.
Kent.   Mortimer shall know that he hath wrongèd me.
   Hence will I haste to Killingworth Castle
   And rescue agèd Edward from his foes,   120
   To be revenged on Mortimer and thee.
              Exeunt [on one side Queen Isabella, Prince Edward,
                     and Mortimer Junior; on the other, Kent].

✳

---

82 *enlarged* liberated.

Enter Matrevis and Gurney [and Soldiers, with King Edward].
Matrevis.   My lord, be not pensive; we are your friends.
  Men are ordained to live in misery.
  Therefore come; dalliance dangereth our lives.
King Edward.   Friends, whither must unhappy Edward go?
  Will hateful Mortimer appoint no rest?   5
  Must I be vexèd like the nightly bird
  Whose sight is loathsome to all wingèd fowls?
  When will the fury of his mind assuage?
  When will his heart be satisfied with blood?
  If mine will serve, unbowel straight this breast,   10
  And give my heart to Isabel and him;
  It is the chiefest mark they level at.
Gurney.   Not so, my liege; the queen hath given this charge
  To keep your grace in safety.
  Your passions make your dolors to increase.   15
King Edward.   This usage makes my misery increase.
  But can my air of life continue long
  When all my senses are annoyed with stench?
  Within a dungeon England's king is kept,
  Where I am starved for want of sustenance.   20
  My daily diet is heart-breaking sobs,
  That almost rents the closet of my heart.
  Thus lives old Edward not relieved by any,
  And so must die, though pitièd by many.
  O, water, gentle friends, to cool my thirst   25
  And clear my body from foul excrements.
Matrevis.   Here's channel water, as our charge is given.
  Sit down, for we'll be barbers to your grace.
King Edward.   Traitors, away! What, will you murder me,
  Or choke your sovereign with puddle water?   30
Gurney.   No, but wash your face and shave away your beard,
  Lest you be known and so be rescuèd.
Matrevis.   Why strive you thus? Your labor is in vain.
King Edward.   The wren may strive against the lion's strength,
  But all in vain; so vainly do I strive   35
  To seek for mercy at a tyrant's hand.
        They wash him with puddle water, and shave his beard away.
  Immortal powers, that knows the painful cares
  That waits upon my poor distressèd soul,
  O level all your looks upon these daring men,
  That wrongs their liege and sovereign, England's king.   40
  O Gaveston, it is for thee that I am wronged;
  For me both thou and both the Spencers died,

V,iii.
  6 *nightly bird* owl.   27 *channel* See note at IV,iv,12.

And for your sakes a thousand wrongs I'll take.
The Spencers' ghosts, wherever they remain,
Wish well to mine; then tush, for them I'll die.   45
Matrevis.   'Twixt theirs and yours shall be no enmity.
Come, come away. Now put the torches out;
We'll enter in by darkness to Killingworth.
                         Enter Kent.
Gurney.   How now, who comes there?
Matrevis.   Guard the king sure; it is the Earl of Kent.   50
King Edward.   O gentle brother, help to rescue me.
Matrevis.   Keep them asunder; thrust in the king.
Kent.   Soldiers, let me but talk to him one word.
Gurney.   Lay hands upon the earl for this assault.
Kent.   Lay down your weapons, traitors; yield the king.   55
Matrevis.   Edmund, yield thou thyself, or thou shalt die.
Kent.   Base villains, wherefore do you gripe me thus?
Gurney.   Bind him and so convey him to the court.
Kent.   Where is the court but here? Here is the king,
And I will visit him. Why stay you me?   60
Matrevis.   The court is where Lord Mortimer remains;
Thither shall your honor go; and so farewell.
          Exeunt Matrevis and Gurney, with King [Edward].
Kent.   O miserable is that commonweal, where lords
Keep courts, and kings are locked in prison!
Soldier.   Wherefore stay we? On, sirs, to the court.   65
Kent.   Ay, lead me whither you will, even to my death,
Seeing that my brother cannot be released.
                              Exeunt.

                    Enter Mortimer [Junior] alone.   V,iv.
Mortimer Junior.   The king must die, or Mortimer goes down;
The commons now begin to pity him.
Yet he that is the cause of Edward's death
Is sure to pay for it when his son is of age,
And therefore will I do it cunningly.   5
This letter, written by a friend of ours,
Contains his death, yet bids them save his life.
                              [He reads.]

'*Edwardum occidere nolite timere bonum est;*
Fear not to kill the king, 'tis good he die.'
But read it thus, and that's another sense: 10
'*Edwardum occidere nolite timere bonum est;*
Kill not the king, 'tis good to fear the worst.'

Unpointed as it is, thus shall it go,
That, being dead, if it chance to be found,
Matrevis and the rest may bear the blame,   15
And we be quit that caused it to be done.
Within this room is locked the messenger
That shall convey it and perform the rest.
And by a secret token that he bears,
Shall he be murdered when the deed is done.   20
Lightborn, come forth!

[Enter Lightborn.]

Art thou as resolute as thou wast?
Lightborn.   What else, my lord? And far more resolute.
Mortimer Junior.   And hast thou cast how to accomplish it?
Lightborn.   Ay, ay, and none shall know which way he died.   25
Mortimer Junior.   But at his looks, Lightborn, thou wilt relent.
Lightborn.   Relent! Ha, ha! I use much to relent.
Mortimer Junior.   Well, do it bravely, and be secret.
Lightborn.   You shall not need to give instructions;
'Tis not the first time I have killed a man.
I learned in Naples how to poison flowers,   30
To strangle with a lawn thrust through the throat,
To pierce the windpipe with a needle's point,
Or whilst one is asleep, to take a quill
And blow a little powder in his ears,   35
Or open his mouth and pour quicksilver down.
But yet I have a braver way than these.
Mortimer Junior.   What's that?
Lightborn.   Nay, you shall pardon me; none shall know my tricks.
Mortimer Junior.   I care not how it is, so it be not spied.   40
Deliver this to Gurney and Matrevis.   *[He gives a letter.]*
At every ten miles' end thou hast a horse.
Take this. *[He gives money.]* Away, and never see me more.
Lightborn.   No.
Mortimer Junior.   No,   45
Unless thou bring me news of Edward's death.
Lightborn.   That will I quickly do. Farewell, my lord.

[Exit.]

Mortimer Junior.   The prince I rule, the queen do I command,
And with a lowly congé to the ground,
The proudest lords salute me as I pass;   50
I seal, I cancel, I do what I will.
Feared am I more than loved; let me be feared,
And when I frown, make all the court look pale.

V,iv.

13 *Unpointed* without punctuation.
21 *Lightborn* The name, invented by
Marlowe, may be a translation of Lucifer.

24 *cast* See note at II,iii,8.
32 *lawn* thread.
49 *congé* bow.

I view the prince with Aristarchus' eyes,
Whose looks were as a breeching to a boy.   55
They thrust upon me the protectorship
And sue to me for that that I desire.
While at the council-table, grave enough,
And not unlike a bashful Puritan,
First I complain of imbecility,   60
Saying it is *onus quam gravissimum;*
Till, being interrupted by my friends,
Suscepi that *provinciam* as they term it;
And to conclude, I am Protector now.
Now is all sure; the queen and Mortimer   65
Shall rule the realm, the king, and none rule us.
Mine enemies will I plague, my friends advance,
And what I list command who dare control?
Major sum quam cui possit fortuna nocere.
And that this be the coronation day,   70
It pleaseth me, and Isabel the queen.
                              [*Trumpets sound within.*]
The trumpets sound; I must go take my place.
     *Enter the young King, [Edward III], [the] Bishop [of Canter-
         bury,] Champion, Nobles, [and] Queen [Isabella].*
Canterbury.   Long live King Edward, by the grace of God,
     king of England and lord of Ireland.
Champion.   If any Christian, Heathen, Turk, or Jew,   75
     Dares but affirm that Edward's not true king,
     And will avouch his saying with the sword,
     I am the champion that will combat him.
Mortimer Junior.   None comes, sound trumpets.
                                     [*Trumpets sound.*]
King Edward III.   Champion, here's to thee.
                                     [*He gives a purse.*]
Queen Isabella.   Lord Mortimer, now take him to your charge.   80
            Enter Soldiers, with the Earl of Kent prisoner.
Mortimer Junior.   What traitor have we there with blades and bills?
Soldier.   Edmund, the Earl of Kent.
King Edward III.   What hath he done?
Soldier.   'A would have taken the king away perforce,
     As we were bringing him to Killingworth.
Mortimer Junior.   Did you attempt his rescue, Edmund? Speak.   85
Kent.   Mortimer, I did; he is our king,
     And thou compell'st this prince to wear the crown.

---

54 *Aristarchus* Greek grammarian and
schoolmaster of the second century B.C.
55 *breeching* beating.
60 *imbecility* weakness.

61 *onus quam gravissimum* a very heavy
load.
63 *Suscepi that provinciam* I accepted
that province (undertook the task).
69 *Major . . . nocere* I am too great
for fortune to harm me.

Mortimer Junior.   Strike off his head! He shall have martial law.
Kent.   Strike off my head! Base traitor, I defy thee.
King Edward III.   My lord, he is my uncle and shall live.   90
Mortimer Junior.   My lord, he is your enemy and shall die.
Kent.   Stay, villains!
King Edward III.   Sweet mother, if I cannot pardon him,
  Entreat my Lord Protector for his life.
Queen Isabella.   Son, be content; I dare not speak a word.   95
King Edward III.   Nor I, and yet methinks I should command;
  But, seeing I cannot, I'll entreat for him.
  My lord, if you will let my uncle live,
  I will requite it when I come to age.
Mortimer Junior.   'Tis for your highness' good and for the realm's.   100
  How often shall I bid you bear him hence?
Kent.   Art thou king? Must I die at thy command?
Mortimer Junior.   At our command. Once more away with him.
Kent.   Let me but stay and speak; I will not go.
  Either my brother or his son is king,   105
  And none of both them thirst for Edmund's blood.
  And therefore, soldiers, whither will you hale me?
    [Soldiers] hale Kent away, and carry him to be beheaded.
King Edward III.   What safety may I look for at his hands,
  If that my uncle shall be murdered thus?
Queen Isabella.   Fear not, sweet boy, I'll guard thee from thy foes.   110
  Had Edmund lived, he would have sought thy death.
  Come, son, we'll ride a-hunting in the park.
King Edward III.   And shall my uncle Edmund ride with us?
Queen Isabella.   He is a traitor; think not on him; come.
                                         Exeunt.

                Enter Matrevis and Gurney.   V,v.
Matrevis.   Gurney, I wonder the king dies not,
  Being in a vault up to the knees in water,
  To which the channels of the castle run,
  From whence a damp continually ariseth,
  That were enough to poison any man,   5
  Much more a king brought up so tenderly.
Gurney.   And so do I, Matrevis. Yesternight
  I opened but the door to throw him meat,
  And I was almost stifled with the savor.
Matrevis.   He hath a body able to endure   10
  More than we can inflict, and therefore now
  Let us assail his mind another while.
Gurney.   Send for him out thence, and I will anger him.

Matrevis.   But stay, who's this?

Enter Lightborn.

Lightborn.   My Lord Protector greets you.

[He gives letter.]

Gurney.   What's here? I know not how to conster it.   15
Matrevis.   Gurney, it was left unpointed for the nonce;
  '*Edwardum occidere nolite timere,*'
  That's his meaning.
Lightborn.   Know you this token? I must have the king.

[He gives token.]

Matrevis.   Ay, stay awhile; thou shalt have answer straight.   20
  This villain's sent to make away the king.   [*Aside.*]
Gurney.   I thought as much.   [*Aside.*]
Matrevis.   And when the murder's done,
  See how he must be handled for his labor.
  Pereat iste! Let him have the king.   [*Aside.*]
  What else? Here is the key, this is the lake;   25
  Do as you are commanded by my lord.
Lightborn.   I know what I must do. Get you away.
  Yet be not far off; I shall need your help.
  See that in the next room I have a fire,
  And get me a spit, and let it be red-hot.   30
Matrevis.   Very well.
Gurney.   Need you anything besides?
Lightborn.   What else? A table and a feather-bed.
Gurney.   That's all?
Lightborn.   Ay, ay; so, when I call you, bring it in.
Matrevis.   Fear not you that.   35
Gurney.   Here's a light to go into the dungeon.

[He gives a light, and then exit with Matrevis.]

Lightborn.   So now
  Must I about this gear. Ne'er was there any
  So finely handled as this king shall be.
  Foh, here's a place indeed, with all my heart.   40
King Edward.   Who's there? What light is that? Wherefore comes thou?
Lightborn.   To comfort you and bring you joyful news.
King Edward.   Small comfort finds poor Edward in thy looks.
  Villain, I know thou com'st to murder me.
Lightborn.   To murder you, my most gracious lord?   45
  Far is it from my heart to do you harm.
  The queen sent me to see how you were used,
  For she relents at this your misery.
  And what eyes can refrain from shedding tears
  To see a king in this most piteous state?   50

V,v.
24 *Pereat iste* Let him perish.   38 *gear* business.
25 *lake* pit or dungeon.

King Edward.   Weep'st thou already? List awhile to me
     And then thy heart, were it as Gurney's is,
     Or as Matrevis', hewn from the Caucasus,
     Yet will it melt ere I have done my tale.
     This dungeon where they keep me is the sink   55
     Wherein the filth of all the castle falls.
Lightborn.   O villains!
King Edward.   And there in mire and puddle have I stood
     This ten days' space; and, lest that I should sleep,
     One plays continually upon a drum.   60
     They give me bread and water, being a king;
     So that, for want of sleep and sustenance,
     My mind's distempered, and my body's numbed,
     And whether I have limbs or no I know not.
     O, would my blood dropped out from every vein,   65
     As doth this water from my tattered robes.
     Tell Isabel, the queen, I looked not thus,
     When for her sake I ran at tilt in France
     And there unhorsed the Duke of Cleremont.
Lightborn.   O speak no more, my lord; this breaks my heart.   70
     Lie on this bed, and rest yourself awhile.
King Edward.   These looks of thine can harbor nought but death.
     I see my tragedy written in thy brows.
     Yet stay awhile; forbear thy bloody hand,
     And let me see the stroke before it comes,   75
     That even then when I shall lose my life,
     My mind may be more steadfast on my God.
Lightborn.   What means your highness to mistrust me thus?
King Edward.   What means thou to dissemble with me thus?
Lightborn.   These hands were never stained with innocent blood, 80
     Nor shall they now be tainted with a king's.
King Edward.   Forgive my thought for having such a thought.
     One jewel have I left; receive thou this.

                                   [*He gives a jewel.*]

     Still fear I, and I know not what's the cause,
     But every joint shakes as I give it thee.   85
     O, if thou harbor'st murder in thy heart,
     Let this gift change thy mind and save thy soul.
     Know that I am a king. O, at that name
     I feel a hell of grief! Where is my crown?
     Gone, gone, and do I remain alive?   90
Lightborn.   You're overwatched, my lord; lie down and rest.
King Edward.   But that grief keeps me waking, I should sleep;
     For not these ten days have these eyes' lids closed.
     Now as I speak they fall, and yet with fear
     Open again. O wherefore sits thou here?   95

91 *overwatched* exhausted from lack of sleep.

Lightborn.   If you mistrust me, I'll be gone, my lord.
King Edward.   No, no, for if thou mean'st to murder me,
   Thou wilt return again, and therefore stay.   [*He sleeps.*]
Lightborn.   He sleeps.
King Edward.   [*waking*]   O let me not die yet. Stay, O stay a while!   100
Lightborn.   How now, my lord?
King Edward.   Something still buzzeth in mine ears
   And tells me if I sleep I never wake.
   This fear is that which makes me tremble thus;
   And therefore tell me, wherefore art thou come?   105
Lightborn.   To rid thee of thy life. Matrevis, come!
                    [*Enter Matrevis and Gurney.*]
King Edward.   I am too weak and feeble to resist.
   Assist me, sweet God, and receive my soul!
Lightborn.   Run for the table.
King Edward.   O spare me, or dispatch me in a trice.   110
                    [*Matrevis brings in a table.*]
Lightborn.   So, lay the table down, and stamp on it,
   But not too hard, lest that you bruise his body.
                    [*King Edward is murdered.*]
Matrevis.   I fear me that this cry will raise the town,
   And therefore let us take horse and away.
Lightborn.   Tell me, sirs, was it not bravely done?   115
Gurney.   Excellent well. Take this for thy reward.
                    Gurney stabs Lightborn, [who dies].
   Come, let us cast the body in the moat,
   And bear the king's to Mortimer our lord.
   Away!
                    Exeunt [with the bodies].

                    Enter Mortimer [*Junior*] and Matrevis.   V,vi.
Mortimer Junior.   Is't done, Matrevis, and the murderer dead?
Matrevis.   Ay, my good lord; I would it were undone.
Mortimer Junior.   Matrevis, if thou now growest penitent
   I'll be thy ghostly father; therefore choose
   Whether thou wilt be secret in this   5
   Or else die by the hand of Mortimer.
Matrevis.   Gurney, my lord, is fled, and will, I fear,
   Betray us both; therefore let me fly.
Mortimer Junior.   Fly to the savages.
Matrevis.   I humbly thank your honor.   10
                    [*Exit.*]

V,vi.
   4 *ghostly father* priest (who brings sacraments to one about to die).

Mortimer Junior.   As for myself, I stand as Jove's huge tree,
　And others are but shrubs compared to me.
　All tremble at my name, and I fear none;
　Let's see who dare impeach me for his death.
　　　　　　Enter Queen [Isabella].
Queen Isabella.   Ah, Mortimer, the king my son hath news　　15
　His father's dead, and we have murdered him!
Mortimer Junior.   What if he have? The king is yet a child.
Queen Isabella.   Ay, ay, but he tears his hair, and wrings his hands,
　And vows to be revenged upon us both.
　Into the council chamber he is gone　　　　　　20
　To crave the aid and succor of his peers.
　Ay me, see where he comes, and they with him.
　Now, Mortimer, begins our tragedy.
　　　Enter King [Edward the Third,] with the Lords, [and
　　　　　　　　　Attendants].
First Lord.   Fear not, my lord; know that you are a king.
King Edward III.   Villain!　　　　　　　　　　　25
Mortimer Junior.   How now, my lord?
King Edward III.   Think not that I am frighted with thy words.
　My father's murdered through thy treachery,
　And thou shalt die, and on his mournful hearse
　Thy hateful and accursèd head shall lie　　　　　30
　To witness to the world that by thy means
　His kingly body was too soon interred.
Queen Isabella.   Weep not, sweet son.
King Edward III.   Forbid not me to weep; he was my father;
　And had you loved him half so well as I,　　　　35
　You could not bear his death thus patiently.
　But you, I fear, conspired with Mortimer.
First Lord.   Why speak you not unto my lord the king?
Mortimer Junior.   Because I think scorn to be accused.
　Who is the man dare say I murdered him?　　　40
King Edward III.   Traitor, in me my loving father speaks
　And plainly saith, 'twas thou that murdered'st him.
Mortimer Junior.   But hath your grace no other proof than this?
King Edward III.   Yes, if this be the hand of Mortimer.
　　　　　　　　　　　　[He shows letter.]
Mortimer Junior.   False Gurney hath betrayed me and himself.　45
　　　　　　　　　　　　　[Aside.]
Queen Isabella.   I feared as much; murder cannot be hid.
　　　　　　　　　　　　　[Aside.]
Mortimer Junior.   'Tis my hand; what gather you by this?
King Edward III.   That thither thou didst send a murderer.
Mortimer Junior.   What murderer? Bring forth the man I sent.
King Edward III.   Ah, Mortimer, thou knowest that he is slain;　50
　11 *Jove's huge tree* the oak.

And so shalt thou be too. Why stays he here?
Bring him unto a hurdle, drag him forth;
Hang him, I say, and set his quarters up;
But bring his head back presently to me.
Queen Isabella.   For my sake, sweet son, pity Mortimer.   55
Mortimer Junior.   Madam, entreat not; I will rather die
Than sue for life unto a paltry boy.
King Edward III.   Hence with the traitor, with the murderer!
Mortimer Junior.   Base Fortune, now I see that in thy wheel
There is a point, to which when men aspire,   60
They tumble headlong down. That point I touched,
And, seeing there was no place to mount up higher,
Why should I grieve at my declining fall?
Farewell, fair queen; weep not for Mortimer,
That scorns the world, and, as a traveler,   65
Goes to discover countries yet unknown.
King Edward III.   What! Suffer you the traitor to delay?
                    [*Mortimer Junior is taken away by the First Lord
                                        and Attendants.*]
Queen Isabella.   As thou received'st thy life from me,
Spill not the blood of gentle Mortimer!
King Edward III.   This argues that you spilt my father's blood;   70
Else would you not entreat for Mortimer.
Queen Isabella.   I spill his blood? No!
King Edward III.   Ay, madam, you; for so the rumor runs.
Queen Isabella.   That rumor is untrue; for loving thee,
Is this report raised on poor Isabel.   75
King Edward III.   I do not think her so unnatural.
Second Lord.   My lord, I fear me it will prove too true.
King Edward III.   Mother, you are suspected for his death,
And therefore we commit you to the Tower
Till further trial may be made thereof;   80
If you be guilty, though I be your son,
Think not to find me slack or pitiful.
Queen Isabella.   Nay, to my death, for too long have I lived,
Whenas my son thinks to abridge my days.
King Edward III.   Away with her. Her words enforce these tears,   85
And I shall pity her if she speak again.
Queen Isabella.   Shall I not mourn for my belovèd lord,
And with the rest accompany him to his grave?
Second Lord.   Thus, madam; 'tis the king's will you shall hence.
Queen Isabella.   He hath forgotten me; stay, I am his mother.   90
Second Lord.   That boots not; therefore, gentle madam, go.
Queen Isabella.   Then come, sweet death, and rid me of this grief.
                              [*Exit with Second Lord.*]

52 *hurdle* cart on which condemned   91 *boots* avails.
criminals were taken to the gallows.

[Enter First Lord, with the head of Mortimer Junior.]
First Lord.   My lord, here is the head of Mortimer.
King Edward III.   Go fetch my father's hearse where it shall lie,
And bring my funeral robes.
                              [Exeunt Attendants.]
                    Accursèd head,   95
Could I have ruled thee then, as I do now,
Thou hadst not hatched this monstrous treachery!
Here comes the hearse; help me to mourn, my lords.
      [Re-enter Attendants with the hearse and funeral robes.]
Sweet father, here unto thy murdered ghost
I offer up this wicked traitor's head,   100
And let these tears, distilling from mine eyes,
Be witness of my grief and innocency.
                              [Exeunt.]

101 *distilling* falling slowly.

Textual Notes

Our earliest extant text of *Edward II* is an octavo printed for William Jones in 1594, two copies of which today survive, the one in the Landesbibliothek in Cassel, Germany, and the other in the Zentralbibliothek in Zurich, Switzerland. Another printing, in quarto, was issued by Jones in 1598, and additional quartos followed by Roger Banes in 1612 and Henry Bell in 1622. Each of these editions was printed from the one previous to it.

There was in the possession of Alexander Dyce, and now in the Dyce Collection at South Kensington, an imperfect copy of the 1598 quarto, in which the title page and first seventy lines of the play have been supplied in a seventeenth-century handwriting, the manuscript title page bearing the date of 1593. That this could have been a mistake for 1598 is very unlikely because the manuscript lines bear a much closer resemblance to the 1594 text than they do to the 1598, and yet they diverge from the 1594 sufficiently to make it likely that they were, in fact, transcribed from a 1593 printing, no copy of which today is extant. The present text is based upon the Zurich copy of the 1594 octavo which has been departed from only in the following instances:

I,i.

22 *fawn* (Eds.) fanne (1594)
37 *Third Poor Man* Sold. (1594)
47 *Poor Men* Omnes (1594)
49 *Poor Men* Omnes (1594)
73, SD *and others* &c (1594). *King* the King (1594)
107 *Kent* Edm. (1594)
133, SD Exeunt Nobiles (1594)

142 *Why . . . am* Why . . . kneele,/ Knowest . . . am (1594)
176 *Coventry* Bish. (1594) and throughout scene

I,ii.

35 *Canterbury* Bish. (1594) and throughout scene
45, SD *Queen* the Queene (1594)
77 *Canterbury* omitted in 1594

I,iv.

SD Enter Nobiles (1594)
3 *Canterbury* Bish. (1594) and throughout scene
7, SD *King* the King (1594)
93, SD Exeunt Nobiles (1594)
115 *ne'er* (Eds.) neare (1594)
143, SD *Enter* Enter Edmund and (1594)
186, SD Enter the Nobles to the Queene (1594)
267 *murderer* murtherer (1594)
346 *embroidery* imbrotherie (1594)
384, SD *all except the* Manent (1594)
392 *Hercules* (Eds.) Hector (1594)
415 *While others* whiles other (1594)

II,i.

1–2 *Spencer . . . dead* one line in 1594
56, SD *King's Niece* Ladie (1594) and throughout scene

II,ii.

SD *Queen* the Queene (1594)
50–51 *My . . . friend* one line in 1594
69 *Kent* Edm. (1594) and throughout scene
81–82 *Here . . . him* (Eds.) one line in 1594. *Edward* omitted in 1594
99, SD *King* the King (1594)
110, SD *Messenger* Poast (1594)
197, SD Exeunt Nobiles (1594)
217–218 *Away . . . me* one line in 1594
222, SD *Queen* the Queene (1594). *two Ladies* Ladies 3 (1594)
224 *'em* (Dyce) him (1594)
226 *Niece* La. (1594) and throughout scene
246–247 *Ay . . . allied* one line in 1594
263, SD Exeunt omnes (1594)

II,iv.

SD *King* the king (1594)
11 *Niece* Lad. (1594)
15, SD *all but Queen* omnes, manent (1594)
21, SD *Lancaster . . . Others* the Barons (1594)
69, SD *Exit* Exeunt (1594)

II,v.

7, SD Enter the Nobles (1594)
14–17 *Monster . . . death* Monster . . . strumpet/ Traind . . . Warres,/ So . . . knights,/ Looke . . . death (1594)
18 *King* (1598) Kind (1594)

20–22 *Go . . . cause* (Eds.) Go . . . hence,/ For . . . off:/ Gaveston . . . turne:/ It . . . cause (1594)
34–35 *His . . . Gaveston* one line in 1594
41 *Renownèd* Renowmed (1594)
49–50 *Shalt . . . him* Shalt . . . graunt?/ Souldiers . . . him (1594)
69–70 *We . . . thief* (Eds.) We . . . so,/ To . . . Theefe (1594)
72 *renown* renowm (1594)
98, SD Manent Penbrooke, Mat. Gauest. & Penbrookes men, foure souldiers (1594)
104 *Arundel* Mat. (1594)
110, SD Exit cum seruis Pen. (1594)
111, SD Exeunt ambo. (1594)

III,i.

17, SD Manet Iames cum caeteris (1594)

III,ii.

10 *Spencer Junior* Spencer (1594) and throughout scene.
31, SD *Spencer Senior* Hugh Spencer an old man, father to the young Spencer (1594)
32 *Spencer Senior* Spen. pa. (1594) and throughout scene
58, SD *Queen* the Queene (1594)
88, SD *Arundel* Lord Matre (1594) and throughout scene
125 *murder* murther (1594)
128 *He kneels* kneeles, and saith (1594)
148 *here's* (Eds.) heres is (1594)
179 *murdering* murthering (1594)

III,iii.

SD *King* the king (1594). *Senior . . . Junior* the father . . . the sonne (1594)
10, SD *and others* cum caeteris (1594)
12–13 *And . . . company* one line in 1594
17 *Thou'd* Th'ad (1594). *them* (Brooke) thee (1594)
41 *murder* murther (1594)
45 *Kent* Edm. (1594)
62–63 *I . . . Away* one line in 1594
70–71 *Do . . . gone* one line in 1594
77, SD *with all except* Manent (1594)
97, SD Exeunt omnes (1594)

IV,i.

SD *Kent* Edmund (1594) and throughout scene
10–11 *Thy . . . device* one line in 1594
11–12 *Holla . . . lord* one line in 1594
12–13 *Mortimer . . . happily* one line in 1594

IV,ii.

SD *Queen* the Queene (1594)
20 *share of* (Brooke) shake off (1594)
34, SD *Kent* Edmund (1594) and throughout scene

IV,iii.

SD *King* the king (1594). *Arundel* Matr. (1594)
23, SD *Messenger* Post (1594) and in line 25
28 *reads* reads the letter (1594). *premised* (1598) promised (1594)

IV,iv.

SD *Queen* the Queene (1594). *Kent* Edmund (1594)
13–14 *Of* . . . *thou* one line in 1594

IV,v.

SD *King* the King (1594). *Junior* the sonne (1594)
9 SD *Kent* Edmund (1594) and throughout scene
14 *Vile* vilde (1594)
27 SD *Queen* the Queene (1594)
36 *unfortunate* infortunate (1594)
54, SD *Senior* the father (1594)
71 *Unhappy* is Vnhappies (1594)
80 *Senior* pa. (1594)
88, SD Exeunt omnes (1594)

IV,vi.

26–27 *Your* . . . *abode* prose in 1594

V,i.

SD *King* the King. *the Bishop of Winchester* with a Bishop for the crowne (1594)
13 *And highly* (Eds.) highly (1594)
38 *Winchester* Bish. (1594) and throughout scene
47 *vine* (Eds.) vines (1594)
55 *murdered* murthered (1594)
101 *murderer* murtherer (1594)
111, SD Enter Bartley (1594)
112 *Winchester* (Eds.) Bartley (1594)
113–114 *Call* . . . *lunatic* (Eds.) Call . . . lorde,/ Away . . . me,/ Greefe . . . lunatick (1594)
129 *Berkeley* Bartley (1594) and throughout scene
155, SD Exeunt omnes (1594)

V,ii.

28 *Winchester* Bish. (1594)

30 *ere* (Charleton and Waller) or (1594). *Berkeley* Bartley (1594) and throughout scene
47 *Matrevis* . . . *presently* one line in 1594
60 *Till* (Eds.) And (1594)
73, SD Manent Isabell and Mortimer (1594)
81 *Kent* Edmun. (1594) and throughout scene
121, SD Exeunt omnes (1594)

V,iii.

SD *King* the king (1594)
29 *murder* murther (1594)
48, SD *Kent* Edmund (1594 and throughout scene)
62, SD *King* the king (1594) Manent Edmund and souldiers (1594)
67, SD Exeunt omnes (1594)

V,iv.

21–22 *Lightborn* . . . *wast* one line in 1594
45–46 *No* . . . *death* one line in 1594
54 *Aristarchus'* Aristorchus (1594)
59 *Puritan* (Eds.) paretaine (1594)
73 *Canterbury* Bish. (1594)
86 *Kent* Edm. (1594) and throughout scene
106 *them* then (1594)
107, SD *Soldiers* They (1594)
109 *murdered* murthered (1594)
114, SD, Exeunt omnes (1594)

V,v.

37–38 *So* . . . *any* one line in 1594
44 *murder* murther (1594) and in lines 45, 86, 97
116, SD *Gurney* Then Gurney (1594)
118–119 *And* . . . *Away* one line in 1594
119, SD Exeunt omnes (1594)

V,vi.

1 *murderer* murtherer (1594)
14, SD *Queen* the Queene (1594)
23, SD *King* the king (1594)
24 *First Lord* Lords (1594)
38 *First Lord* Lords (1594)
46 *murder* murther (1594)
48 *murderer* murtherer (1594) and in line 49
89 *Second Lord* Lords (1594) and in line 91
93 *First Lord* Lords (1594)

The Major Critics

MICHEL POIRIER

EDWARD II

The drama that remains to be examined holds a very peculiar place in Marlowe's production. Apart from *Tamburlaine*, it is the only one that has come down to us in its original condition. The text is correct, of normal length and without any visible signs of collaboration or revision. This is probably the result of its early publication. Unless a play were pirated—and the purity of the text precludes such an hypothesis in the present case—its manuscript used to be handed to the printer only when it could no longer fill the house. This means that *Edward II* cannot have been written in the last months of Marlowe's life. Since the title-page states that it was acted by the Earl of Pembroke's company, who seem not to have performed in London between 1576 and the end of 1592, the play was probably written in 1592.

It is a chronicle play in its purest form, without the least admixture of comical elements. Here, as elsewhere, Marlowe runs counter to the Elizabethan tradition, even at the risk of jeopardizing the success of his tragedy.

Like most chronicle plays, it is the history of a king rather than of a reign. The plot can be summed up in one sentence: it is the story of a feudal monach who attempts to govern as an absolute sovereign and fails. By his relations with Gaveston and Spenser, by the extravagance to which those two minions lead him, by his indifference and incompetence, he creates dissatisfaction and rebellion in the nobles. The blunder he makes in bullying a prelate sets the Church against him. The struggle into which he is thus drawn ends with his defeat; he loses his crown and is /**173**/ finally put to death. To this

Reprinted from *Christopher Marlowe* (London: Chatto & Windus, 1951).

subject-matter must be added a secondary plot developed in the course of that conflict: Queen Isabella, spurned by her husband, rallies Mortimer, the leader of the feudal lords, to whom she gives her support and also her love.

Once more we must admire the conscientiousness with which the author has gathered information concerning that reign. His chief source is Holinshed's chronicle, which he kept before his eyes throughout the course of his work, and from which he drew many almost textual borrowings. But whereas Shakespeare in his historical dramas generally contents himself with that chronicle, Marlowe studies others also, those of Fabyan and Stow, whence he derives further details.

The facts he has related extend from Edward's accession in 1307 to the execution of Mortimer in 1330. It stands to reason it was necessary to prune and condense. From the matter supplied by history, too abundant and diverse to fit into a drama, Marlowe deliberately sets aside all that refers to foreign politics: the long wars with Scotland, the most famous episode of which was the battle of Bannockburn, as well as the conflict with France, which is but summarily dealt with. He also leaves out many other events that would have overburdened the play or entailed repetitions, such as Edward's voyage to France, his marriage, Gaveston's second exile and that of the Spensers, to mention only a few of them. The civil war between the King and the great noblemen is compressed into the single battle of Boroughbridge. Yet it sometimes happens that this condensation leads to improbabilities similar to those we have pointed out in *The Massacre at Paris*. Whereas Gaveston was exiled in Ireland from May 1308 to July 1309, a single scene is devoted both to his banishment and his recall. It is difficult to understand how, at the close of that scene, /174/ Edward can send a messenger to his favourite in Ireland, considering that the latter was standing in front of him a few moments before. Farther on, the nobles request the King to dismiss his new minion Spenser, who in that very same scene has just received the first token of the royal favour. Without referring to the sources, it is impossible to set a date to most scenes or appraise the length of the interval that elapses between them. This lack of precision tends to make the action appear much swifter than it actually was.

Some liberties taken with chronology are more serious, though they may always be justified by some psychological or artistic reason. Thus the battle of Bannockburn, fought two years after Gaveston's death, is placed before the latter event in order better to display the disastrous consequences of his rule. Similarly, Mortimer, whose intervention Holinshed mentions only after the fall of Gaveston, is introduced at the very beginning of the play instead of the Duke of Lancaster, who was then the most powerful of the King's enemies. Edward's brother, the Duke of Kent, joins the lords at a time when he was only six years old. Were it not liable to become wearisome, this enumeration of chronological inaccuracies could easily be extended.

On the other hand, very few fictitious episodes are to be noted. The most important one concerns Mortimer's capture by the Scots and the King's refusal to ransom him. The incident may have been inspired by Henry IV's attitude towards another Mortimer. It is meant to make the audience feel the full measure of the King's indifference to the affairs of the State and to his most distinguished servants.

The masterly, swift and essentially dramatic exposition at once reveals Gaveston's and Edward's characters and at the same time displays the opposing forces about to engage: on one hand, the King invested with the glamour /175/ of his rank, and supported by his favourite, on the other hand the temporal and spiritual lords. The plot starts in the first scene with the arbitrary arrest of the Bishop of Coventry. The noblemen and prelates retort by demanding Gaveston's banishment. After a time they consent to his being recalled. According to Holinshed, they did so in the illusory hope that the King would mend his ways. In the play, their decision is more clearly motivated and founded upon more selfish considerations: they fear lest Gaveston should increase his power in Ireland and it occurs to them that they will be able to dispatch him more easily if he comes back to England, for the people will then side with them. The favourite's return does not ease the situation as the King had expected, and the first part of the conflict ends with Gaveston's murder. Meanwhile, Edward II has already found a new minion in Spenser, who becomes the object of a new struggle from which the King comes off victorious. But the Queen and such lords as have fled to France land at the head of an army and rout the loyalist forces. At the end of the play, the whole interest centres upon the unfortunate King, whose arrest, abdication and murder are staged. In the last scenes, Edward II's successor sends to the scaffold Mortimer the regicide.

From a dramatic standpoint, the chief drawback of this subject lay in the lack of cohesion between its different parts. The conflict between the King and the feudal lords might easily have resolved itself into a series of clashes forming so many separate episodes. Marlowe has obviated that danger by interconnecting the various stages of the struggle, by foreshadowing its rebound every time it seems about to end. Before Gaveston comes back from Ireland, we know that the noblemen will not endure him any more patiently than in the past. Before he is killed we know that his successor will become a new cause of conflict. Lastly, /**176**/ as Queen Isabella opposes her husband from the beginning, we guess she will take advantage of her stay in France to raise an army against him. The whole play consequently reveals qualities of dramatic construction of which no other drama by Marlowe, except maybe *The Jew of Malta*, could let us surmise the existence and which we appreciate all the more as the printed text is exceptionally correct. The well-knit plot is a logical development proceeding inevitably from the initial situation and from the characters. Nothing is fortuitous, nothing is arbitrary.

The sober staging of the war is also to be praised. As in *Tamburlaine*, we see the results of the battles, not the battles themselves. The play does not lay itself open to reproofs such as those of Sidney, who wrote ironically: "Two Armies flie in, represented with foure swords & bucklers, and then what hard hart wil not receive it for a pitched field?"[1]

Yet the dramatic technique is not always faultless. One source of weakness the playwright has not removed, namely the existence of two successive favourites, which entails regrettable repetitions. The vassals demand Spenser's disgrace in terms very similar to those they had already used in connection with Gaveston. The attempt made by Kent to deliver the King is presented in such a way that it seems childish and doomed to failure. If the events are in general duly condensed, one incident has been developed out of all proportion; the request sent to the feudal lords by the King, who wished to have a last interview with their prisoner Gaveston, leads to endless dis-

---

[1] *The Defence of Poesie, Works*, ed. Feuillerat, III, p. 38.

cussions on the expediency of granting it. Lastly, here as in *The Jew of Malta*, stage-asides are used too grossly in order to disclose to the audience the favourite's and the King's double dealing. Far more dexterous is the use of another /**177**/ device, the whispered conversation by which the Queen persuades Mortimer to consent to Gaveston's recall. Not only does it avoid useless repetitions, but it arouses much curiosity as to the reason for his sudden and unexpected change.

Astonishing as this may seem in the light of his other dramas, Marlowe has achieved a still greater success in the characterization than in the construction of the tragedy. Yet the task was more important and more difficult. Apart from the facts, Holinshed supplied him only with a few succinct estimates of the King's character, considered from a moral rather than psychological standpoint. It was the playwright's task to recreate the latter's personality, to endow him with a character whence all his actions would proceed logically. This he has done far better than in any other drama, which gives *Edward II* a rank far above all earlier chronicle plays.

The king he has portrayed is an unintelligent man who allows himself to be swayed by his emotions, in whom the least incident is liable to cause a sudden alteration of mood. Now he falls a prey to violent and ineffectual fits of anger, now he displays an extraordinary need of affection. On hearing that the lords consent to recall his exiled favourite, he is filled with a naive joy and puerile optimism. Like a child, he lays his head on the lap of the abbot who shelters him in his flight.

He is also a sodomite whose whole life is subordinated to the exclusive passion he feels first for Gaveston, then for Spenser, and which will be the cause of his downfall. Consequently, he harbours no love at all for his wife. Indeed, his behaviour towards her is odious. He takes an interest in her only in so far as she can help his unnatural passion. Just as he rebukes her for being too intimate with Mortimer, so he urges her to use her influence with the latter /**178**/ on his behalf. He threatens to banish her if she does not succeed in keeping Gaveston at court. When she secures the recall of the favourite, he takes her hand as if to ratify their nuptials, which will not prevent him from being as unfaithful as in the past.

This man is also a king imbued with the greatness and dignity conferred upon him by his crown, a premature champion of the theory of divine right. What grandeur in the oath he takes to revenge himself upon the revolted noblemen:

> By earth, the common mother of us all,
> By heaven, and all the moving orbs thereof,
> By this right hand, and by my father's sword,
> And all the honors 'longing to my crown,
> I will have heads and lives for him as many
> As I have manors, castles, towns, and towers.
>
> [III. ii. 128–33]

What stress he gives to the words "king", "England's king", often emphasized by their position at the end of the line! Yet if he enjoys all the privileges his title gains him, he does not acknowledge the least duty. Claiming to act as he chooses, he unscrupulously and unreservedly puts into practice the doctrine of the King's good pleasure. He values his pre-eminent position chiefly for the benefits his passion derives from it. Wealth, honour, power appeal to him only because he can bestow them upon Gaveston. He looks upon his kingdom as personal property which he can share with his friend [I, i, 164–65]. At other times, his wavering mind contemplates a spontaneous abdication that would enable him to devote himself entirely to his minion; he is ready to assent to the disruption of his kingdom

> So I may have some nook or corner left
> To frolic with my dearest Gaveston.
>
> [I. iv. 72–3]/**179**/

The affairs of government bore him. He refuses to examine the political problems that arise, under-estimates the seriousness of his dispute with the King of France and shows himself ungrateful to his most faithful servants.

This despot is entirely devoid of realism and even of intelligence. The full-length portrait of him painted by Marlowe curiously resembles his sketch of Cosroe in *Tamburlaine*. The King of England is neither cowardly nor ridiculous, like the King of Persia, but he displays the same stupidity and the same illusions about the scope of his power. He forgets that a sovereign cannot be free in his private life, that the Church and the nobility, towards whom he is violent and insolent, are forces with which he has to reckon. In medieval England his desire to rule as an autocrat could have been fulfilled only if it had been furthered by an exceptional statesmanship. But Edward cannot even prevent Gaveston from being arrested in his presence. He goes his own way without ever concerning himself about the consequences of his actions, and in speeches full of dramatic irony he delights in visualizing the future over which he has no command. His destiny is implied in his character; the fall of such a sovereign was a foregone conclusion.

Thus does Edward II appear in the first part of the play. As usual, Marlowe refrains from passing a moral judgement on his hero. On the contrary, far from disapproving of his paederasty, he clothes it with whatever is noblest and purest in friendship. All the same, Edward is too deficient in moral conscience and above all in intelligence for his career to be followed with sympathy.

And yet, although he paints him with such unflattering colours, Marlowe succeeds in making the King likable at the end of the play. In a way, this is a dramatic defect like the one to be observed in Shakespeare's tragedy, where /**180**/ Julius Caesar, belittled and almost ridiculous during his life-time, takes on a gigantic and impressive aspect after his death. Even though it brings about a sudden change of perspective in the course of the action, such an alteration is none the less a feat of skill which the characterization of Marlowe's previous dramas did not foreshadow. By what means has it been carried out? In the first place by the talk of the other characters as soon as Edward's defeat has been consummated. Kent reproaches himself with having betrayed his brother and most opportunely recalls the Queen's hypocrisy and adultery. The Abbot of Neath bewails the fate of the royal fugitive. His tyranny, selfishness, frivolity and even stupidity are henceforth deliberately toned down; his favourites are dead. Losing his power, he is thereby divested of everything that made him weak. At the same time, the poet takes care to stress the eminent majesty of the King's person even more than before and, to develop that idea, he draws on all the resources of his language and verse. Like Lear wandering on the blasted heath, Edward is now every inch a king. Hence we are all the more moved by the ill-treatment he must bear and we instinctively take his side against his tormentors.

We now come to the two greatest scenes in the drama, the abdication and the murder, both admirable, especially the first. It is almost entirely a long soliloquy spoken by the King. Some of his opponents urge him to hand over the crown to them, but they seem so anxious to carry it away that they are sparing of their words. Edward, on the contrary, discloses at length the various thoughts and emotions that fill his mind and heart. More than at any other time he speaks like a poet, as will speak Shakespeare's Richard II, who owes much to him. His faults and foibles are now a thing of the past. We watch with compassion the pangs of the sovereign compelled to give up something /**181**/ more precious than his life, now he has lost his favourites. As Shakespeare's Charmian said

> The soul and body rive not more in parting
> Than greatness going off.[2]

To bring home to his listeners the full value of his sacrifice, he first recalls the greatness of his rank which in adversity as well as in prosperity sets him above other men.

> The griefs of private men are soon allayed,
> But not of kings. The forest deer, being struck,
> Runs to an herb that closeth up the wounds,
> But when the imperial lion's flesh is gored,
> He rends and tears it with his wrathful paw,
> And highly scorning that the lowly earth
> Should drink his blood, mounts up into the air.
> And so it fares with me.

[V. i. 8–15]

Now that misfortune has opened his eyes, he casts a clear glance upon his impotence. Convinced as he is that Mortimer wants to succeed him on the throne, he finds it all the more difficult to comply and abdicate. Then, like Faustus at the hour of his death, alone in front of destiny, he feels an unescapable doom weighing upon him. He wants to ward it off, to delay it at least, to postpone his decision by a few hours. The King's reaction in front of his fall is almost identical with the scholar's in front of death:

> But stay awhile; let me be king till night,
> That I may gaze upon this glittering crown;
> So shall my eyes receive their last content,
> My head, the latest honor due to it,
> And jointly both yield up their wishèd right./**182**/

---

[2] *Antony and Cleopatra*, IV. xi. 5–6.

Continue ever thou celestial sun;
Let never silent night possess this clime,
Stand still you watches of the element;
All times and seasons, rest you at a stay,
That Edward may be still fair England's king.

[V. i. 59–68]

Realizing the futility of such wishes, he is seized with a brief fit of anger which is equally vain. When someone points out to him that if he delays too long, his son may be deprived of his right to the throne, he at last brings himself to abdicate, but—and this is the last tremor of the dying lion—he refuses to take off the crown from his head himself. Yet he must drain the cup to the dregs. He finally complies and seeks comfort in the thought of the hereafter. It is unfortunate that this grand and moving scene should end on a discordant note: the incident of the handkerchief soaked with his tears and dried by his sighs is a grievous offence against taste which causes this fine soliloquy to sink into the most ridiculous and ill-timed preciosity.

This pathetic climax is followed by the frightful horror of the murder scene. Outdoing Holinshed, Marlowe has given free play to that morbid instinct for cruelty which is the most displeasing feature of his personality. Pent up in a sewer whose waters reach up to his knees and send forth an unbearable stench, Edward must keep standing and cannot sleep. After some grim preparations, the murderer draws him out. Confronted with this sinister-looking visitor, he realizes he is lost. He tries to move him to pity, to bribe him, but all in vain. He struggles against sleep, he struggles against fear, and falls at last after commending his soul to God.

As Edward II's character is a development of Cosroe's, so his fate is similar to Bajazet's, but depicted in an /183/ altogether different light. In *Tamburlaine* all the interest centred upon the superman. The playwright had no sympathy to waste upon the victims. Here, on the contrary, the subject-matter is not the rise of a strong man to power but the fall of a weak man from power. The place of honour is given to the victim of a conspiracy caused by his own mistakes. Marlowe can therefore afford to make him attractive.

The success this play achieves as a psychological study cannot make us forget that the same method is followed in it as in the others. A single character is minutely depicted; the others are mere sketches, often hastily and clumsily drawn. A few exceptions do not invalidate

that statement. Torn between his brotherly love and his duty to the
State, Kent is faced with an interesting point of conscience, but his
chief function is to serve as a foil to the protagonist, his own change
of attitude being designed to modify the spectator's towards the
King. Gaveston's words and actions have just the minimum of
reality required. On the contrary, some of Prince Edward's speeches
sound absurd in the mouth of a child. As to the Queen, she is a mere
puppet. At the beginning, her fawning love for Edward turns her
into his slave: she is ready to do anything to remain in favour with
him, even to plead the cause of her male rival in front of the noblemen. It is true she seems to be on fairly intimate terms with Mortimer, but she denies she has had any sinful intercourse with him. She
is obviously truthful when she says so since, left alone on the stage,
she takes heaven to witness she loves only the King [II. iv. 15]. How
can we, then, believe her when in the same scene, forty-five lines
farther on, she tells Mortimer she could live for ever with him, inas-
much as she has known him for a long time and so has not fallen in
love at first sight? Such /**184**/ a sudden volte-face has nothing in
common with the usual workings of a human heart. She is one more
instance of that negligence or clumsiness we have already noted in
Marlowe's delineation of minor characters. Once more, the dramatist's attention and art have been focused too exclusively on the
protagonist.

At first sight this historical drama has an objective quality that
contrasts with the lyricism which fills *Tamburlaine* or *Doctor Faustus*.
The subject chosen and to a certain extent the technique used no
longer correspond to the same self-centred preoccupations. The hero
no longer embodies the poet's high aspirations. It is all the more
interesting to determine how far *Edward II* may nevertheless be
connected with his personality. Leaving aside a possible influence
of Shakespeare, to which we shall return later, he has been attracted
by an historical personage showing a homosexual tendency similar to
his own. Once more he allows himself to be allured by the initial
situation of an action that may be used as material for a dream. As
a consequence, he accepts and develops the rest of the plot. As a
matter of fact, Holinshed hardly lets the true character of the relationship between the King and his minions be surmised, and many
readers would certainly miss it. But Marlowe, guided by an exceptional flair, does not fail to notice it. Unlike the chronicler, he dwells

complacently upon that unnatural passion, describes it in a congenial manner, haloes it with the glamour of illustrious precedents. He links it to vows of friendship—a feeling far more intense in the sixteenth centruy than nowadays—which would enhance and almost excuse it. Faithful to Edward until death, Gaveston stands, it could could be said, as the hero and martyr of sodomy.

Thus, contrary to his custom, Marlowe is led to give the leading part to a weakling who lets himself be tossed about /185/ by circumstances and is at no time master of his fate. Yet Edward resembles the heroes of the other dramas by his complete indifference to good and evil and also by intensity of passion, which is always the strong and sole driving power. But that passion is no longer the same. The others' ambition is only repeated by a weak echo, especially in the lines in which Mortimer speaks of his "virtue that aspires to heaven" [III. iii. 72] which is somewhat startling in such a cynical man. On the other hand, his career illustrates the fickleness of fortune as effectively as those wheels carved on the porch of cathedrals:

> Base Fortune, now I see that in thy wheel
> There is a point, to which when men aspire,
> They tumble headlong down. That point I touched,
> And seeing there was no place to mount up higher,
> Why should I grieve at my declining fall?
>
> [V. vi. 59–63]

How remote all this is from *Tamburlaine*!

The love of gorgeous ornaments and splendid entertainments, the taste for everything sumptuous whereby Marlowe stands as the perfect representative of his time, again appear in this drama, not only in some of the comparisons and metaphors but chiefly in the description of the festivities and pastimes that are to fill Gaveston's and his royal friend's lives:

> Therefore I'll have Italian masks by night,
> Sweet speeches, comedies, and pleasing shows;
> And in the day, when he shall walk abroad,
> Like sylvan nymphs my pages shall be clad.
> My men, like satyrs grazing on the lawns,
> Shall with their goat-feet dance an antic hay. /186/
> Sometime a lovely boy in Dian's shape,
> With hair that gilds the water as it glides,

> Crownets of pearl about his naked arms,
> And in his sportful hands an olive tree,
> To hide those parts which men delight to see,
> Shall bathe him in a spring; and there, hard by,
> One like Actæon peeping through the grove,
> Shall by the angry goddess be transformed,
> And running in the likeness of an hart,
> By yelping hounds pulled down, and seem to die.

[I. i. 55–70]

It is obvious that Marlowe is thinking not of the entertainments at the court of Edward II but of the masques and plays at that of Elizabeth. Similarly, when he describes the *imprese* chosen by the noblemen, he refers to a custom of his own time and conforms to the vogue of euphuism.

Anachronisms are equally conspicuous in passages dealing with religion. Walter de Langton, in whom Holinshed sees chiefly the Lord Treasurer, appears in the play only as the Bishop of Coventry. Thus, when the King insults him, the offence strikes not a statesman but a prelate. To give more authority to the Archbishop of Canterbury, Marlowe has made him the Papal legate. Through him, the Church, still more than the feudal lords, compels Edward II to a humiliating capitulation. So the King is not master in his own kingdom: he has to submit to the intolerable interference of a foreign power. This gives rise to a violent anti-Catholic tirade, two lines of which repeat almost word for word Henry III's words in *The Massacre at Paris*:

> Why should a king be subject to a priest?
> Proud Rome, that hatchest such imperial grooms,
> For these thy superstitious taper-lights,
> Wherewith thy antichristian churches blaze, /**187**/
> I'll fire thy crazèd buildings and enforce
> The papal towers to kiss the lowly ground.
> With slaughtered priests may Tiber's channel swell,
> And banks raised higher with their sepulchers.

[I. iv. 96–103]

Such invective is all the more unjustified as the two prelates, conscious of the dignity of priesthood, indifferent to threats and trusting in divine Providence, are portrayed in a very objective manner.

The references to Puritans [II. i. 31–43] are equally unexpected in a drama taking place in the fourteenth century. They are doubly interesting as one of the earliest anti-puritan satires on the stage and as one of the very few passages wherein Marlowe draws on his observations of contemporary society. Finally, the dramatist has ascribed to Edward II a wavering religious attitude which seems somewhat similar to his own. At times the King denies the existence of Providence and speaks of the life hereafter like a pagan, in words borrowed from mythology [IV. vi. 73–5 and 86–9]; now he sees in death the be-all and end-all, now the beginning of everlasting felicity [V. i. 153 and 107–9]. As to Baldock's half-Christian, half-Stoical attitude, it is typical of the age more than of the dramatist [IV. vi. 104–11].

Like *The Jew of Malta* and *The Massacre at Paris, Edward II* is a Machiavellian or rather pseudo-Machiavellian play, although to a lesser extent. It partakes of the same character in the first place by what is furthest from the true Machiavelli, the art of killing. Lightborn has learnt it in Italy, as Barabas did. He would be ashamed of using the same method twice. He avoids shedding blood, likes his /188/ work to be quickly and neatly done. He practises murder as one of the fine arts and admires his own virtuosity. Spenser and Baldock, two men of unscrupulous ambition, choose the King's side because they deem it the more profitable one. But Edward II wins them over so that they soon give up their own selfish schemes, become faithful to their master, and evince the same disinterestedness as Gaveston; so they prove bad disciples of the Florentine thinker.

The same cannot be said of Mortimer, especially after his victory. The protector of the kingdom, who is in fact omnipotent, is a perfect embodiment of Machiavellism. He practises dissimulation and admires the Queen's. He pretends he has not sought after power and, under the guise of "a bashful Puritan" [V. iv. 59], he cleverly clothes himself with the cloak of religion, as Machiavelli prescribes. He is entirely devoid of moral conscience. The King having abdicated, he wants to kill him in order not to be killed himself, for, as Machiavelli says, "it is a speciall poynte of Government to wynne men with smooth woordes, or rowndly to cutt them of". Even in such a circumstance, when he seems to run but little risk, he acts most warily. He conveys his order by a Latin sentence with a twofold meaning and causes the murderer to be dispatched as soon as he has done his work. Once his ambition is gratified, he notes, in one of those long soliloquies so dear to Marlowe, that he is feared more than loved and he rejoices therein. "I thincke it more safetie", wrote Machiavelli, "to be feared then loved", and Harvey made him say: "Plebs amor nihil est." Yet, despite all his cleverness, his crime is found out and he must atone for it. For the sake of poetic justice which happens to be also historical justice, Marlowe has ended the play not with Edward's death but with /189/ Mortimer's. Like Barabas, like Guise, the latter fails through applying the maxims of *The Prince* too faithfully.

By its style and verse as well as by its subject-matter and dramatic technique, *Edward II* stands in contrast with Marlowe's other important plays. Ornate passages, such as the account of the entertainments at court quoted above, are rare; rare too are lines standing out for their musical quality and their magical value, such as this one:

> Because he loves me more than all the world [I. iv. 77].

The sentences are clear, the dialogue is quick, often made up of short retorts clashing against one another and at times drawing close to stichomythia. In short, the style is subordinated to the action more than anywhere else. Lyricism nevertheless reappears after Edward's defeat. The speeches grow longer, the comparisons more frequent and more elaborate, the poetry more abundant. We may quote as an example:

> But what are kings when regiment is gone,
> But perfect shadows in a sunshine day?
>
> [V. i. 26–7]

Generally speaking, the prosody is marked by more flexibility than in any other play. The percentage of feminine endings, of lines beginning with a stressed syllable and of lines including fewer than five feet is perceptibly higher. The enjambements nevertheless remain scarce, which may be accounted for by the shortness of the speeches, some of which are not more than one or two lines long. The flourishes of trumpets which sounded so often in *Tamburlaine* are heard no longer. The verse as well as the language is made to serve exclusively dramatic purposes.

Edward II is unquestionably the first chronicle play that is a great work of literature. Apart from Shakespeare's it /190/ is indeed the greatest achievement in that genre. If we leave aside the two anonymous dramas on the Wars of the Roses, it is also the one in which Shakespeare's influence is most apparent. The example of the second and third parts of *Henry VI* in their final form, whose composition Shakespearean scholars ascribe to the year 1590 or 1591, must have induced Marlowe to change his manner considerably. Thanks to that influence, he has greatly improved his dramatic technique.

In its turn, *Edward II*, together with the Machiavellian dramas, is the play through which Marlowe has exerted the strongest influence upon Shakespeare. It is certainly not by accident that very soon afterwards he too staged a King of England who loses his throne and life owing to incompetence. The comparison between *Edward II* and *Richard II* has become almost a commonplace of criticism. As a matter of fact, their resemblance is limited to the subject-matter and to the poetical utterances of the two kings. Their qualities are very different; so are the characters of the respective heroes. Edward II is prompted by his passion for his favourites; he neglects his duties as a sovereign, but he knows what he wants. More sentimental, more refined, above all more passive and more inclined to narcissism, Richard II on the contrary shows himself unable to take a decision and hold on to it. The opposition between the king and the leader of the rebels is more strongly marked by Shakespeare, which does not prevent the hero, contrary to all expectation, from being more lyrical than Marlowe's. Edward II in adversity claims our sympathy; Richard II does not, and seems to feel an unhealthy satisfaction in divesting himself of his royal privileges. Shakespeare, who in the blinding of Gloucester will put on the stage an unbearable scene worthy of the *Grand Guignol*, here shows nothing so horrible as Edward's death. /**191**/ In spite of all this, the last scenes of Marlowe's drama are more impressive and moving.

It is more difficult to assess the value of this play than that of any other by Marlowe. Critics are divided. Some look upon *Edward II* as his best drama. In actual fact, if judged according to the usual standards, it is certainly the most successful one he wrote. Better built than the others, it also evinces a more perfect harmony between the characters and the action; it stands closer to the Shakespearean conception of the chronicle play. Others, with whose opinion we concur, find *Edward II* less attractive than the great lyrical dramas. Owing to the more conscientious workmanship and also to the

correctness of the text that has come down to us, the play unquestionably remains on a more uniform level throughout. It is less
glaringly faulty, but also less poetic save in the last two great scenes.
Whatever may be said on its behalf, the characterization remains
sketchy except in the case of the King. Nor does Marlowe's strong
personality reveal itself so completely. The author of *Tamburlaine*
and *Doctor Faustus* is a more original writer, a greater genius than
that of *Edward II*. This last drama is nevertheless most valuable, for
it proves that Marlowe was not a pure lyrical poet who had chosen
an unsuitable medium, that he was not the victim of the infatuation
of his age for the drama, but rather a genius capable of renewing
himself and who might have disclosed still other aspects had he not
met with such an untimely death. /**192**/

IRVING RIBNER

EDWARD II
As Historical Tragedy

In Shakespeare's *Richard III* we have seen perhaps the ultimate development of the Senecan mode in English historical drama. For the genre to progress further, the history play had to follow other avenues, and in the year or so before *Richard III* was written another play had appeared which was to open new vistas for development. This was Christopher Marlowe's *Troublesome Reign and Lamentable Death of Edward the Second*, written probably in 1591 or 1592 and influenced somewhat by Shakespeare's own *Henry VI* plays which appear to have preceded it.[1] The title-page of the earliest extant edition, printed for William Jones in 1594, tells us that it was 'sundrie times publiquely acted in the honourable citie of London, by the right honourable the Earle of Pembrooke his servants'. There is some evidence, moreover, for a now lost edition of the play in 1593.[2] Just as Marlowe's *Tamburlaine* had heralded in and shaped the tone of a wave of historical drama which was to reach its heights in Shakespeare's first tetralogy, Marlowe's *Edward II* gave rise to another wave which was to culminate in Shakespeare's Lancastrian plays.[3]

Reprinted from *The English History Play in the Age of Shakespeare* (London: Methuen & Co., 1965).

[1] H. B. Charlton and R. D. Waller, eds., *Edward II* (London, 1933), argue convincingly that the play was written in the autumn of 1591 but that it was not played in London until December, 1592, although it may have been earlier played in the provinces (p. 20).

[2] *Ibid.*, p. 4.

[3] It is possible that *Edward II* had already begun to influence Shakespeare in *Richard III*, but there is really little Marlovian quality in that play which cannot be attributed to the influence of *Tamburlaine*.

In Marlowe's *Edward II* we have the beginning of a type of historical tragedy not based upon the Senecan formula, although the play displays a horror more moving than the Senecan clichés ever could, because it is more realistic. We have in *Edward II*, perhaps for the first time in Elizabethan drama, a tragedy of character in which a potentially good man comes to destruction because of /**123**/ inherent weaknesses which make him incapable of coping with a crisis which he himself has helped to create. And in his downfall he carries with him the sympathies of the audience. Marlowe is deeply concerned with the personal tragedy of Edward as a man, and he forges upon the stage a vision of human suffering whose realism and intensity have rarely if ever been equalled, while at the same time in the parallel tragedy of Mortimer he presents the fall of aspiring humanity from high place which had long been the theme of *de casibus* story. It has been held by some[4] that Marlowe's only interest in this play was in presenting a vision of the suffering of which mankind is capable, that he saw his characters only as persons, without regard to their political roles, and thus that there is in the play no probing of the political or moral implications in the fate of Edward, Mortimer or Isabella. But it is impossible to separate these dramatic characters from their historical roles. The fate of Edward is not only that of a man but that of an English king, and thus his tragedy is involved inextricably with the life of the state.

In making Edward's disaster the subject of a play Marlowe is exploring an earlier political situation of much interest to Elizabethan Englishmen, as we can tell from the many treatments of it in prose and verse, one which mirrored the kind of civil war of which they lived in constant dread. In choosing this story from the chronicles Marlowe was obliged to assume the role of historian. Suffering humanity in this play is a suffering English king, with the ends of tragedy and those of history entirely fused, for Edward's sins are sins of government, the crisis he faces is a political one, and his disaster is not merely death but the loss of his crown and the ruin of his kingdom by civil war.

---

[4] See, for instance, Clifford Leech, 'Marlowe's Edward II: Power and Suffering,' *Critical Quarterly*, I (1959), 181–96; Douglas Cole, *Suffering and Evil in the Plays of Christopher Marlowe*, pp. 161–90; J. B. Steane, *Marlowe, A Critical Study*, pp. 204–35. The contrary has been held by Reese, *The Cease of Majesty*, pp. 80–81, who writes: 'Edward is a king, his failings are the failings of a ruler, and the crisis of his reign is political; Marlowe recognizes that the sins of the man cannot be separated from the sins of his government."

The historical implications of his story were an essential part of it which Marlowe could scarcely have avoided even if he had chosen to do so, and there is little reason for us to assume that he would so choose, for Marlowe was occupied with the problems of /**124**/ the nature and limitations of political power through much of his career. He had explored the subject in *Tamburlaine* and in *The Massacre at Paris*; that his vision of the effects of human power is so different in *Edward II* from that in *Tamburlaine* indicates no less a concern with the problem, but merely that Marlowe has grown immensely as a tragic artist and can see the implications of his subject more fully than ever before.[5] He is now able to create characters who change and develop under the pressure of events and thus to reveal a fuller vision of human potential, for good as well as evil, than had ever before been realized upon the English stage. Mortimer and Isabella, the traitor and the adultress of the final scenes, are hardly recognizable for the long-suffering wife and brave patriot of the opening scenes, and King Edward grows and develops under the pressure of disaster, with his brother Edmund, serving as a kind of chorus to guide the shifting sympathies of the audience. That these characters are not the rigid symbols of abstract political positions we may find in *Tamburlaine* does not mean that the political implications of their fates are less real or less fully explored. That there is in the play much besides its political issues is obvious, but these issues are what make *Edward II* a history play, and it is with them that I am here primarily concerned.

Marlowe's play covers a long and involved period of history, from the accession of Edward II in 1307 to the execution of Roger Mortimer in 1330. For almost all of his material he went to Holinshed, but he also consulted Stow, from whom he took the episode of the shaving of Edward in puddle water, and Fabyan, from whom he took the jig quoted by the Earl of Lancaster on England's disgrace at Bannockburn.[6] It has been suggested that Marlowe's first interest in the subject may have been aroused by the tragedy of 'The Two Mortimers' in the 1578 *Mirror for Magistrates*.[7] Marlowe approached his

[5] I have suggested a view of Marlowe's development as a tragic artist in 'Marlowe's "Tragicke Glasse,",' *Essays on Shakespeare and Elizabethan Drama in Honor of Hardin Craig*, pp. 91–114. On the development of the play's characters as they react to one another, and on the shifting sympathies involved, see E. M. Waith, '*Edward II*: The Shadow of Action,' *Tulane Drama Review*, VIII (1964), 59–76.

[6] II, ii, 188–93.

[7] Alwin Thaler, 'Churchyard and Marlowe,' *MLN*, XXXVIII (1923), 89–92.

sources with a sure /125/ awareness of his purposes and perhaps a
keener dramatic skill than had ever before been exercised in the
dramatizing of English history. For out of the great mass of material
in Holinshed he carefully selected only what he needed for a well
integrated tragedy. He omitted most of Edward's long and involved
relations with the barons, his wars in France and Scotland, with the
disastrous defeat at Bannockburn. He condensed the events of almost thirty years into what appears to be about one year, although
the play gives us little real indication of the passage of time. The
resulting inconsistencies and errors in chronology are too numerous
to list, but all of Marlowe's manipulation of his sources serves the
functions of his play, and there is very little invented matter. By
this compression and rearrangement, Marlowe achieved an economy and effectiveness which had not before been seen in the history
play.

In many respects Marlowe prepared the way for Shakespeare's
great historical tragedy of *Richard II*, and not least in that he gave a
new tragic significance to the *de casibus* theme of rise and fall which
we have already noted in the *Henry VI* plays and in *Richard III*. As
Edward falls, young Mortimer rises in his place, only to fall himself
as the new King Edward III assumes his position.[8] Edward and
Mortimer are fashioned by Marlowe as parallel characters, each
serving as foil to the other. All of Edward's weaknesses are mirrored
in Mortimer's strength; what private virtue Edward may acquire is
set off by Mortimer's corresponding loss. Those elements which
cause Edward to fall cause Mortimer to rise. This use of two con-
trasting and complementary characters in tragedy Shakespeare was
to learn from Marlowe in his *Richard II*, and he was to continue to
use it in some of the greatest of his later plays.

The denial to providence of any role in human affairs, which we
have noted as Marlowe's position in *Tamburlaine*, persists in *Edward
II*, although it is not so strongly emphasized, and it is tempered by
a kind of medieval fatalism which is wholly absent from the earlier
play. This is most evident in Mortimer's final speech: /126/

> Base Fortune, now I see that in thy wheel
> There is a point, to which when men aspire,
> They tumble headlong down. That point I touched,

[8] See R. Fricker, 'The Dramatic Structure of *Edward II*,' *English Studies*,
XXXIV (1953), 204–17.

And, seeing there was no place to mount up higher,
Why should I grieve at my declining fall?

(V, vi, 59–63)

There is nothing here of the Christian attitude which would emphasize man's fall as divine retribution for his sins, merely a calm acceptance of the inevitable destruction at the hands of fate of all who
aspire beyond a certain point. What we have is a stoical acceptance
of fortune in the manner of the classical historians.

It is largely in this pessimism that the view of history to which
Marlowe came in *Edward II* differs from that in *Tamburlaine*, where
there are no limits to what the ever-triumphant superman may
attain, where ruthless self-sufficiency may create empires, and where
human attainments are limited only by the death which must
inevitably come to all, and which to the hero like Tamburlaine will
come at the very height of his achievement. The flamboyant optimism of the earlier play is now replaced by a more tragic view of life
most evident in the decline of Mortimer. For as he achieves success
his character steadily degenerates. His initial concern for England
soon becomes a concern only for his own aggrandizement, and to
further his aims there is no baseness to which he will not resort.
When he is cut off by fortune, he has lost all sympathy the audience
may have had for him at the play's beginning. Marlowe has thus
moved some distance from the Machiavellian position he had
espoused in *Tamburlaine*.[9] Mortimer is destroyed in spite of the fact
that he embodies a Machiavellian self-sufficiency, strength and
aspiring will. Edward and Mortimer are each endowed with those
qualities the other lacks and each nevertheless is destroyed. Edward
is ruined by his lack of public virtue; Mortimer declines because as
his public virtues manifest themselves in action his private virtues
are slowly eroded and destroyed. Perhaps Marlowe is suggesting the
Aristotelian rather than the Machiavellian ideal: that the king's
public morality must be grounded upon a private humanity, and
perhaps he is adding /**127**/ the pessimistic observation that it is
virtually impossible for this personal humanity to survive in the
wielder of absolute public power. In short, although Machiavelli's
humanistic non-providential view of history is still in *Edward II*,
Marlowe's enthusiasm for the Machiavellian superman is consider-

[9] See Irving Ribner, 'Marlowe and Machiavelli,' *Comparative Literature*, VI
(1954), 349–56.

ably diminished. He has come to see the moving spirits of history not as prototypes of an impossible ideal, but as men who are themselves moulded by the pressure of events, who develop and change. He has come to recognize that to control power in the secular absolutist state, the Machiavellian brand of virtù will not suffice.

There is thus a kind of ambivalence in the play, for while Edward's shortcomings as a king are fully detailed there is little assurance that had he been otherwise he might have fared better. This feeling the parallel tragedy of Mortimer, who begins with all of the appurtenances of kingship, does much to enforce. *Edward II* reflects in a political setting that pessimism which in Marlowe's last plays came gradually to succeed the flamboyant optimism of *Tamburlaine*, and which is reflected also in *Doctor Faustus* where while the terrible results of the hero's apostasy are portrayed, there is no emphasis upon the goodness of the religious system he rejects. While Marlowe in *Edward II* dwells upon political failure, he is able to offer no real formula for political success. This feeling persists in spite of the appearance at the end of Edward III who Marlowe's audience knew would grow up to be one of England's greatest kings.

Tillyard has commented that there is in *Edward II* 'no sense of any sweep or pattern of history' such as we find in Shakespeare's history plays,[10] and F. P. Wilson has made essentially the same observation.[11] Marlowe sees no pattern in history because, unlike Shakespeare, he does not see in history the working out of a divine purpose, and therefore he cannot see in it any large scheme encompassing God's plans for men and extending over many decades. Marlowe sees history as the actions of men who bring about their own success or failure entirely by their own ability to cope with events. This is the humanistic attitude of both the classical and the Italian Renaissance historians, and if it is not /**128**/ proclaimed in *Edward II* as loudly and as flamboyantly as it is in *Tamburlaine*, it is nevertheless present.

Tillyard (pp. 107–8) has called the political doctrine in *Edward II* impeccably orthodox. But if this were so, it would be indeed strange to note, as Alfred Hart has pointed out,[12] that there is in *Edward II* not a single reference to the divine right of kings. Nor is there any mention of the king's responsibility to God, a cornerstone of orthodox

[10] *Shakespeare's History Plays*, p. 108.
[11] *Marlowe and the Early Shakespeare*, p. 125.
[12] *Shakespeare and the Homilies*, p. 25.

Elizabethan doctrine. The truth is that the political milieu of *Edward II* is the same as that of *Tamburlaine*, in which the unquestioned absolutism of the king is based not upon divine ordination, but upon human power, and in which the king is not controlled by any responsibility to a God who will destroy him if he neglects his duties to his people, but only by the limits of the king's own ability to maintain his power in spite of any opposition.[13] The tragedy of Edward II is that he is born into a position where he must be capable of controlling absolute power in order to survive, and since he is not he is doomed to destruction. Michel Poirer has called the play 'the story of a feudal monarch who attempts to govern as an absolute monarch and fails'.[14] But we must note that it is not in the divinely sanctioned absolute monarchy of Elizabeth that he attempts to rule, but rather in the powerful secular autocracy of Italian Renaissance political theory. In his failure to maintain his position in such a state, Edward loses all of the appurtenances of kingship, as he himself affirms:

> But what are kings when regiment is gone,
> But perfect shadows in a sunshine day?
>
> (V, i, 26–27)

In the tragedy of Edward II Marlowe accomplishes the political purposes of the Elizabethan historian, for while the play embodies no assurance that any human king can survive in an absolute state, the downfall of Edward is nevertheless explained in terms of his violation of political principles. Some of Edward's shortcomings in this respect had already been indicated by Holinshed: /**129**/

> . . . he wanted judgment and prudent discretion to make choice of sage and discreet counsellors, receiving those into his favour, that abused the same to their private gain and advantage, not respecting the advancement of the commonwealth.[15]

It was the 'covetous rapine, spoil and immoderate ambition' of these favourites which alienated the nobles and caused them to rise up against their king. Marlowe thus warns that a king must be prudent in his choice of counsellors. He must further be strong, able to

[13] See Paul H. Kocher, *Christopher Marlowe: A Study of His Thought, Learning and Character*, p. 189

[14] *Christopher Marlowe*, p. 173.

[15] *Chronicles* (London, 1587), III, 327.

control his nobles, cut off those who oppose him, which Edward manifestly cannot do. But a successful king does not alienate his nobles in the first place, for they are an important bulwark of his power. At Edward's brief reconciliation with the barons, Queen Isabel directs an important bit of didacticism to the audience:

> Now is the king of England rich and strong,
> Having the love of his renowned peers.

(I, iv, 365–6)

This theme of a king's relation to his nobles is an important political theme in *Edward II*.

Edward II would be an absolute ruler. He regards his kingdom as personal property which he is free to give to his parasitic Gaveston if he chooses:

> If for these dignities thou be envied,
> I'll give thee more; for but to honour thee,
> Is Edward pleased with kingly regiment.
> Fearst thou thy person? Thou shalt have a guard.
> Wantest thou gold? Go to my treasury.
> Wouldst thou be loved and feared? Receive my seal;
> Save or condemn, and in our name command
> Whatso thy mind affects or fancy likes.

(I, i, 163–70)

He places his personal pleasures above the interests of his government, and perhaps worst of all, he has no real desire to rule. He will see England quartered and reduced to chaos rather than forgo his attachment to his minion: /**130**/

> Make several kingdoms of this monarchy
> And share it equally amongst you all,
> So I may have some nook or corner left
> To frolic with my dearest Gaveston.

(I, iv, 70–73)

If a Renaissance absolute monarch required anything to maintain himself in power, it was a paramount desire to rule and a concern above all else with the maintenance of his power in spite of all opposition.

Paul H. Kocher has found in *Edward II* two new political considerations which are not in *Tamburlaine*: 'one is the fundamental principle of Renaissance political science that the sovereign must observe justice. The second is the elementary awareness that the nobles and commons are political forces of prime importance'.[16] Edward's sins are violations of political ethics which the Renaissance had come generally to accept. The absolute ruler must rule justly, and this Edward does not. His people, both noble and common, are a potent political force which may make its pressure felt in a kingdom, no matter how absolute the ruler may be. An absolute monarch must be aware of this force, as Machiavelli's prince always is, for if he does not learn to handle it properly it may overwhelm him. Marlowe thus incorporates into *Edward II* some awareness of the parliamentarianism which had been a part of his own English government for several centuries. An absolute ruler may continue to be one only so long as he knows how to rule: with strength, justice, and an awareness of both the power and the needs of his subjects.

There are further at least two minor political issues in *Edward II*. In one important passage Marlowe disposes of the ever-present problem in Elizabethan England of the relation of king to pope, and his statement is one to gladden the hearts of patriotic Elizabethan Protestants:

> Proud Rome, that hatchest such imperial grooms,
> For these thy superstitious taper-lights,
> Wherewith thy antichristian churches blaze,
> I'll fire thy crazèd buildings and enforce
> The papal towers to kiss the lowly ground. /131/
> With slaughtered priests may Tiber's channel swell,
> And banks raised higher with their sepulchers.
> As for the peers that back the clergy thus,
> If I be king, not one of them shall live.
>
> (I, iv, 97–105)

A second minor issue is the relation of kingship to noble birth. In *Tamburlaine* Marlowe had proclaimed that there was no relation between the two, that it was in the nature of every man to aspire to kingship, that only the man of merit could achieve it. In *Edward II* this notion has been greatly modified and tempered, but a slight note of it nevertheless persists. Although Marlowe probably shares the abhorrence of the barons for Piers Gaveston, he does not scorn Gaveston for his lowly birth, as Mortimer does (I, iv, 41, 402). We

---

[16] *Christopher Marlowe*, p. 207.

detect a note of sympathy in Edward's defence of the lowly born against the overbearing barons:

> Were he a peasant, being my minion,
> I'll make the proudest of you stoop to him.
>
> (I, iv, 30–31)

One wonders why Marlowe insisted that Gaveston be of lowly birth, when the chronicles report no such thing, if it were not for the opportunity which this afforded him to repeat, although in a greatly subdued manner, the doctrine he had so loudly and defiantly proclaimed in *Tamburlaine*: that kingship and nobility have small relation to birth.

In dramatic structure *Edward II* marks a new departure in that for the first time in an English history play all of the elements are completely integrated. Every incident furthers the total effect of the play, which is concentrated in the downfall of Edward. To accomplish this Marlowe had to abandon the episodic survey treatment we have found in earlier history plays,[17] and notably in his own *Tamburlaine*. Of the morality influence there is little in *Edward II*, although it is possible to conceive of Edward as faced with a choice between his barons and his favourites and choosing his favourites to his own destruction. There is none of the awareness of error and consequent regeneration which is so much a part of the morality tradition; Edward never really learns the cause of /132/ his downfall, and he is not penitent at the end.[18] There is little thematic statement by means of ritual: the washing of Edward in puddle water, which might be interpreted to have some such significance, was merely rendered literally from his sources. The morality play, which appears to have influenced Marlowe strongly in *Doctor Faustus* had little effect upon *Edward II*. /133/

[17] See W. D. Briggs, *Marlowe's Edward II*, pp. cviii–cix.
[18] F. P. Wilson, *Marlowe and the Early Shakespeare*, p. 99.

WILBUR SANDERS

History Without Morality:
EDWARD II

Perhaps the most remarkable thing about Marlowe's *Edward II* is
the fact that, although it has every appearance of being a play on a
national and political theme, a play about kingship, it is yet an intensely personal play in which the public issues hardly arise. It's
true that there is a fair deal of talk about 'our country's good' (see
II. iii. 1; IV. i. 2; IV. v. 74–7; and V. i. 38), and no scarcity of criti-
cisms against Edward's mode of ruling, but on these occasions one is
primarily conscious either of the slackness of unfelt platitude, or of
a very bald sophistry on the part of egocentric power-seekers. The
sentiments do not seem to mesh with any larger scheme of political
morality in the drama. When Isabella exults,

> Successful battles gives the God of kings
> To them that fight in right and fear His wrath,   IV. v. 28

one's first impulse is to sneer, for the introduction of providential
sanctions seems quite gratuitous in the world of this play. It is not
that Marlowe has created a dramatic context, like the world of
Richard III, within which the rationalisations of violence stand na-
kedly revealed for pious cant: what would have been clearly placed,
in *Richard III*, as a sophistical cloak for unscrupulous opportunism,
remains, in *Edward II*, oddly unplaced. Like the frequent appeals to
an overriding common good, the queen's theology is neither imaginatively ratified nor used to expose the egocentricity of her motiva-
tion: it is simply a statement thrown up in the course of conflict.

Reprinted from *The Dramatist and the Received Idea: Studies in the Plays of Marlowe & Shakespeare* (Cambridge University Press, 1968).

This strange moral indeterminacy—and it is thoroughly typical of the play—is a quality that is familiar enough to readers of modern newspapers: it is the reporter's studious policy of non-involvement, the uncommitted neutrality that operates by means of the reported speech and the eye-witness account. It is an early essay in the documentary mode. But it is rather startling to find it in an Elizabethan play. Marlowe appears to have assimilated the naturalistic trend of Renaissance historiography so thoroughly as to exclude altogether the providential tradition. As Irving Ribner puts it, /**121**/

Marlowe sees no pattern in history simply because . . . he does not see in history the working out of a divine purpose, and therefore he cannot see in it any large scheme encompassing God's plans for men and extending over many decades. Marlowe sees history entirely as the action of men who bring about their own success or failure entirely by their own ability to cope with events.[1]

Though I am unconvinced by the rest of Ribner's argument, this is, I think, an accurate charting of the sphere of action in *Edward II*; and it might seem to imply a very proper concentration on the dimension of human behaviour which lends itself naturally to dramatisation. And yet it is a very different kind of naturalism from the Shakespearian; for it is without moral anchorage. Marlowe displays no faith in the natural order; he does not seem to regard it, indeed, as anything more than material to be reported, and the play, consequently, provides us with an interesting test case for the question raised in the last chapter: whether a fundamental faith in the morality of nature is not a necessary faith for the dramatist? We can examine here, in a particular context, the consequences that ensue when a playwright chooses to put 'providential' thinking resolutely behind him.

But because Marlowe 'sees no pattern in history', it is exceedingly difficult to get hold of the pattern in the play. Theoretical views of monarchy bear on it only to the negative extent that they are largely ignored. The shape of the dramatic movement does not in any obvious way reveal a general conception lying behind the plotting. We cannot even take our bearings in the historical theorising of Marlowe's contemporaries, for his apparent obliviousness to providential-

---

[1] I. Ribner, *The English History Play in the Age of Shakespeare* (Princeton, 1957), p. 131.

ism makes him a veritable phoenix of Elizabethan thought—though many were prepared to challenge it, few could affect to be unaware of the existence of providential historiography. The only way into the play seems to lie in an attempt to discover the personal sources from which it stems—the thematic nodes in the source material which could account for Marlowe's interest in it.

F. S. Boas pointed out some time ago the remarkable similarity between the political and personal situations of the king in *Edward II* and Henry III in *The Massacre at Paris*. It is a parallelism which extends, as he shows, as far as a number of quite close verbal echoes.[2] He was not, however, the first to note the analogy:

The Duke [of Espernon] was then in his Cabinet, attending the houre of masse: where hee red the history of *Pierce Gaueston*, in old time deerely fauored by *Edward* the second King of *England*, prefered before all others in Court, in- /122/ riched with the Kings treasure, and the people's wealth, but after banished the realme, and in the end beheaded at the sute of the Parliament.

This slanderous libell being printed at *Paris*, not so much against the Dukes honour as the Kings, compared the Duke with *Gaueston*, and concluded that vnder Henry the third, hee should ende his daies by the like tragedie . . .[3]

Since the first recorded printing of these words was after Marlowe's death, it is most unlikely that he saw them—though he may have read the scurrilous pamphlet to which De Serres refers.[4] Be that as it may, the connexion made libellously by Espernon's enemies in the Holy League indicates that some assumptions, which have been very much in dispute in the interpretation of Marlowe's history play, may legitimately be made: first, that there is a path leading directly from the weak beminioned king of *The Massacre* to King Edward II, and that to see a common preoccupation with homosexual friendship in both plays is not a post-Freudian delusion, but the kind of thing a contemporary might have noticed; secondly, that an allegation of this kind (*pace* L. J. Mills and his scholarly contentions about the normality of such relationships for platonically enlightened

[2] F. S. Boas, *Christopher Marlowe* (Oxford, 1940), pp. 172–91.

[3] Jean de Serres, *A general Inventorie of the History of France*, tr. E. Grimestone (London, 1607).

[4] P. H. D. T., *Histoire Tragique et memorable, de Pierre de Gauerston Gentilhomme Gascon jadis le mignon d'Edoiiard 2 . . . Dediée a Monseigneur le Duc d'Espernon* ([Paris?], 1588).

Elizabethans[5]) was regarded as 'slanderous', even in those broad-minded days. It is thus, from an historical point of view, entirely possible that Marlowe was attracted to the reign of Edward by the opportunity it offered him to treat a forbidden sexual deviation. Whether this is really what the play is about is a critical question that I shall try to answer by critical methods. All I want to establish here is the historical admissibility of such a view.

A second possible point-of-entry for Marlowe is one which has been frequently noted—the overreaching figure of Mortimer, who so clearly swims in the mainstream of the Marlovian heroic tradition; though (I am bound to add) one is more conscious of the consider-able amplification which takes place in dramatisation, than of the fitness of Holinshed's Mortimer for the role.[6] For in Holinshed, the man is a fairly conventional aspirant for temporal power, and his method of ascent is undivulged. We are told simply that 'what he willed the same was doone, and without him the queene in all these matters did nothing'. The fullest account we get of his career is in the five articles of his Attainder, by which time it is at an end.[7] The character of Mortimer, it would seem, is less dependent on source material and more truly Marlowe's creation than most of the other characters in the play. Consequently he reveals very little about the preoccupations which sent Marlowe to this particular section of English history.

There is, however, one striking passage in Holinshed which cannot /**123**/ have escaped his notice, and which also forms the most ob-vious climax in the play—the murder of Edward. Here is Holinshed's rather too circumstantial account:

they came suddenlie one night into the chamber where he laie in bed fast asleepe, and with heauie featherbeds or a table (as some write) being cast vpon him, they kept him down and withall put into his fundament an horne, and through the same they thrust vp into his bodie an hot spit, or (as others haue) through the pipe of a trumpet a plumbers instrument of iron made verie hot, the which passing vp into his intrailes, and being rolled to and fro, burnt the same, but so as no appearance of any wound or hurt out-wardlie might be once perceived . . .[8]

[5] 'The Meaning of "Edward II",' *Modern Philology*, **XXXII** (1934), 11–31.

[6] For the primacy of Holinshed as Marlowe's source, see *Edward II*, ed. H. B. Charlton and R. D. Waller (London, 1933), pp. 31–52.

[7] *Hol.* III, 340/1, 349/1.

[8] *Ibid.*, III, 341/2.

This is strong meat, so strong that the play's most recent editors question whether Marlowe dared to stage it.[9] Yet it is a fact that he specifies feather-bed, table *and* spit in Lightborn's instructions to his assistants (V. v. 29–32) and it seems gratuitous to assume that the spit was requisitioned yet not used. Clearly the whole gruesome scene is enacted unexpurgated in full view of the audience. After all, the cry of a man smothered under a feather-bed is not so horrific as to provoke fears that it 'will raise the town' (V. v. 113), nor does it leave that indelible mark in the memory of a spectator which would account for a strange digression in a State Poem by Peele—

> Edward the Second, father to this king,
> Whose tragic cry even now methinks I hear,
> When graceless wretches murder'd him by night . . .[10]

Since no stage direction describes the actual performance of the murder, we are justified in assuming that this ferocious execution was performed as Holinshed gives it. This is disturbing enough.

But if we look more closely at the murder we see that the physical horror masks a more profound psychological horror; for the spit of Lightborn is a diabolic phallic parody of the perversion which is hinted at in the rest of the play—the so-called 'talion' punishment which psychoanalysis has diagnosed as one *modus operandi* of a guilt-ridden mind revenging itself on the world or on itself.[11] One does not have to accept the Freudian account of such matters to feel the malign fascination of this symbolic torture, and the ferocious concept of justice which lies behind it. And it is hard to believe that a man who could pretend to read sodomy into the intimacy of Christ with St John—and on this point Kyd and Baines corroborate each other— and who accounted those 'that loue not Tobacco & Boies' 'fooles', would have been /**124**/ totally insensible to the significance of the punishment which a plodding Holinshed dutifully reports.[12] Though such extrinsic arguments are always inconclusive, it seems

---

[9] *Edward II*, ed. Charlton and Waller (London, 1933), note to V. v. 30.

[10] 'The Honour of the Garter' [1593], ll. 222–4. Charlton and Waller (p. 21 note) are dubious whether this passage in fact refers to Marlowe's play. But its complete irrelevance in context—it is suggested by the mention of a sixteenth-century Mortimer whom Peele is eulogising—is best explained as the irruption of a theatrical memory still fresh and powerful. It is the *cry* he remembers, which would be odd if he had only read about it.

[11] Cf. W. Empson, 'Two Proper Crimes', *The Nation*, CLXIII (1946), 444–5.

[12] See C. F. Tucker Brooke, *Life of Marlowe* (London, 1930), pp. 99 and 107.

that in Edward's symbolic torture we have another at least plausible reason for Marlowe's interest in this chapter of English history.

If I say that this last point-of-entry—the murder of Edward—raises doubts in my mind, I hope I shall not be suspected of merely scenting perversion afar off and evading the issue. Partly it's an uneasiness I have about the internal balance of the play: such a blazing *fortissimo* of physical and psychic horror runs in peril of destroying whatever dynamic integrity the drama possesses. But the climax also raises questions about the pressures under which Marlowe writes. Does he, in short, *use* the homosexual motif, or does it use him? Does it simply gush up from that great storehouse of insurrectionary compulsions that goes by the name of the Unconscious? Clifford Leech, less disturbed by the death-scene than I am, has remarked,

Here in *Edward II* [Marlowe] stages the ultimate physical cruelty. He was a man who speculated on, and brought alive to his mind, the furthest reaches of human power and human suffering and humiliation. These things, he saw, men could do and had done, could suffer and had suffered, and his wondering mind gave them dramatic shape.[13]

My problem with *Edward II*, to try to crystallise the matter, is that Marlowe's mind in this play does not strike me as a 'wondering' one. Rather it is alternatively a wandering one, playing over an historical landscape in which he finds nothing to stimulate his imagination, and a compulsively driven one, delivered up to deep internal drives which he cannot bring into any satisfactory relation with the world of the human and the historical. It is as if the concerns which, in the first place, directed his attention to this reign—the weak homosexual king, the sensational violence of his death, the Machiavellian ambition of a Mortimer—take charge of his pen; and when their momentum is spent, he is obliged to trace meaningless patterns on the paper until the imaginative fit seizes him again.

This, it seems to me, is what happens to the Gaveston-Edward liaison, colourfully (if somewhat inconsistently) adumbrated in Gaveston's early soliloquies: before very long it has sunk into a lethargy of barren and repetitive protestations of love, from which it never recovers. If one must choose, the quartan fever of imaginative possession seems preferable to the lethargy. But neither is the mark of /**125**/ 'a man in his wholeness wholly attending'—to borrow a

13 'Marlowe's "Edward II": Power and Suffering', *CQ*, I (1959), 195.

phrase from Lawrence. There seems a singular absence of any guiding and shaping intelligence behind the presentation of the historical
material.

Perhaps I can focus this dissatisfaction by asking in what sense this
is an historical play at all. We have seen that it is not historical in the
religious-providential way—Marlowe is largely indifferent to the
great epochal tides in human affairs, and certainly does not see them
in theological terms—but this is only one way of looking at history
and can hardly be regarded as the *sine qua non* of historical drama.
A more serious lack in *Edward II*, as an historical play, is its consistent
subjugation of the political and the public to a very narrowly conceived pattern of personal conflict. It is not, as with Shakespeare, a
simultaneous vision of the political and private dimensions of the
public man, but a determined attempt to ignore the political sphere.
The king's fatal defiance of the duties imposed by his position ('for
but to honor thee, / Is Edward pleased with kingly regiment'—I. i.
164–5) is a violent insurrection against the exigencies of political
existence which, though eloquent, merely comes into collision with
those exigencies, without generating any new insight either in the
king or in the play.

Edward II is indeed (as so many of the commentators find themselves saying) a play about a man who happens also to be a king; and
the chief use to which his kingly status is put is to enhance the pathos
of his situation as a man:

> Within a dungeon England's king is kept.   V. iii. 19

> They give me bread and water, being a king.   V. v. 61

This indifference to the possible significances of kingship, except as
a personal cross to be borne by Edward, is one side of the coin; its
obverse, by an apparent paradox, is the absence of any common
human context for the political action that *is* presented. How unusual
(and how refreshing) it is to find Pembroke making a little detour in
order to visit his home:

> We that have pretty wenches to our wives,
> Sir, must not come so near and balk their lips.   II. v. 102

This kind of placing of the action in a context of everyday reality,
which is integral to Shakespeare's historical vision, is a stranger to
Marlowe's. There is only one other scene in *Edward II* where we are

made aware, as we constantly are in *Richard III*, that high-level
political decisions devolve infallibly on the backs of the commonalty.
This is in /**126**/ the joint attack that Mortimer and Lancaster
launch against the king in Act II, Scene ii:

Mortimer Junior: The idle triumphs, masks, lascivious shows,
                    And prodigal gifts bestowed on Gaveston,
                    Have drawn thy treasure dry and made thee weak,
                    The murmuring commons overstretched hath.

    . . . .

Lancaster: Thy garrisons are beaten out of France,
                    And, lame and poor, lie groaning at the gates.
                    The wild O'Neil, with swarms of Irish kerns,
                    Lives uncontrolled within the English pale.
                    Unto the walls of York the Scots made road
                    And unresisted drave away rich spoils.

    . . . .

Mortimer Junior: Libels are cast against thee in the street,
                    Ballads and rhymes made of thy overthrow.
Lancaster: The Northern borderers seeing their houses burnt,
                    Their wives and children slain, run up and down,
                    Cursing the name of thee and Gaveston.   II. ii. 155 f.

This, though rhythmically wooden, is effective enough in the way it
plots Edward's movements against the coordinates of a larger social
necessity; but it is also quite uncharacteristic. Indeed it would not be
so effective if it were not so different from the writing that surrounds
it. One feels that a great weight is being lifted off the play, and that
its terms of reference are being radically enlarged. The claustropho-
bic constriction of a political action which is no more than an admin-
istrative extension of obsessive personality patterns (as much in the
barons as in Edward) begins to break up and there is movement in
the air. But it is a false dawn. The nearest we get to action on the
basis of a conception of the common weal is in the last scene, with
young Edward's belated bout of pruning in the garden of the State,
and his recognition that there is a clash between the public function
and the private nature of a king:

        If you be guilty, though I be your son,
        Think not to find me slack or pitiful.   V. vi. 81–2

No doubt this is to get priorities straight, but the rest of the play has
recognized the dilemma only to deny it. Although it provides a for-

mal coda to the piece, this final scene has no organic relation to the action it concludes. Moreover, its function as a resolving cadence is subverted /**127**/ by two very different gestures which, theatrically speaking, dominate the last few moments—Mortimer's of stoic defiance, 'Weep not for Mortimer, / That scorns the world . . .' and Isabella's of despair, 'Then come, sweet death, and rid me of this grief'. Marlowe's uneasiness with the kind of monarchic synthesis, which Shakespeare indulges at the end of *Richard III*, is apparent in the unfinished air of the concluding lines, which merely recapitulate a pathos of which we've already had a good deal too much:

> And let these tears, distilling from mine eyes,
> Be witness of my grief and innocency.   V. vi. 101–2

Young Edward's grief and innocency are neither in question nor to the point.

Of course, I am not deploring the absence of a platitudinous Richmond to tie all up in a neat parcel and bow himself out, but rather recognising the justice of the instinct which leads Shakespeare to attempt such a summation. For if we are to have more than a psychological study of faction war, if the moral meaning is to encompass more than a personal ethical dilemma, the action must be placed in a larger frame. It must be seen to have both context and consequences. The crown must become more than a symbol of personal power-lust, more than a piece of jewellery which one wears or gives away as the caprice takes one: for the abdication scene (v. i), with its now-you-see-it, now-you-don't whimsy, surely borders on the burlesque. Such a performance would be unthinkable if the crown had been imaginatively clothed with the kind of significance Shakespeare gives it—

> Here, cousin, seize the crown.
> Here, cousin,
> On this side my hand, and on that side thine.
> Now is this golden crown like a deep well
> That owes two buckets . . .   *Richard II*, IV. i. 181

Edward's crown is not 'a deep well' but a glittering bauble (V. i. 60), another in the long line of theatrical properties with which he has adorned himself as the player-king. It sparkles; but one cannot look down into it, glimpsing at the bottom that ghostly reflection of one's own face which is a haunting presence behind so many lines of Shakespeare's play. Nor is there any cross-fertilisation between Edward's vacillating anguish and the moral awareness of his tormentors—no more than he, can they learn anything from the experience, frozen as they are in postures of stereotyped and uncomprehending revolt. One /**128**/ has only to recall Bolingbroke tensed in unwilling fascination on the edge of this throne—'Mark, silent king, the moral of this sport . . .'—to realise how two-dimensional Marlowe's dramatic imagination really is.

Now of course many admirers of the play have noted the abdication of social responsibility implicit in the barons', and more especially in Edward's, behaviour. The difference is that they have seen it as a Marlovian insight and a masterly piece of dramatic analysis. And so it might have been, if certain conditions had been fulfilled: if, for instance, Edward's weakness had been firmly placed, if he had been presented through a dramatic verse subtle and poised enough to permit a consistent ironic detachment in the audience, if his manner of speech had made us aware of the things he didn't know at the very moment he enunciated those he did—poetic refinements, all of them, largely foreign to the verse of this play; or if there had been a dramatically realised social context which provided an implicit critique of Edward's imperfect adjustment to his public responsibilities—something we have already seen to be sadly lacking; or if Edward had been attended by a Gaunt or a York, instead of by the faceless ciphers Lancaster, Mortimer Senior, Warwick: *then* we might have had the penetrating study of royal weakness and baronial faction that these critics credit Marlowe with producing. But the activities of power are not, in *Edward II*, given a fully human context.

The serious limitations of Marlowe's conception of the human can be illustrated by a small piece of source-study. The episode in Act V, Scene iii, where Edward is shaved with puddle water, is one of the few occasions in the play where Marlowe goes outside his Holinshed for material, and it can be traced indirectly to the Latin chronicle of Geoffrey le Baker (though we cannot be sure how the passage in question was actually transmitted to Marlowe).[14] In the play, the king requests water to cool his thirst and to clear his body of 'foul excrements'. His warders offer him 'channel water' and proceed to shave off his beard, to prevent recognition and rescue. The emphasis

[14] A Latin version is printed as *Vita et Mors Edwardi Secundi* in W. Stubbs (ed.), *Chronicles of the Reigns of Edward I, and Edward II*, Rolls series, vol. 76, p. ii.

of this short scene is principally on the humiliation and indignity of
the operation—

> Traitors, away! What, will you murder me,
> Or choke your sovereign with puddle water?   V. iii. 29–30

and the chief effect generated is one of a generalised pathos attendant
on the contrast between Edward's status and the treatment he receives. In Marlowe's source, however, there is much more./**129**/

These champions bring *Edward* towardes Barkeley, being guarded with a
rabble of helhoundes, along by the Grange belonging to the Castle of Bris-
towe, where that wicked man *Gorney*, making a crowne of hay, put it on his
head, and the souldiours that were present, scoffed, and mocked him beyond
all measure, saying, Tprut auaunt sir King . . . [Since] they feared to be met
of any that should knowe *Edward*, they bent their iourny therefore towardes
the left hand, riding along the Marish grounds lying by the riuer of Seuerne.
Moreouer, deuising to disfigure him that hee might not bee knowne, they
determined for to shaue as well the haire of his head, as also of his beard:
wherefore, as in their iourny they travailed by a little water which ranne in a
ditch, they commaunded him to light from his horse to bee shauen, to whom,
being set on a moale hill, a Barbar came vnto him with a basen of colde
water taken out of the ditch, to shaue him withall, saying vnto the king, that
that water should serue for that time. To whom *Edward* answered, that
would they, noulde they, hee would haue warme water for his beard; and,
to the end that he might keepe his promise, hee beganne to weepe, and to
shed teares plentifully.[15]

It is possible to see why a playwright chary of official vengeance on
blasphemy might omit the suggestive scene of the mock-crowning.
But why, having decided to present the shaving sequence, does
Marlowe suppress that intensely human gesture of Edward's as he
demands—in the midst of the desolate 'Marish grounds'—warm
water for his beard? Or why is nothing made of the incipiently
powerful identification of warm water and tears? One is tempted to
mutter piously, 'What a scene Shakespeare would have made of it!'
But perhaps the truth is that Marlowe ignores these details because
they are nothing to his point: this is not the kind of drama he is writing. He does not want to take us into that inner world of poignant
self-delusion where royalty can only assert itself in a ludicrous demand for the luxurious appurtenances of kingship, nor to make us see

[15] As given by Stow, *Annales* (London, 1615), p. 226.

in a single vision the absurdity and the dignity of Edward's nature. The marriage of the incongruous with the tragic implicit in the conceit of a king who provides his own shaving water by weeping is too deeply disturbing to subserve the effects of generalised pathos at which Marlowe is aiming here. The marriage may be native to Shakespeare's art—

> That bucket down and full of tears am I,
> Drinking my griefs . . .   *Richard II*, IV. i. 188

—but Marlowe is content with, indeed he is committed to, a surface pathos founded upon the simple opposition of good and evil, tyrannical oppression and innocent suffering—/**130**/

> The wren may strive against the lion's strength,
> But all in vain; so vainly do I strive
> To seek for mercy at a tyrant's hand.   V. iii. 34–6

The activities of power are not given a fully human context: instead they are schematised in a kind of vectorial diagrammatic reduction. The world is populated by wrens and lions. The metaphor implies a kind of imaginative extremism—since there are, after all, intermediate beasts—which is magnified when we recall that only two scenes earlier it was Edward, not Mortimer, who was 'the imperial lion' (V, i. 11 f.). It seems largely a matter of convention which way the arrows in the force-diagram point; and whichever way it is, they are always the generalised components, not the unique human force they set out to account for. It is this breaking up of a complex conflict into its vectorial components, which explains those violent reversals of feeling, those inversions of the moral 'sense' of a character, of which Isabella's infamous desertion is the most familiar, and the most frequently deplored, example. For if one is committed to this kind of diagrammatic representation there can be no gradual transitions—the only angles are right-angles, and the third dimension must be systematically suppressed.

And yet, to do the play justice, the tyranny of the schematic is not ubiquitous; indeed, it is precisely because there are signs of a very human ambivalence in the first two acts that the supervention, in the second half, of over-systematic moral conceptions is disappointing. This is particularly true of the two characters who, in the last act, have hardened into mere monsters of turpitude—Isabella and Mortimer. Listen to the Isabella of Act I, pleading with the barons for the repeal of Gaveston:

Mortimer Senior:	Plead for him he that will; I am resolv'd.
Lancaster:	And so am I, my lord. Dissuade the queen.
Queen Isabella:	O Lancaster, let him dissuade the king,
	For 'tis against my will he should return.
Warwick:	Then speak not for him; let the peasant go.
Queen Isabella:	'Tis for myself I speak, and not for him.
Pembroke:	No speaking will prevail, and therefore cease.
Mortimer Junior:	Fair queen, forbear to angle for the fish
	Which, being caught, strikes him that takes it dead.

I. iv. 214–22

Despite a certain metrical inflexibility, much of Isabella's torturing dilemma has been captured in the sharp reciprocating movement of the /131/ stychomythia, and the whole agonising ambivalence of Gaveston's lethal attractiveness is precipitated in Mortimer's metaphor. But the precariousness of the achievement is sufficiently indicated by the next two lines, in which the tight knot of meaning is unravelled with pathetic explicitness:

> I mean that vile torpedo, Gaveston,
> That now, I hope, floats on the Irish seas.

The metaphorical fusion of ideas has given place to their whimsical association, and Mortimer's tone of earnest compassion and admonition relapses into the old monotone of inflexible opposition.

Yet however violent may seem Isabella's transition from a dogged, doomed loyalty to a conscienceless callousness (see especially V. ii. 68–74), the germs of the dramatic implausibility are already present in the verse Marlowe gives her in Act I:

> Like frantic Juno will I fill the earth
> With ghastly murmur of my sighs and cries,
> For never doted Jove on Ganymede
> So much as he on cursèd Gaveston.
> But that will more exasperate his wrath;
> I must entreat him, I must speak him fair,
> And be a means to call home Gaveston.
> And yet he'll ever dote on Gaveston,
> And so I am for ever miserable.   I. iv. 178–86

Soliloquy in this vein may sketch the outline of a conflict but it can-

not present it. Instead of an imaginative initiation into the inner
condition of the speaker ('How weary, stale, flat, and unprofitable /
Seems to me all the uses of this world'), we are given a succession of
hypothetical reconstructions which replace each other like cards in a
shuffled pack ('But that will . . . I must . . . And yet . . . And
so . . .'). Figurative language does not so much explore and deepen
the sense of inner conflict ('Oh, that this too too solid flesh would
melt, / Thaw, and resolve itself into a dew . . .'), as give a kind of
enamelled fixity to a rhetorical posture already chosen ('Like
frantic Juno . . .'). The style of the verse is the poetic counterpart in
unrealised intention of a dramatic action which is often no more
than 'a good idea for a play'. Those who, with Clifford Leech, wish
to see the Queen's betrayal as 'one of the most perceptive things in
Marlowe's writing', are obliged to add, 'at least in the planning' for
it is a dramatic perception deprived of a poetic body.[16]

There is a similar disappointment in the treatment of Mortimer,
/132/ whose sturdy masculinity and bursts of impetuosity reveal
something of an embryonic Hotspur.[17]

Queen Isabella: Ah, Mortimer! now breaks the king's hate forth,
                     And he confesseth that he loves me not.
Mortimer Junior: Cry quittance, madam, then, and love not him.

I. iv. 193–5

Or this—

Warwick: Bridle thy anger, gentle Mortimer.
Mortimer Junior: I cannot, nor I will not; I must speak.
                   Cousin, our hands I hope shall fence our heads
                   And strike off his that makes you threaten us.
                   Come, uncle, let us leave the brain-sick king
                   And henceforth parley with our naked swords.

I. i. 121–6

Yet this is another of the play's unfulfilled promises. Just as Isabella's

---

[16] C. Leech, 'Marlowe's "Edward II": Power and Suffering', *CQ*, I (1959),
190–1.

[17] W. D. Briggs, in his edition (London, 1914) of *Edward II*, was the first to
point out the similarity. If Shakespeare was a Pembroke's man, and acted in
Marlowe's history-play—a fact which would explain the odd and unauthorised
appearance of 'Tressel' (Trussel) and 'Berkeley' as attendants on Lady Anne in
Richard III, when Shakespeare was casting about for a couple of incidental
names—there could be more than coincidental resemblance involved.

divided loyalties are resolved by transforming her into the ferocious caricature of Act V, so Mortimer's irascible ambivalence is reduced to a monolithic and herculean Machiavellism—

> Mine enemies will I plague, my friends advance
> And what I list command who dare control?   V. iv. 67–8

> Feared am I more than loved; let me be feared,
> And when I frown, make all the court look pale.   V. iv. 52–3

> As for myself, I stand as Jove's huge tree,
> And others are but shrubs compared to me.   V. vi. 11–12

This is familiar Marlowe country and the playwright seems to be very much at home in the facilities of the old rhodomontade; but dramatically and poetically it is as much of a blind alley as the earlier characterisation of Mortimer was fraught with possibilities.

The one determined attempt Marlowe makes to grapple with the complexities of self-division—in the person of Kent—yields only a hectic series of changes-of-heart, whose rapid succession is very nearly comic. In Kent's soliloquies we are presented, not with the process of moral debate, but with its end-product, which is submitted to the usual varieties of rhetorical embellishment and inflation:

> Rain showers of vengeance on my cursèd head,
> Thou God, to whom in justice it belongs
> To punish this unnatural revolt . . .   IV. v. 16–18 /133/

Since, on the last occasion we heard from him in this vein (IV. i)' Kent was performing the same operation to the extenuation of the rebellion he now abhors, there is a singular lack of conviction in this apostrophe. In any case, the worthy earl barely has time to establish which side he is on now, before he is whisked away to vacate the stage for those monuments of undeviating will in whom Marlowe is so much more interested.

Yet the preoccupation with Mortimer and his kind is hardly justified. They are not so much characters as character-postulates, aggregations of certain selected characteristics, like a child's drawings with the guiding lines left in, or, in Rossiter's phrase, 'fractional-distillations of Man, not men'.[18] This bondage to generalised and

---

[18] A. P. Rossiter in the 'Introduction' to *Woodstock: a Moral History* (London, 1946), p. 65. (Of Marlowe's characters generally, not of this play specifically.)

simplified outline is apparent even in Marlowe's attempts to represent complexity of motive—Gaveston, within forty lines of declaring himself desirous of dying on Edward's bosom, is busy devising means to 'draw the pliant king which way I please' (I. i. 53), and there is no dramatically realised 'self' in the lines which could mediate between the passionate lover and the cynical opportunist in his character. The two traits are simply juxtaposed and we (or the actor) must make of it what we can. (A skilful director can indeed make a great deal of it, but he should not fool himself that he is interpreting Marlowe. He is merely making up Marlowe's mind for him.) Anyway, it's not long before the genuinely individual in Gaveston—his superb effrontery, for instance, when he parries Isabella's 'Villain! 'tis thou that robb'st me of my lord', with 'Madam, 'tis you that rob me of my lord' (I. iv. 160)—is submerged by the spring tide of lamentation which laps about the whole play, until the characters can only 'stand metaphorically back-to-back and bawl and counterbawl about their fates to the stars'.[19]

With many of the characters there is not even as much raw material of human ambiguity as we find in Gaveston. The baronial opposition is from the start frozen in the least interesting of postures, and condemned in its utterances to a monotone of recrimination, as they inveigh interminably against 'that base and obscure Gaveston', 'accursed Gaveston', 'that villain Gaveston', 'that base peasant', 'hateful Gaveston', and so on. Succumbing to the creeping paralysis, Edward responds with equally tedious praises of 'my Gaveston', 'sweet Gaveston', 'my dearest Gaveston', thus bogging the action down in the elaboration of feelings which have passed beyond all possibility of modification or growth.[20] It is hard to imagine anything less instructive than this head-on collision of meaningless obsessions. Nor are we much further forward when the Spencers replace Gaveston, /**134**/ for the same peevishly repetitive malice is diverted into the new channel with hardly a break in the steady flow of abuse. The Spencers, we are told (twice), are revelling in 'England's wealth and treasury' (IV. iv. 27 and IV. v. 61), but since Marlowe ignores Holinshed's fairly detailed accounts of these depredations, the hostility of the barons remains a mere postulate, a piece of creaking plot

[19] Rossiter again, *op. cit.* p. 65.
[20] Harry Levin counted 110 usages of this kind. See *The Overreacher* (London, 1954), p. 115.

machinery unrelated to the favourites we actually see on the stage.

I suppose there are admirers of *Edward II* who would be prepared to admit most of these charges, but who would, at the same time, invite us to consider the crucial case of Edward himself as an exception to such strictures. This view is sufficiently general to demand consideration and I had best begin by indicating the extent to which it is true. For there are several points, in the first two acts particularly, where Marlowe strikes a chord rich with possibilities of development. In each case the suggestiveness derives from an objectification of feeling, an ironic detachment, which makes it possible for us to contemplate Edward steadily and dispassionately, instead of being swamped in a hot wave of generalised emotion.

In the fourth scene, Edward has been raining titles and offices on the implacable barons in a vain attempt at conciliation. He goes on, in the stony silence which has greeted his concessions,

> If this content you not,
> Make several kingdoms of this monarchy
> And share it equally amongst you all,
> So I may have some nook or corner left
> To frolic with my dearest Gaveston.   I. iv. 69–73

In these lines, the extravagance of Edward's affection ('Ere my sweet Gaveston shall part from me, / This Isle shall fleet upon the Ocean, / And wander to the unfrequented Inde'—I. iv. 48–50) makes a decisive break with an extravagance native to Marlowe's style (the 'fleeting land' conceit is an old weapon in the Marlovian armoury— See *Dido*, IV. iv. 134–5) and stands firmly in its own dramatic right. For the first time we begin to *see* Edward, to sense that appalling inner vacuum which makes him fling kingdoms about like dust in the wind. We see that his dedication to the personal values of friendship is a neurotic dedication to pure nullity—that telling verb 'frolic' occurs several times in this connexion (cf. I. ii. 67 and II. iii. 17)—a last frantic attempt to build banks against the black wave of emptiness and self-doubt that rises against him. The poignancy of the last two lines is due in part to /**135**/ his unadmitted knowledge that no such 'nook or corner' exists in the real world. An intense personal anguish is released a few lines further on, when Mortimer questions in exasperation, 'Why should you love him whom the world hates so?' and the king replies,

> Because he loves me more than all the world.   I. iv. 77

This is a genuine *cri de coeur* (contrast the rhetorical posturing implicit in a line like 'O shall I speak, or shall I sigh and die!'—III. ii. 122) and its effect is arresting. Again we find ourselves really *hearing* Edward on the emotional level where human sensitivity is activated. The vision of agonising *ab*normality functions normatively in directing attention to the springs of true feeling, here irremediably fouled and muddied.

The other example I would like to adduce is an external and hostile view of the same internal turmoil; yet its visual immediacy and precision of observation make it an imaginative gateway to the same insight:

> When wert thou in the field with banner spread?
> But once, and then thy soldiers marched like players,
> With garish robes, not armor, and thyself,
> Bedaubed with gold, rode laughing at the rest,
> Nodding and shaking of thy spangled crest,
> Where women's favors hung like labels down.   II. ii. 180–5

Through the lens of Mortimer's contemptuous masculinity—'When wert thou in the field . . . But once, and then . . .'—our doubts about Edward are sharply focused in details of costume, in diction keen as a scalpel—'bedaubed', 'spangled', 'labels'—and in a verse movement which is superbly gestural—'nodding and shaking of thy spangled crest'. The tinsel flimsiness of Edward's very triumphs revives again the sense that he treads a thin crust of glittering ice which, if it cracks, will plunge him into the black waters of self-negation—though here it is the political implications of his psychic malady that are stressed.

If we put these two passages together we have the germ of a powerful tragic encounter, in which neither the personal dimension is sacrificed to the political, nor the social vision obscured by the inward vision, but in which they exist in a mutually enriching symbiosis. Why then do we not get it—for even the play's loudest advocates talk of pathos rather than tragedy?

Pathos, indeed, has a great deal to do with the failure of *Edward II*; for pathos is a paralysed form of imaginative sympathy, a self-imposed embargo on all ways of looking at the subject but one—the pathetic. Before I attempt to give an account of the 'why' of this substitution of /**136**/ pathetic *attitude* for tragic *insight*, it would be well to examine the 'how'. What means does Marlowe use to elicit this pathos?

The process can be studied most fully in the Neath Abbey scene (IV. vi), where the king is finally overtaken by his pursuers.

> O, hadst thou ever been a king, thy heart,
> Piercèd deeply with sense of my distress,
> Could not but take compassion of my state.
> Stately and proud, in riches and in train,
> Whilom I was powerful and full of pomp;
> But what is he whom rule and empery
> Have not in life or death made miserable?
> Come, Spencer; come, Baldock, come, sit down by me;
> Make trial now of that philosophy
> That in our famous nurseries of arts
> Thou sucked'st from Plato and from Aristotle.
> Father, this life contemplative is heaven.   IV. vi. 9–20

The chief effect of this passage—and it is entirely representative of the Edward of Acts IV and V—is to force us to surrender the tragic insights given in the kind of writing I've just been discussing. We, through the Abbot whom Edward addresses, are urged insistently to abandon that hard-won detachment, and to indulge in a very simple kind of identification—'O, hadst thou ever been a king . . .'—'Put yourself in my shoes'; and the moral duty of a 'compassion' which swallows up all distinct apprehension of its object is made to supersede the more painful obligation to see weakness for what it is. A generalised, and so anaesthetising capitulation to the *de casibus* cycle is to replace our very clear perception of what it really means to be 'stately and proud, in riches and in train'—that is, to be 'bedaub'd with gold . . . laughing at the rest, / Nodding and shaking of thy spangled crest . . . '. It is only by dint of forgetting that it is '*mis*rule and empery' that has made Edward miserable, that we can receive fully the voluptuous gratification of indulged emotion which this passage offers (and I take it that Marlowe wants us to receive it, since he repeats the strategy so often as the play draws to an end). Philosophy, we note, is not the art of understanding reality, but simply a means of keeping an intolerable reality at bay, a 'life contemplative' conducted in monastic isolation from the world. The very personalities of the real world are taboo here:

> Mortimer! Who talks of Mortimer?
> Who wounds me with the name of Mortimer,
> That bloody man? /**137**/

And then follows a most revealing passage:

> Good father, on thy lap
> Lay I this head, laden with mickle care.
> O might I never open these eyes again,
> Never again lift up this drooping head,
> O never more lift up this dying heart!

Friends and foes of Marlowe alike regard this as a central passage; but what does it amount to? Isn't it the old, old song of the lotus-eaters, the drug-pedlars, the death-worshippers? Certainly it presents nothing precisely, with its 'drooping heads' and 'dying hearts'; its rhythms are the rhythms of rhetorical anaesthesia—'O might I never . . . Never again . . . O never more . . . '; it is the child's lapse out of responsibility on the lap of a 'good father'.

In the nature of things, it is difficult to demonstrate (what I believe to be the case) that Marlowe is trying to carry us, along with Edward, into the phantasmic world of oblivion. But we are entitled to ask where else, if not in the broken king, the imaginative centre of gravity is located. Is it in Mortimer? Isabella? in vacillating Kent? Clearly not, yet all the other central characters are mere shadows of Edward's grief. Nor is the answer to be found in the energies of the verse; for it has lost its capacity for dramatic presentment and has become either enervated and bonelessly 'lyrical', meandering in a despairing arc of subordinate appendages—

> I wear the crown, but am controlled by them,
> By Mortimer, and my unconstant queen,
> Who spots my nuptial bed with infamy,
> Whilst I am lodged within this cave of care,
> Where sorrow at my elbow still attends,
> To company my heart with sad laments,
> That bleeds within me for this strange exchange.

> V. i. 29–35

or violently emotional, with such drastic imprecision that one is hard put to it to guess what effect was aimed at—

> For such outrageous passions cloy my soul,
> As with the wings of rancor and disdain

> Full often am I soaring up to heaven,
> To plain me to the gods . . .   V. i. 19–22

or (a short step) we are back in the old 'Stygian vein' of *Tamburlaine*
—/**138**/

> A litter hast thou? Lay me in a hearse,
> And to the gates of hell convey me hence.
> Let Pluto's bells ring out my fatal knell
> And hags howl for my death at Charon's shore. IV. vi. 86–9

Much of this is no more than Marlowe's familiar stylistic vices at large again. As Mortimer is made to remark, in an attempt to apply the brakes to the runaway carriage of high-astounding diction, '*Diablo*! What passions call you these?' But when the verse does get a grip on itself, it does so primarily to enforce our acquiescence in Edward's self-destructive pilgrimage to Killingworth:

> Whither you will; all places are alike,
> And every earth is fit for burial.   V. i. 145–6

It is not 'Whither you will, so I were from your sights'—Richard's anguished protest against an intolerable humiliation—but 'Whither you will; all places are alike . . .'—a capitulation so complete that Edward almost ceases to exist as a human entity. To call this tragic is to strain the word too far from its proper usage.

With the explicit emergence of this strain in the play, the life-denying stoic abdication of the human, we are very near to grasping the central failure of *Edward II*. Wilson Knight has observed that 'Marlowe, like Tamburlaine, is a king-degrader';[21] but *Edward II* sets me (for one) wondering whether he is not also a man-degrader. What other motive can be advanced for staging the exquisite humiliation of Edward's death? Why else the long enumeration of the squalid conditions of his incarceration in Act V, Scene v? What possible satisfaction can the spectator derive from that scene, unless it is the satisfaction of seeing 'inhuman cruelty presented more or less for its own sake'?[22]

Several attempts have been made to resist the force of this argument. Miss Mahood would have us believe that Marlowe is display-

---

[21] *The Golden Labyrinth* (London, 1962), p. 58. The whole section on Marlowe, though brief, is extremely penetrating.

[22] Thus Charlton and Waller in the Introduction to their edition, p. 63.

ing, with impartial tragic insight, the self-destructive dynamic of
'false humanism'. But such a demonstration would require a moral
framework within which the self-destructive dynamic worked itself
out, and to which it was referred, and this Miss Mahood fails to
locate.[23] Clifford Leech claims for Marlowe's exhibition of suffering,
a dispassionate scientific objectivity:

There is no theory here which Marlowe illustrates, no warning or programme for reform, no affirmation even of a faith in man. The playwright
merely directs our attention on certain aspects of the human scene . . .[24]/**139**/

But if this is what it means to have 'no theory', it can hardly be
claimed as a virtue in a playwright. It seems almost indistinguishable
from having no point of view—and indeed this is the clearest impression I have of the Marlowe who wrote *Edward II*, that he has no
firmly-grounded centre of consciousness from which to conduct his
exploration of human life. And thus the obsessive and the compulsive
is free to burst into surface conflagration until it has burnt itself out—
as in the anti-papist frenzy of Act I, Scene iv, the anti-clerical animus
of the bishop of Coventry sequence (I. i), or in the images of violent
destruction which need surprise only those readers unacquainted
with Marlowe's chronic partiality for circumstantial bloodiness:

> If I be England's king, in lakes of gore
> Your headless trunks, your bodies will I trail,
> That you may drink your fill, and quaff in blood,
> And stain my royal standard with the same,
> That so my bloody colors may suggest
> Remembrance of revenge immortally . . .   III. ii. 135–40

We cannot pretend that the mild Edward is the real speaker of these
lines.

But the most disturbing thing that bubbles up in the dark pool of
the playwright's consciousness is an ecstatic impulse to 'do dirt on
humanity', to humiliate and grind into the dust, and then again to
humiliate. I am not disputing that the process generates a good deal
of theatrical power—though that power is somewhat dissipated by
the bludgeoning monotony of it all—I am questioning the health of
the imagination which so dwells on it.

---

[23] *Poetry and Humanism* (London, 1950), p. 86 and preceding pages.
[24] 'Marlowe's "Edward II": Power and Suffering', *CQ*, I (1959), 195.

It was known before the age of psychoanalysis that misanthropy was the uneasy bedfellow of self-contempt and guilt, and I am making no revolutionary proposal if I suggest that there is a strange congruency in the fates of Edward, the dabbler in sodomy, and of Faustus, the religious sceptic, which might be accounted for as a neurotic desire for symbolic punishment and expiation. If this were merely a matter of biographical curiosity, such a theory might well remain unexpressed. But it is worth serious consideration if it enables us to offer an account of puzzling features in the play *qua* play—the unbalanced and apparently motiveless violence of its catastrophe, for instance; or Marlowe's fascinated circling around objects in his consciousness which Wilson Knight has characterised as 'things at once hideously suspect yet tormentingly desirable',[25] things like the homosexual theme, or the sadistic horrors /**140**/ of Edward's last days (Swinburne, disciple of de Sade, once observed that Marlowe was not exempt from a certain 'hideous lust of pain').[26] It's precisely because it is a 'circling' that the psychodynamic hypothesis is so tempting, since one distinguishing mark of neurosis is a simultaneous incapacity either to leave the painful subject alone or to do anything constructive about it. The irrelevant outbursts of violence are similarly intelligible if we posit a creative process disrupted by explosions and eruptions of the unresolved tensions below the level of consciousness.

But there is another way in which a 'psychiatric' explication of the play is useful. We are confronted in *Edward II* with a drama which, despite its manifest crudities and its obsessive repetitiousness, has an unholy fascination. I have tried to show that the fascination, whatever else it may be, is not the fascination of maturity and genius, and I am accordingly bound to offer some explanation of opinions like Hazlitt's that the final scenes are 'not surpassed by any writer whatever'.[27] Such views have gained wide currency. Now we are familiar enough with the fascination exercised by a psychological aberration which is also intelligent and articulate—the reputation of the later Tennessee Williams (to name only one case) is almost entirely founded on his fascination with disease. When we succumb to the

[25] *The Golden Labyrinth*, p. 58.

[26] Quoted (without a reference) by Mario Praz, 'Christopher Marlowe', *Eng. Studs.* XIII (1931), 211.

[27] Quoted by Charlton and Waller, *op. cit.* p. 54. Lamb had a similarly high opinion of the play. See his *Complete Works*, ed. E. V. Lucas (London, 1903), I, 42.

fascination, we confuse the deep satisfactions of great imaginative literature with the idle pleasure of indulging our curiosity about the fringes of human sanity. Delirium is, so to speak, mistaken for the authentic poetic 'frenzy', and neurotic intensity is confounded with imaginative power.

This, I submit, is the kind of mistaken response which leads critics to place a high *literary* value on the last two acts (particularly) of *Edward II*. They have been led by the fascination of the neurotically intense to ignore the extent to which it is dependent on imaginative malfunction—on a neurotic over-insistence on a half-truth about the human condition. It is the function of criticism, however, to stand for health in the broadest sense of that term: and I wonder, as I read those critics who give way to the fascination of *Edward II*, whether they have not abandoned this function and constituted themselves apologists for the neurotic elements that, in an imperfect world, are to be found in the best of us.

Be that as it may—and I do not claim to have demonstrated anything—*Edward II* fails to address itself to much that is human in us; it uses a shrunken language to tell a tale of men who are less than men. Which makes me the more surprised to find the editors of this play Charlton and Waller, who have hitherto sturdily resisted the blandishments of /**141**/ the critical establishment, agreeing at the end of their (otherwise) excellent Introduction that *Edward II* is superior to *Richard II*—though, to their credit, they do so grudgingly:

It is no doubt futile to make too close a comparison between Shakespeare's loosely-built drama with its wealth of discursive poetry and Marlowe's grimly realistic tragedy. No doubt the latter is the better play and leaves the sharper impression on the mind; it has less grace, less poetry, less humanity, but more power and a better form . . .[28]

This is astounding. These editors have shown themselves alive to the 'formalist fallacy' which has led to so exaggerated an estimate of *Edward II*; they have conceded that the play has 'no moral pattern', that it operates by means of a 'complete detachment from ordinary human sympathies', and that it displays 'the inhumanity of *Tamburlaine* or *The Jew*, without the *élan*, the poetry, the *amour de l'impossible* which makes us forget temporarily their extreme exaggeration'.[29]

[28] *Edward II*, ed. Charlton and Waller, p. 64.
[29] *Ibid*. pp. 55 and 56.

And then we are exhorted to prefer it to *Richard II*! What can 'power' mean, if it is independent of 'grace', 'poetry', and 'humanity'? It would seem that it is as I have argued: the 'grim realism' is a function of inhumanity.

But this is a degradation of the term 'realism' as much as it is of the term 'humanity'. Marlowe's is no more than the reporter's realism, the kind which finally shirks a whole dimension of the real—the moral. The equable tone in which Marlowe enunciates his horrors, the strange bareness of diction, is not the result of a classical restraint, or of some new discipline of art: it is a kind of indifference both to humanity and to art. The play is amoral, not by intention, but by default.

One cannot finally avoid making moral discriminations: one can only be betrayed into superficial and inconsistent ones, by pretending not to be making them. One cannot dispense with the concept of purpose in human affairs: one can only become an unwitting apostle of meaninglessness by affecting to ignore it. Marlowe's attempt to do without the conceptions of moral order of his own day deprived him of dramatic, as well as moral, logic. It left his play a prey to all the disordered forces of personality which lie in wait for the man who loses sight of the elusive and fine-drawn filament of purposiveness, without which life is a mere labyrinth, and consciousness a Minotaur. /**142**/

ROBERT FRICKER

The Dramatic Structure of
EDWARD II

It has been generally recognised that the structure of Marlowe's chronicle play differs from that of his other dramas in many respects, but the question in what exactly this difference consists, has not been thoroughly examined so far. Kocher, in his valuable biographical interpretation of Marlowe's work,[1] sees it in, and explains it by, the growing interest of the poet in the human world outside his ego which led him to abandon the one-man structure of *Tamburlaine* and, first, to take into consideration the ethical code and the religious opinions of this world and, secondly, to extend his sympathy to a number of other dramatis personae. In its ultimate result this opinion coincides with the one offered by Charlton and Waller in the introduction to their edition of *Edward II*, but they explain the change of Marlowe's technique not by a corresponding development of his character but by the example set by his contemporary and disciple Shakespeare in *2* and *3 Henry VI*, which made him rely less on 'transport and rhetoric' than on 'the interplay of human character'.[2]

Both explanations of the same phenomenon may be right, and each ultimately rests on a hypothesis, the hypothesis namely that Marlowe—like a romantic poet and unlike what seems to have been the attitude of the Elizabethan playwrights—expressed himself through his work so that his plays may be regarded as the mirror of his thought, and on the hypothesis that Shakespeare wrote his

Reprinted from *English Studies*, XXXIV (1953).
[1] Paul H. Kocher: 'Christopher Marlowe, a Study of his Development' (*Phil. Q.* XVII, 1938); *Christopher Marlowe, a Study of his Thought, Learning, and Character*. Chapel Hill, 1946.
[2] P. 25.

chronicle plays before Marlowe created his *Edward II*. The aim of this paper is not to discuss the question /**204**/ whether the change of dramatic technique in *Edward II* was the result either of the development of Marlowe's character or of the influence of Shakespeare, but to investigate some aspects of the dramatic method which he used in this play. I shall be less concerned with Marlowe's verse and his character-drawing than with the structure of the play, though in a highly organic work of art like *Edward II*, the three aspects are inextricably mixed and cannot be completely isolated from one another. The study of the verse and the characters should therefore yield results similar to those obtained by the study of the structure of the play.

The dramatic method which Marlowe used in his other plays[3] may be roughly summed up in the following way: he juxtaposed a number of episodes which form the body of the drama, and linked them together by the figure of the hero, which he represented by means of either a lyrical portrait as in *Tamburlaine* or, as in *Doctor Faustus*, a spiritual conflict which is clearly separated from the rest of the play. The different episodes are further connected by their causal relationship as in *The Jew*, where Barabas revenges himself on the Governor through the death of the latter's son and then tries to rid himself of those who know about the part he played in the duel between Lodowick and Matthias; or by a common religious and political interest as in *The Massacre*, where the play deals with the struggle between the Catholics and the Huguenots.

Thus the principle of the construction of these plays is rather juxtaposition than subordination to a central idea or motif, although the will to create a whole can be felt even in *Tamburlaine*. But, in his earlier dramas, Marlowe never achieved the impression of unity by the handling of the plot; he rather achieved it by the dominant position he gave to the hero. The impression is left that character and plot exist side by side and do not completely explain each other. Nowhere is the character fused into the action of the play and revealed by the action alone. There still remains a part of his portrait which is not, and cannot be, expressed by the plot and therefore exists for its own sake.

[3] Unfortunately I have not been able to consult G. P. Baker: 'Dramatic Technique in Marlowe' (*Essays and Studies by Members of the Eng. Ass.* IV, 1913) and G. I. Duthie: 'Dramatic Structure of "Tamburlaine" ' (*English Studies*, New Series I, 1948).

This is no longer the case, however, in *The Massacre*, where the Guise's aspirations are purely political and are completely absorbed by the drama. Boas[4] was the first to insist on the importance of this play because it represents in many respects a precedent to *Edward II*. He limits his observations, however, to parallels between characters and to verbal echoes, whereas the relationship includes the structure of the plays: *The Massacre* shows the same merging of the character into the plot, the violent clash between the hero (Guise) and at least one antagonist (Henry III) which leads to the death of both, and the high speed of the action. But this play—leaving aside the question of the artistic level—still falls into two episodes, the massacre and the struggle between the Guise and Henry III, /**205**/ and the only links between them—the figure of the hero and the politico-religious nature of the conflict—are not strong enough to make it an organic whole. *Edward II* possesses the dramatic qualities of the earlier play without sharing its weaknesses, and it has the further advantage that it is preserved in a good text.

Most readers will find it difficult to get a clear idea of the plot of the other plays, whereas it is comparatively easy to sum up the action of *Edward II:* it is the struggle between a king and his peers about a minion, which leads to the latter's death and is followed, first, by the king's revenge and, secondly, by the struggle for power carried on by his antagonist which ends with the death of both the hero and his adversary. This clear outline of the plot is the result of the envisagement and subsequent handling of the material not as a series of episodes but as a whole. Marlowe did not merely condense the material which he found in Holinshed and other chroniclers with a view to reducing the events of 23 years to the 'two hours traffic of the stage', but he selected only those episodes which fitted into the pattern of the play as he conceived it, bound them together and gave prominence to certain minor characters, while he rejected other events which would have made excellent theatre.[5] He eliminated all that would have spoilt his design, namely the prolonged conflict lifting up now the king and now the barons, while it inevitably draws to its tragical conclusion.

This pattern differs widely from that of the other plays where the

---

[4] F. S. Boas: *Christopher Marlowe*. Oxford 1940; chapt. XI, pp. 172–91.

[5] Cf. Charlton and Waller, *op. cit.*, pp. 31 ff., and J. Bakeless: *The Tragicall History of Christopher Marlowe* (1942), vol. II, pp. 8 ff.

hero, as in *Tamburlaine* and *The Jew*, inflicts a series of defeats on those who successively oppose him, and finally is either 'hoist with his own petar' or meets with his accidental or tragical fate. In *The Massacre* alone the Guise is defeated by a human antagonist; his death is not, however, the result of the development of a uniform action, but is dealt out to him by a man who rises to eminence only in the second half of the play and only at the end identifies himself with the religious and political forces against which the Guise has spent his fury. Nor is Henry of Navarre his antagonist in the proper sense of the word; although he represents the party hostile to him, he is not the direct cause of his overthrow and his character is too dimly conceived for this part. In *Edward II* the man and the cause are identical from the beginning, and for the first time in Marlowe's plays the hero is confronted with an enemy of equal stature, namely Mortimer, who, as will be shown by the analysis, fully deserves this title.

The play opens, not with a clamorous state scene or the aftermath of a pitched battle as in *2* and *3 Henry VI*, but with Gaveston's soliloquy, which is skilfully broken in the middle by a dramatic passage. This quiet and strictly personal opening is significant in that it prepares the way for a play which is not concerned with political issues and warlike events alone, but with private and intimate relations as well that will lead to actions in the /**206**/ heroic sphere. At the same time this opening focuses our interest on the man who is the object of strife and the cause of the hero's tragical overthrow. With the exception of this scenic section Gaveston remains in the background of the play; his is a passive part and his activity is limited to being banished, recalled and hunted to death, and to cynical sallies of his Gascon wit. Marlowe reveals his character only so far as it concerns the King, to whom he is devoted, though his devotion is not free from egoistical motives. His treatment of the three Poor Men shows that he does not care for the people, whom he considers only so far as they serve his selfish interests. His thoughts are centred in the King

> . . . upon whose bosom let me die,
> And with the world be still at enmity.   [I, i, 14–15]

In order to remain in his lord's favour he will gladly risk the hatred of all other men, and he will separate the King from them by his love. In the second part of his soliloquy he gives free rein to the sensuous imagination with which he will satisfy Edward's craving for 'music and poetry'. It is just the kind of entertainment he describes here that fascinates the King, and it is important that we should recognise the dramatic function of this soliloquy because it silences the possible objection that nowhere in the play does Marlowe give any reason for the infatuation of the King. The principle of economy which Marlowe observes strictly in this drama, is responsible for the fact that this is the only place where he introduces any motive.[6] The comparative amplitude of the passage—one of the very few descriptions in *Edward II*—is fully justified by its dramatic function.

On this quiet introductory section of the first scene which, translated into musical terms, might be called sostenuto, follows the violent clash between the king and his rebellious peers which, for all its conciseness, recalls the numerous scenes of this kind in the first chronicle plays of Shakespeare. Here Edward shows his headstrong character and professes his determination to have his will and Gaveston. Among his opponents the interest at once concentrates on the young Mortimer who, by his impetuous temperament and craving for immediate action, resembles Richard, the later Duke of Gloucester, in *3 Henry VI*.

This rapid and stormy section of I, i is followed by the meeting of the two friends. The king has his wish and feels he has reached the height of bliss. Transported as they are they take to swift action and mishandle the Bishop of Coventry who was the main cause of Gaveston's banishment. By ill-treating the spiritual peer they add fuel to the fury of the nobles whose cause slowly gathers impetus in I, ii. The speed of the counteraction, however, is checked by the short intervention of the Queen who, siding /**207**/ with her husband, acts as a clog and, at the same time, prepares us for the part she is to play later on.

The controlled movement of this scene is interrupted by the ironic thumbnail sketches of the nobles which Gaveston gives in I, iii. After this brief suspense, and rendered more effective by it, I, iv begins at top speed: the peers hurriedly put their signatures to the order banishing the favourite. The counter-action thus reaches a first culminating point, and by its concentrated power and momen-

---

[6] It would be more to the point to speak not of a motive but of the poetic equivalent to a motive, because it is not the psychological adequacy but the poetic function that counts here and elsewhere in poetic drama.

tum the two friends are separated, the King being forced to sign the order. Edward who had his will in the first scene now has to bow to the barons; but he is not prepared to brook the insult and it is he who keeps the action going through the Queen. He threatens not to acknowledge her as his wife if she does not succeed in making the peers recall Gaveston. So she sets about accomplishing this difficult task. It is the young Mortimer whom she selects among the nobles to plead for her cause and through him she effects the recall of the King's minion. Thus this scene witnesses, in its first half, the triumph of the antagonists and, in the second half, the swift rise of the hero to a state of generosity and glad expectancy. At the end of act I the dramatic struggle seems to be decided in his favour.

The dialogue of the two Mortimers which ends the scene, and II, i where Baldock and Spencer make up their minds to offer their services to Gaveston, and the King's niece expects the return of her betrothed, mark the time which elapses between his sailing to Ireland and his return. It is a period of political inactivity—although Mortimer Senior departs for the Scottish wars—and a lull in the movement of the drama, the interest being shifted to the private sphere of life. A minimum of tension is preserved, however, by the aristocratic pride of the young Mortimer, who emphasizes his determination not to 'yield to any such upstart' and 'dapper Jack so brisk' as Gaveston. Rebellion is still smouldering.

The tension becomes more acute in II, ii where Edward impatiently expects his minion, while the nobles vent their hatred of Gaveston. The latent conflict at once explodes into open hostility after the King has saluted his friend. It is the lords who take the initiative and Mortimer who, first, wounds Gaveston and then forces his way into the King's presence to denounce his disastrous foreign policy. Thus, from a complete lull, the counter-action breaks out in its most violent form. Compared to the similar situation in I, iv the development of the play is marked by the change from threats and more or less peaceful means to immediate action and war. The section of this scene which is devoted to the open conflict is again followed by one of comparative quiet: after the indignant Kent has left his brother, Baldock and Spencer are accepted into Edward's service, and the King thinks not of war but of the marriage of Gaveston to his niece. The interest once more shifts to the private sphere of life and the tempo slackens.

Action is resumed with increasing speed in the following scenes

(II, iii–III, i): they sketch the renewed and successful attempt of the barons to separate the King from his minion—this time not by written order but /208/ by an act of force. The assault on Tynmouth Castle and the succeeding separation of Edward and Gaveston is represented against the background of Isabella's feelings; the infatuated King neglects her entirely and it is she who directs the peers in their pursuit of the favourite. Her two short soliloquies interrupt the speed of the action and create a fine rubato movement. The private and the political elements are skilfully combined and the first serves as a lyrical or emotional foil to the latter. At the same time the Queen's affection is shown to shift definitely towards Mortimer, although Marlowe has taken care not to hurry this process, as is witnessed by her resolution in the second soliloquy once more to attempt to gain Edward's favour.

It is characteristic of the technique used in this play that the author has prepared this development from the moment when the Queen first appears on the stage in I, iv. Here she is immediately addressed by Mortimer and it is to him that she speaks last. The accusations of Edward and Gaveston concerning her intimacy with the young lord —which have no foundation in the play so far—and her choosing Mortimer as a means to change the minds of the peers, are the stages which lead up to the open declaration of love in this scene. From now on she ceases to clog the activity of the lords and becomes, next to Mortimer, the main antagonist of the King and a decisive factor in his overthrow.

Marlowe has skilfully regulated the movement of Gaveston's downfall in II, v and vi where, immediately after his capture, Arundel asks the barons for a last interview of the King with their prisoner. The auther thus brings about, on the one hand, a conflict among the nobles similar to that in I, iv, where the Queen entreats them to re-call Gaveston, on the other hand a slight delay of the counter-action and a corresponding upward movement of the cause of Edward and his friend. The lull at the end of II, v where Pembroke and Arundel, in whose custody the prisoner has been left, decide to visit the former's wife, is immediately followed by the vigorous movement of III, i: Warwick forces Pembroke's servants to yield Gaveston up to him and has him hurriedly put to death. The considerable space Marlowe has allowed for this episode is fully justified when we consider its rhythmical function in the pattern of the play. It can be understood as an experiment in the regulation of dramatic speed which is repeated—on a larger scale—in the series of scenes representing the hero's fall from power.

III, ii develops with increasing speed. Edward is uncertain about Gaveston's fate and apprehends the worst. The two Spencers are trying, not without success, to rouse him from his dejection. The Queen takes leave to go to France and thus introduces at an early date the territory which is to serve as a jumping-board for the final onset of the counter-action. When Arundel announces the death of Gaveston, the King temporarily relapses into his humour:

> O shall I speak, or shall I sigh and die! /**209**/ [III, ii, 122]

It is again young Spencer who urges him to resist so that Edward vows a terrible vengeance for the death of his friend. When therefore the rebels' herald asks him to deliver up his new minion, he sends the messenger back, promising to follow 'with sword and fire at (his) heels'. He is now the revenger of Gaveston and bent on swift and ruthless action.

The next scene opens with a breathing pause during the battle of Boroughbridge. It shows Edward ready to 'pour vengeance with (his) sword On those proud rebels', fretting to get back into action. The defiant speeches of the leaders of the two hosts which follow lead the conflict at once to its intellectual pitch. The King will sacrifice everything, even his country, to revenge; he is firmness itself and resolved 'rather to Make England's civil towns huge heaps of stones' than to give in. This 'desperate and unnatural resolution', as Warwick calls it, leads to immediate victory and in the following section of the scene Edward is shown as the implacable judge of his adversaries.

It is again Mortimer on whom Marlowe focuses the interest by placing his speech last when the barons are led to their respective dooms:

> What, Mortimer, can raggèd stony walls
> Immure thy virtue that aspires to heaven?
> No. Edward, England's scourge, it may not be;
> Mortimer's hope surmounts his fortune far. [III, iii, 71–4]

The cause of his rebellion has been removed by Gaveston's death, but imprisonment becomes a new cause for further resistance—if we are allowed to speak of a cause, for he rather follows an irrational

yearning which revolts against the prison-bars and will not be satisfied until he has annihilated the tyrant. His aristocratic pride which
made him hate the upstart Gaveston, transforms itself into the deadly
hatred of the soaring intellect against its oppressor.

To make Edward's victory more complete Spencer, in the last
section of III, iii, frustrates the efforts of the Queen to win the French
King for her cause. The counter-action thus is at a standstill at the
beginning of act IV, the heart of the resistance lying 'immured' in
the Tower. Then it gathers force slowly.

Marlowe begins the new act with two scenes which are marked by
their parallel structure—an andante followed by an allegro—and by
a significant increase of size and implication. Kent, in a soliloquy
which is set in a fine lyrical frame—'Fair blows the wind for France:
blow, gentle gale'—is waiting for Mortimer to escape from the
Tower. When he arrives they set sail for France. Here the Queen is
shown in a state of dejection after the French King's refusal of her
demand for help. As soon as Mortimer joins her and Hainault, the
action takes a directed course and gains speed.

In IV, iii the King revels in his victory and he makes up his mind
at once /**210**/ when he hears of the activity of his enemies in France.
Like his antagonist Mortimer he thirsts for immediate action and
expresses his impatience in the time-devouring verses:

> Gallop apace, bright Phœbus, through the sky,
> And dusky night, in rusty iron car,
> Between you both shorten the time, I pray,
> That I may see that most desirèd day,
> When we may meet these traitors in the field.
>
> [IV, iii, 45–9]

The onward urge of these words is at once bridled by the speeches
of the Queen and Mortimer who, in the following scene, land in
England. It is significant that the latter no longer primarily thinks
in terms of action but of policy. His verse has lost the youthful ring of
the earlier scenes and it is strange to hear him gently rebuke the
Queen:

> if you be a warrior
> You must not grow so passionate in speeches.
>
> [IV, iv, 15–16]

And then follows his own speech on the legality of their enterprise which, by its formal coldness, rings false and shows the Machiavellian man of power hiding behind the mask of the loyal subject. As long as the King was governed by his minions, the sympathy of the audience was rather drawn towards his antagonist. Now Mortimer is shown as a usurper and therefore appears in a less favourable light. The development of his character should, no doubt, be understood primarily as a necessity to which the dramatist had to submit in order to have his play performed on the public stage; it is less motivated by the lapse of time because Marlowe, at least up to this moment, does not create the impression that a period of many years is covered by the play. The perfunctory delineation of Mortimer's development causes a flaw in his dramatic portrait which shows that the author was not interested in this aspect but rather hurriedly proceeded to what was of more concern to him: Mortimer's Machiavellian rule and the tragedy of the hero.[7]

Thus he does not dwell on Edward's attempt to oppose his enemies but represents, in the rapid opening of IV, v, his reluctant flight to Ireland. Then, after the quiet movement of Kent's soliloquy, who is shown to waver in his allegiance and thereby prepares us, in time, for his part in act V, we see the victorious antagonist having the old Spencer put to death and giving order, in spite of the compassion of Kent, the Queen, and the Prince for the fugitive King, to trace him to his hiding place. It is again Mortimer who represents the driving force of the counter-action which, in the course of this scene, gradually gathers speed. /**211**/

IV, vi opens quietly with the King seeking 'this life contemplative' in the Welsh Abbey of Neath. That the lull in the action is going to be of short duration only and the calm introduces the tempest, is shown by Edward's haunting suspicion and the uneasy remark of Spencer about 'a gloomy fellow in a mead below' who 'gave a long look after (them)'. When the hero's spirits have drooped lowest and he puts his head 'laden with mickle care' in the abbot's lap, wishing he may 'never again lift up this drooping head', the emissaries of Mortimer, led by the very mower who had watched the fugitives, intrude into this pseudo-idyll which, by its unique mixture of quiet and unrest, of fearful apprehension and an intense craving for se-

[7] The Machiavellian element in certain of Marlowe's characters has been emphasized by M. Poirier in *Christopher Marlowe* (London 1951) (see my review in *English Studies*, June 1953).

curity, belongs to the finest rubato scenes of the play. Edward is separated from his friends and forced back into the political strife. This time he stands alone.

Act V witnesses the continuation, on the one hand, of the slow but steady decline of the hero and, on the other, the gradual rise to supreme power of the antagonists. In the abdication scene we still hear the Edward who could scarcely await Mortimer's coming to England in order to crush him. He compares himself to the 'imperial lion' who

> Highly scorning that the lowly earth
> Should drink his blood, mounts up into the air.
>
> [V, i, 13–14]

He feels 'pent and mew'd in a prison' while his wings carry him 'soaring up to heaven'. Thus he strongly resembles his antagonist when put in prison himself in III, iii. At the same time, however, his weaker self is ready to submit to the pressure of the situation and to deliver the crown to the emissaries of his enemy. We have been prepared for this struggle between his nobler and weaker selves already in I, iv where, in a manner as showy as here, he oscillated between furious protest against, and submission to, the exigencies of the hour. But the object or alter ego for which he struggles is no longer his friend whom he stands in danger to lose, but his crown. Like Faustus he clings to something which does not belong to him any more and, like the magician, he asks the 'watches of the elements' to stand still. 'All times and seasons, rest you at a stay,' [V, i, 67] he cries, but time, for Edward as for Faustus, moves on relentlessly and cannot be stopped. Here it is not marked by the striking of a clock but by the short and pressing remarks of Mortimer's emissaries which interrupt the monologue. Having changed his mind six times, the King hands over the crown and expects death as a welcome deliverer.

The steady decline of the hero's fortunes is further interrupted— or lengthened—by the futile effort of Kent to rescue him, for which we have been prepared by his change of sympathy in IV, v and by the mention made of his attempt in V, ii. A last delay in the movement towards the catastrophe occurs in the murder scene where Edward, harping upon his /212/ suffering and trying to bribe Lightborn, strives to escape the clutches of the murderer who is feigning compassion and tears until, throwing off his human mask, he suddenly reveals his murderous intention to his victim and executes it with all speed—an action which is all the more effective because of the delay.

It has been generally recognised that Edward's end is hardly heroic: it is actually as unheroic and pitiful as that of Faustus and reveals, when held against his valorous behaviour in the struggle with Mortimer, the full extent of his bipolar character which mirrors the two-fold vision of man in Renaissance philosophy. Both heroes give a truer, more comprehensive and, at the same time, more objective and dramatic picture of the Renaissance man than Tamburlaine, who illustrates only the optimistic and modern alternative.[8]

In the meantime (V, ii), Mortimer has further strengthened his position, first by taking the young Prince from the protection of his uncle Kent, secondly by giving Lightborn the ambiguous order to kill the imprisoned King, and thirdly by having Prince Edward crowned. He expects to rule through the puppet king and he proves his superiority by sentencing Kent against the will of his sovereign. The latter's resistance, however, when compared to the feeble attempt of the Prince in V, ii to stay under his uncle's protection, shows that the forces antagonistic to Mortimer's rule are increasing and concentrating upon the young King. Marlowe has prepared us for his part by introducing him early into the action (III, ii) and stressing certain features in his character: thus in IV, ii it is he who speaks affectionately of his father while the Queen and Mortimer are taking the first steps towards his ruin.

In the final scene of the play, which follows hard upon the hero's death, Mortimer feels he has reached the goal of his aspiration:

> As for myself, I stand as Jove's huge tree,
> And others are but shrubs compared to me.
> All tremble at my name, and I fear none.   [V, vi, 11–13]

From this zenith of his power he is pushed down by the young King who, supported by the nobles, confronts him and the Queen with a determination which is not to be shaken, though it is distinguished by its humanity.

Thus the play ends with the rapid rise to triumph of the forces

---

[8] Cf. Th. Spencer: *Shakespeare and the Nature of Man* (1945) and E. M. W. Tillyard: *The Elizabethan World Picture* (1943).

which represent poetic justice. Looked at from a distance, *Edward II* shows—in the first two acts or, more exactly, until III, ii—the struggle for Gaveston with the culminating points for the hero in I, i and at the end of I, iv, and the lowest points in the middle of scenes I, iv and III, ii. In the latter scene the struggle for Gaveston is ended and immediately followed by Edward's revenge which is achieved at the end of act III /213/ where, as in a classical tragedy, the hero seems to have secured the victory over his antagonists. The play about Gaveston now changes into the struggle for power which is caused, directly, by this very vengeance (itself rooted in Edward's love of Gaveston) and indirectly by the change of Mortimer's character. During act IV the counter-action gathers force and approaches its climax at the beginning of the last scene of the play where Mortimer exults in his absolute power. This gradual rise is accompanied by the slow decline of the hero's fortunes which, after many oscillations, reach their lowest point in the death scene. Then we witness the swift rise to power of the hero's son which is accompanied, again in a contrasted sense, by the sudden fall of the antagonists.

In spite of a certain weakness of the link between the two movements of the action, the play forms an organic whole. Its structure is characterized by what may be called dramatic rhythm. It would be easy to represent this movement, which I have tried to express in the terms of the drama and—tentatively—of music, graphically by lines tracing, by their varying inclination, the speed with which the actions led by the hero and his antagonist proceed. The result would be, roughly speaking, the rapid fall and rise of the hero's line in the first act, the much slower decline in act II which ends in III, ii and is followed by a vigorous rise in the second half of this act. The last two acts show the undulating falling line of the hero's fate, to which is attached, in the last scene, a steep rise. The line thus described would be accompanied, but in a contrasted sense, by that of the antagonist. The play conceived in this manner would consist of three successive waves and counterwaves which differ from one another only by their growing size. Translating the dramatic structure into terms of music, we may say that the first act gives the tragic theme, which is followed by two variations in each of which the theme is brought nearer to its tragic conclusion.

Thus *Edward II* forms a strongly and closely knit whole from which no part, however loosely joined to the body of the play it may seem, can be separated without either changing the rhythm of the action or weakening its logical structure. It is true that Marlowe might have used a different technique altogether to obtain this result, and given it more outward unity by using, for instance, the messenger's report of classical drama. But the effect would have been entirely different and *Edward II* would not have been acted on the Elizabethan stage for which it was written. Marlowe knew what was expected of him and represented all the episodes of the play on the stage, i.e., he adopted the *ab ovo* technique of the popular drama. Although he selected from the vast body of material offered to him by the sources only those incidents which had a direct bearing on the gradual unfolding of Edward's tragedy, the amount he used is nevertheless enormous when we consider the length of the play. He conquered the difficulties by speed and concentration.

The structural unit of *Edward II* is neither the act nor the scene, but what may be called the scenic section, and in this respect Marlowe was /**214**/ not an innovator but could follow the example set by Kyd in *The Spanish Tragedy*.[9] Yet even from this point of view the difference between the two plays is far greater than their similarity. *The Spanish Tragedy* is a very slow drama in which the action is carried forward simultaneously on three different levels: on the political, where it seems to develop slowly towards a happy ending, namely the marriage of Bel-Imperia and Balthasar: on the private, where Hieronymo gradually changes from a passive into an active hero: and on a level where the fate of Lorenzo's servants is shown.[10] Action and counter-action only meet at the end of the play in the catastrophe. In *Edward II* the private and the political spheres of the action are not separated but mingle from beginning to end, and we witness a rapid series of clashes between the hero and his antagonist. The structure of the two plays is entirely different: the scenic units in *The Spanish Tragedy* help to erect a stately and three-dimensional building, whereas in *Edward II* they form a rapid succession which creates the impression not of space but of time.

The main functions of the scenic units in *Edward II* are the regula-

---

[9] Cf. the excellent study by P. W. Biesterfeldt: *Die dramatische Technik Thomas Kyds* (1936). It speaks for the speed of Marlowe's play that its 24 scenes fall into no less that 90 shorter units, while B. counts only 77 units in the 31 scenes of the original version of the *Sp. Tr.*

[10] A fourth level would of course be that from which the ghosts watch the play.

tion of the rhythm of the action and the reception of a vast material. The action passes swiftly from one unit to the next, and often the impression of speed is heightened by the abrupt opening of scenes which suggests that the action represented has been going on for some time before. The beginning of the play shows Gaveston reading the King's letter. He limits himself to picking out the two most significant lines and proceeds straight to the heart of the matter. Without turning back to what has passed he looks ahead to what is to come. The next section presents the king in the full course of a hot dispute with the barons.

King Edward:	Lancaster !
Lancaster:	My lord.
Gaveston:	That Earl of Lancaster do I abhor. [*Aside.*]
King Edward:	Will you not grant me this? In spite of them
	I'll have my will, and these two Mortimers,
	That cross me thus, shall know I am displeased. [*Aside.*]

[I, i, 74–79]

The essence of the dispute which has taken place before they enter, is contained in these few lines which introduce the hero. We do not know what his will is—but that is of secondary importance: he is crossed in his will by Lancaster and the Mortimers, and Gaveston by his asides shows that he hates them. It is his will the king will have, and it is one of the men he names that will block it. The dramatic conflict is foreshadowed in this breathless passage, the beginning of the drama properly speaking. /**215**/

It has been noticed that Marlowe, true to his classical training and contrary to the stage customs of his time, does not represent the traffic of the battles on the stage. Thus, of the battle of Boroughbridge he only gives a breathing-space filled in with the defiant speeches of the leaders, and the result: the condemnation of the rebels. The second armed conflict between the King and Mortimer he omits completely and proceeds straight to the moment when Edward and his favourites 'shape [their] course to Ireland'. What he gains by this technique is again speed and concentration: the attention of the audience is not diverted by noisy 'alarums and excursions' but remains fixed on the intellectual conflict.

Marlowe's grip on the attention of the audience is further tightened by the reduction to a minimum of the elements creating relief from the forward urge of the action. He gives us neither comic scenes nor descriptions but concise soliloquies which contain a lyrical element, and short scenic sections which do not allow for a lengthy breathing-space. The dynamic force of the play is intensified by the almost complete lack of retrospective passages and descriptions. Rarely do the characters look back on their past experience: their attention—and with it that of the audience—is bent on the immediate future, and when they remember the past it is only in short snatches like Edward's

> Tell Isabel, the queen, I looked not thus,
> When for her sake I ran at tilt in France
> And there unhorsed the Duke of Cleremont.
>
> [V, v, 67–69]

Here, of course, the reminiscence has a dramatic function: by its associations with glorious deeds of chivalry it creates a sharp contrast to the miserable situation in which the King now lives who is timorously facing his murderer.

It is the powerful rhythm of the action which captures the mind of the modern reader perhaps more than the rational exposition of causes and motives. The sacrifice of the earlier heroes' aspiring minds and of the poetry depending on it is compensated for by this dramatic element, and what the characters lack in that respect they gain in outline and impetuosity. The cosmic element gives way to the dynamic; lyrical poetry is transformed into the dramatic poetry of action.

Once we have realized the dynamic quality of this play, the relationship of Shakespeare's first chronicle plays becomes clearer. In both we witness the repeated and violent clash of opposed characters, and the development of Richard, the later Duke of Gloucester, resembles that of Mortimer. The general structure of *3 Henry VI* shows the rise and fall of the conflicting parties in much the same way as that of *Edward II*. But the bareness and onward sweep of the latter play contrast strongly with the breadth of the former, the concise directness of the verse which Marlowe uses here with the exuberant imagery and rhetoric of the early Shakespeare. /**216**/ It is probable that Shakespeare wrote—or rather revised[11]—his plays first, but when he sat down to work he had the clash of defiant

[11] The revision theory has recently been defended with great success by Dover Wilson in the introductions to his edition of *Henry VI* (1952).

speeches and the rhetoric of *Tamburlaine* before him and the aspiring mind, not of the cosmic poet *Tamburlaine*, but of the man who is fascinated by the glittering crown much in the same way as his own Duchess of Gloucester, Jack Cade, the old Duke of York and his two sons. Marlowe, in *Edward II*, seems to have been influenced by the dramatic structure of *2* and *3 Henry VI*—whoever was responsible for that—but it was Shakespeare's turn to fall under the spell of *Edward II* when he wrote *Richard II*, although the total result was something entirely different.[12] Perhaps he got nearest to the dramatic method of *Edward II* in *Romeo and Juliet*, *Othello*, *Macbeth*, and *Antony and Cleopatra*[13]: here we find the dynamic quality of Marlowe's play, and many things besides which we do not get in *Edward II*. /**217**/

[12] Among the main parallels in the structure of the plays I should reckon the facts (1) that *Richard II* is the first chronicle play of Shakespeare's built from beginning to end on the conflict between the hero and one antagonist only, (2) that this conflict is represented by several variations of the tragic theme which, step by step, lead to the catastrophe.

[13] This aspect of *Antony and Cleopatra* has been fully treated by Rudolf Binder in *Der dramatische Rhythmus in Shakespeares 'Antonius und Cleopatra'* (1939) (see my review in *E.S.*, Aug. 1943).

DAVID M. BEVINGTON

The Moral Tradition in
EDWARD II

Edward II, probably first performed in 1592–1593 when Pembroke's company was most active in London, is generally acclaimed as Marlowe's most carefully constructed play, and his most successful in the creation of plausible historical characters. It represents a mature fusion of moral structure with the secular subject matter toward which Marlowe was constantly striving. The play is manifestly more of a chronicle than *The Jew* or *Faustus*, and its personages are historically authentic in a setting more familiar to Marlowe's audiences than the remote and colorful milieu of the Scythian Tamburlaine. Thus *Edward II* is more closely linked to secular reality than any of Marlowe's other plays. Its chief characters contain less generic personification than his other protagonists. Among Marlowe's plays, therefore, it affords least opportunity for a study of indebtedness to the morality drama, and will be discussed least extensively. Nevertheless the moral ambiguity of *Edward II* is not unlike that to be found in Marlowe's other productions, an ambiguity that derives its existence from a pronounced though vestigial moral element within the play.

As is often the case in Marlowe, the ambiguity in *Edward II* arises from the conflict between factual account as it was set down in the playwright's source, and moral causality implied in the structural order of the drama. In this instance Marlowe was guided by Holinshed's chronicle of the reign of Edward II, and the secular element

Reprinted from *From Mankind to Marlowe: Growth of Structure in the Popular Drama of Tudor England* (Harvard Univ. Press, 1962).

in the play is dominant. Marlowe is often so intent on dramatizing what actually took place in history that many critics have found no moral pattern in his reporting of these facts. Charlton and Waller, for example, argue that "We are not asked to consider whether Edward deserved his fate; we are not led either to be sorry for the Queen or to be repelled by her infamous desertion [of /**234**/ Edward]. It is merely the essence of what happened." The play "owes something of its grim power to a certain naturalistic quality."[1] Yet it would be more correct to say that our moral reactions are confused, rather than suspended, as we follow the progress of this crowded narrative. Actually we are both "sorry for the Queen" and "repelled by her infamous desertion," and Marlowe's difficulty is in reconciling these converse impulses. His main problem is to compress the events of twenty-three years into the framework of a single drama, and in doing so to motivate the changes of character indicated in his source.[2] His reliance on the structural formulas of the popular theater to solve this problem creates a conflict between the moral tradition and his factual material.

Edward II chronicles a civil conflict between two political forces represented by the King and Young Mortimer, the leader of the Barons' revolt. Each has his counselors and allies, and the enmity between the two camps is so pervasive that virtually every person in the play is obliged to cast his lot with one or the other. The question of allegiance is a profoundly moral one for the King's brother, Kent, and for the others involved, even if the playwright appears to withhold judgment. In outline, therefore, the play is one of epic confrontation between opposing forces, inviting comparison of their rival claims from both participant and spectator.

Furthermore, these forces move simultaneously in the diverging paths of the homiletic tragedy, such as *Enough Is as Good as a Feast*. Mortimer's fortune exalts him, like the Worldly Man, through a series of triumphs until he topples and is punished. Conversely, King Edward suffers the ignominy of unfavorable reputation and persecution at the hands of Mortimer, until finally his cause wins moral justification like that of Christian Faith in *The Tide Tarrieth* or Just in *Like Will to Like*. By the end of *Edward II*, the moral for-

[1] H. B. Charlton and R. D. Waller, eds., *Edward II*, in the Methuen *Works of Marlowe* (London, 1933), p. 55.

[2] Charlton and Waller, eds., *Edward II*, pp. 32–36.

mula clearly intends retribution for Mortimer as a means of termi-
nating his brief worldly success. Mortimer's period of favor with
Fortune is no more substantial than that of Moros, whom Lady
Fortune exalts for a time in *The Longer Thou Livest* to demonstrate
the temporary reign of Folly. King Edward's claim to ultimate re-
dress is vindicated in the action of his son:

> Sweet father, here unto thy murdered ghost
> I offer up this wicked traitor's head, /235/
> And let these tears, distilling from mine eyes,
> Be witness of my grief and innocency.   [V, vi, 99–102]

In the intermediate morality, this scheme of divided paths for the
opposed protagonists invariably separated the godly from the profane,
and rewarded each according to his merit. Its structural force in
Edward II similarly implies a contrast between a meek but worthy
king and his depraved persecutor. Marlowe's preoccupation with
complexity of character, however, forbids such a plain interpretation
of right and wrong. Just as he sought plausible reasons for Barabas'
viciousness, here he delves into the reasons for King Edward's un-
popularity with the nobles, and is not satisfied with a simple explanation of Mortimer as the Worldly Man. He becomes especially
interested in Queen Isabella's motives for transferring her loyalty to
Mortimer. At the same time he retains the pattern of dual protagonists as a solution for his casting dilemma. The result is that his
characters occupy two spheres, human complexity and moral ab-
straction. The complexity appears chiefly in the exposition, as in
The Jew of Malta, in order to set an historical event in motion,
whereas moral causality leading to a restoration of order figures
increasingly in the play's continuation and denouement.

The technical debt of *Edward II* to popular convention stems
from the necessity of assigning a large number of parts to ten or
so company members, additional hired actors, and two to four boys.[3]
Nearly thirty named adult male roles may feasibly be cast for eleven
actors: (1) King Edward (2) Young Mortimer (3) Edmund Earl of
Kent (4) Gaveston, Hugh Spencer, Trussel, Gurney (5) Lancaster,
Sir John of Hainault, Bishop of Winchester (6) Warwick, Rice ap
Howel, Matrevis (7) Pembroke, Mower, Berkeley (8) Bishop of
Coventry, Beaumont, Young Spencer (9) Archbishop of Canter-

---

[3] See Lawrence, *Stage Studies*, pp. 68–70.

bury, Baldock (10) Levune, Mayor of Bristow, Leicester (11) Mortimer Senior, Arundel, Abbot, Lightborn. The feminine and juvenile
roles call for two experienced boys, one to play Queen Isabella and
the other the King's Niece and Prince Edward. The ladies in attendance on the King's Niece would require only younger boys.

Casting suppression is pronounced. Only four characters are
central to the entire play: Edward, Young Mortimer, Isabella, and
Kent. All the rest exist, in morality fashion, chiefly to highlight /**236**/
a particular phase in the careers of the protagonists. Mortimer Senior,
Lancaster, Warwick, and their peers belong solely to the period of
Young Mortimer's baronial protest against Edward's caprice.
Matrevis, Gurney, and Lightborn seem part of an almost /**237**/ entirely different story of suborned murder and duplicity. Similarly, in
the King's party Gaveston lives as an embodiment of Edward's extravagance for only ten scenes out of twenty-three, whereas Baldock
and the two Spencers occupy the middle portion of the play. Like the
authors of hybrid chronicle, Marlowe treats lesser historical figures
in sequence. He justifies the procedure by moving from phase to
phase in the dual account of contending forces.

Except for an inconsequential appearance of the Archbishop of
Canterbury (V, iv), no suppressed figures return in the final scenes.
Edward II, despite its acclaimed superiority of structure over Marlowe's earlier plays, is still linear in movement. Its sequential plan
thematically illustrates vicious decline for Mortimer and simultaneous deliverance for Edward. The focus in cast moves from the
barons and their ecclesiastical peers in the early scenes of revolt,
to the King's captors, prison-keepers, and murderers in the final
action. At the beginning we see Mortimer surrounded by nobles,
and his cause is identical with theirs: an understandable grievance
against the promotion of sycophants and the neglect of the realm's
defense. As the other lords withdraw, however, the concept of
revolt is increasingly identified with Mortimer and the Queen.
The cause that had previously been the outcry of an entire estate
becomes a crude struggle for personal supremacy. Mortimer's relationship with the Queen, uncertain at first, is enhanced by their
partnership in ambition. In the final scenes Mortimer is surrounded
not by barons but by hirelings and murderers. The few lords remaining, like Leicester, nominally support Mortimer but are
plainly distressed by his highhanded treatment of the King.

Edward's changing fortune is also brought about structurally by a shift of the *dramatis personae*. The all-important presence of Gaveston in the first half of the play continually emphasizes Edward's weakness. Once Gaveston is removed, no matter how much we may have disapproved of the corruption before, we are less apt to dwell upon it. Young Spencer and Baldock, who succeed Gaveston as royal favorites, are perhaps no less dangerous, but they are less in evidence. When they in turn disappear, Edward is left in the hands of Mortimer's hirelings rather than of his own sycophants. Mortimer and the Queen remain without dangerous enemies and without noble allies; Edward is finally friendless and a pitiful victim. His son, young Edward, is also at the mercy of Mortimer /**238**/ until he emerges finally as the avenger of his father and the agent of virtuous recovery.

However much a conventional structure of dual protagonists in *Edward II* may suggest moral victory for the King, the historical "facts" of Edward's reign contradict the simple pattern of right and wrong. The Elizabethans evidently viewed Edward's reign with mixed feelings. In Marlowe's source (Holinshed) and later in Michael Drayton's *Mortimeriados* (1596), for example, much of the blame for civil discord rests with the incompetent and effete King. According to Drayton, young Mortimer is at first the leader of a legitimate and glorious cause. Isabella is originally more victim than wrong-doer, a "poor wife-widowed queen."[4] Only when they carry their cause to the point of regicide do Isabella and Mortimer lose favor with the Elizabethan public.

Marlowe's dramatic problem is to reconcile this historical account of complex characters and shifting sympathies with the structural formula of unrepentant vice. The Worldly Man Mortimer and his consort in rebellion, whose reign of earthly domination must lead to overthrow, are seen at first as human beings with understandable and even laudable motives. Conversely, their "virtuous" victim Edward must appear at first to deserve a large measure of their enmity. These considerations work at cross purposes to the underlying emphasis of the moral formula. The result, as in *The Jew*, is that a highly "naturalistic" exposition yields increasingly to the

[4] Michael Drayton, *Mortimeriados. The Lamentable ciuell warres of Edward the Second and the Barrons*; in *The Works of Michael Drayton*, ed. J. William Hebel (Oxford, 1931), I, 305–392.

pattern of the moral "tragedy" of vice. Characterization, like that of Barabas, begins with plausibility and moves toward viciousness for Marlowe's worldly protagonists. The action of the play descends from a contest between two political powers into a series of cynical intrigues.

Of the central figures, Isabella is perhaps the most perplexing in her extremes of behavior.[5] On first impression one is tempted to suppose her loyal and sincere. She holds onto the hope of reconciliation in spite of Edward's indifference to her. In soliloquy (II, iv) she protests her adoration for her husband, and is in anguish at the prospect of deserting him. Her indecisiveness in this internal monologue is psychologically perceptive and convincing. Isabella thus seems a good-hearted but weak-willed woman who consents reluctantly to accept Mortimer's drive for power only because she has no other choice. Thereafter the lust for power begins to corrupt /239/ her too, until she becomes an adulteress and willing accomplice in murder.

Despite the plausibility of her behavior in the beginning, however, Isabella increasingly conforms to the structural plan of moral decline for the worldly practitioners of vice. A curious suspicion emerges concerning Isabella's supposed relationship with Mortimer. At first she defends her reputation with dignity and seeming candor against Gaveston's charge of adultery. Later, however, this apparently baseless slander turns out to be entirely valid. What is the explanation for this surprising reversal? In retrospect, Marlowe partly suggests that Isabella has been deluding us with her protestations of innocence.

In the later portions of the play Isabella becomes "the subtle queen" (III, iii, 86), an expert intriguer and a hypocrite. The honest Kent laments the dissembling by which Isabella furthers her fortunes:

> But Edmund, calm this rage;
> Dissemble, or thou diest, for Mortimer
> And Isabel do kiss while they conspire;
> And yet she bears a face of love forsooth.
> Fie on that love that hatcheth death and hate.
>
> [IV, v, 20–24]

---

[5] Charlton and Waller, eds., *Edward II*, p. 47.

Isabella's continuing protests of concern for Edward, and her lamentations that circumstances have forced her into reluctant opposition to him ("I rue my lord's ill-fortune; but alas, / Care of my country called me to this war," IV, v, 73–74), are exposed as patent hypocrisy when we learn that she not only acquiesces in Edward's death, but actually proposes it:

> But, Mortimer, as long as he survives,
> What safety rests for us or for my son?
> *Mortimer junior.* Speak, shall he presently be dispatched and die?
> *Queen Isabella.* I would he were, so it were not by my means.
>
> [V, ii, 42–45]

She compounds this duplicity by asking Edward's jailers to convey to him a message of her love and loyalty; Mortimer's delighted comment is "Finely dissembled. Do so still, sweet queen" (V, ii, 74). To Kent she protests her wish to have Edward set at liberty; Kent's aside is "Ah, they do dissemble" (V, ii, 86).

Dissembling is of course one of the stocks-in-trade of the Vice, /**240**/ and although it would be misleading to label Isabella as a vice character, we can see by comparing her with Barabas that Marlowe relies on the moral tradition in his depiction of the Queen's personality. As in the case of *The Jew*, Marlowe suggests that Isabella's piety, loyalty, and humility have been and still are weapons of intrigue, intended to deceive her enemies and her audience at the same time. It must be emphasized that this vice-like quality can explain only a part of her character. After all, Isabella does reveal in soliloquy (II, iv) a convincing display of divided loyalty, and because she is debating with herself the monologue seems perfectly sincere. However, because her critics have found in her later behavior a change too great to be accounted for by Marlowe's psychological analysis of motive,[6] we are left with the impression that Marlowe approaches Isabella from the viewpoint of two dramatic traditions. Insofar as her function is derived from the moral tradition, therefore, Isabella's character is primarily static rather than dynamic.[7] Marlowe proceeds through the revelation of her natural

[6] See Charlton and Waller, eds., *Edward II*, p. 47: "So much devotion and so cruel a desertion, so much gentleness at the beginning and such callous hypocrisy at the end, go badly together; and critics have often complained with some reason of Marlowe's handling of the character."

[7] See Wilson, *Marlowe and Shakespeare*, pp. 95–98.

depravity rather than through development of her human weakness. He uncovers a quality of absolute evil in her nature, and accounts for her apparent change by a gradual unmasking of her true identity.

Mortimer's character undergoes much the same sort of revelation in place of development, and the same transition from rationally motivated behavior to pure viciousness. Marlowe is careful at first to give him plausible motives, as he had done with the Jew. Mortimer professes to hate Gaveston for the ill effects of his corrupt presence on the public weal. As champion of "the murmuring commons" he wins our respect. His subsequent villainy, like that of Macbeth, might be explained in terms of the corrupting effect of power upon a naturally ambitious man. But Marlowe portrays him as representing something more basically evil than ambition. Mortimer becomes a cunning manipulator, a master of duplicity. Although his goal is still personal power, he becomes, like Barabas, more and more concerned with the cleverness of the means of his success. Plotting the death of the King, Mortimer devises in Latin a warrant for Edward's execution, ambiguously worded in such a way that the sender cannot be held accountable. He reads it to the audience for their approval of his diabolical skill, adding:

> And therefore will I do it cunningly.   [V, iv, 5]/**241**/

As an added touch of intrigue, Mortimer arranges the death of the man who is to bear the warrant and commit the assassination, by means of a secret token that will be recognized by Edward's prison-keepers, Matrevis and Gurney.

Having informed the audience of this ingenious plot, Mortimer calls forth the man chosen to do his murder, Lightborn. Their short scene together is appropriately comic in the grim vein of the Vice and his henchmen. Lightborn boasts of his skillful atrocities of the past in a manner that suggests Ithamore's first conversation with Barabas:

> 'Tis not the first time I have killed a man.
> I learned in Naples how to poison flowers,
> To strangle with a lawn thrust through the throat,
> To pierce the windpipe with a needle's point,
>
> .   .   .
>
> But yet I have a braver way than these.   [V, iv, 30–37]

His career in crime is generic, like those of Barabas and Ithamore. Mortimer and Lightborn chuckle appreciatively in admiration of their own cleverness, ignoring all moral consideration. The Baron then sends Lightborn on his way, with a slip of the tongue that almost gives away his own plan for the assassin's subsequent death:

> Take this. Away, and never see me more.
> *Lightborn.* No.
> *Mortimer junior.* No,
> Unless thou bring me news of Edward's death.
>
> [V, iv, 43–46]

Left to himself, Mortimer continues in a jocular vein to unveil his own machinations by which he has cajoled the peers into naming him protector. His bag of tricks includes a show of mock humility and unwillingness to assume so great a task:

> They thrust upon me the protectorship
> And sue to me for that that I desire.
> While at the council-table, grave enough,
> And not unlike a bashful Puritan,
> First I complain of imbecility.
> Saying it is *onus quam gravissimum*;
> Till, being interrupted by my friends,
> *Suscepi* that *provinciam* as they term it;
> And to conclude, I am Protector now. /**242**/ [V, iv, 56–64]

Mortimer's pretended reluctance calls to mind the artistry of another "Vice," Richard III, who so aptly cajoles the London citizens into offering him the crown by following Buckingham's advice: "Play the maid's part, still answer nay, and take it."[8] Mortimer stands revealed as the Worldly Man at the height of his success before inevitable catastrophe, and his last scenes are accordingly a series of comic boasts and triumphs over his victims. Of course there is a great deal more to Mortimer than the type of Worldly Man. Marlowe is concerned, as in his other creations, less with moral example than with human personality. At the same time the moral pattern is undeniably present, and contributes to the restless power of Marlowe's characterization.

The change in King Edward is opposite to that in Mortimer and Isabella. He himself is never regarded as vicious, but only mis-

[8] *Richard III*, III, vii, 50.

guided, inexperienced, and pleasure-seeking. Nevertheless Marlowe
imputes evil to his rule in the persons of his sycophants, who em-
body many vice-like qualities. Gaveston repeatedly identifies
himself as a flatterer and hypocrite. When he encounters three poor
men who hope to find service at court, he promises to aid them but
confides to the audience his insincerity in doing so:

> But yet it is no pain to speak men fair.
> I'll flatter these and make them live in hope.   [*Aside.*]
> [I, i, 42–43]

In a similar manner he boasts of his power over the pliant King.

Young Spencer and Baldock, the parasites who next win their
way into royal favor, are also accomplished in the methods of villainy:

> *Spencer junior:* Then, Baldock, you must cast the scholar off
> And learn to court it like a gentleman.
> 'Tis not a black coat and a little band,
>   . . .
>
> And saying, 'Truly, an't may please your honor,'
> Can get you any favor with great men;
> You must be proud, bold, pleasant, resolute,
> And now and then stab, as occasion serves.
> *Baldock:*   Spencer, thou knowest I hate such formal toys
> And use them but of mere hypocrisy.
>   . . .   /243/
> Though inwardly licentious enough
> And apt for any kind of villainy.   [II, i, 31–51]

The death of these sycophants satisfies the requirement in a moral
play for an intelligible relationship between cause and effect. Once
Edward has been separated from his evil counselors, he becomes the
innocent victim whose suffering must be avenged. Mortimer and
Isabella, who behave increasingly like the unrepentant protagonists
in vice "tragedy," must receive punishment for their crimes. In
meting out these retributions, *Edward II* is more in accord with the
moral formula than is *Tamburlaine* or *The Jew*. Mortimer's death
is not, like Tamburlaine's, the natural end to a busy and successful
life. The young prince Edward is a fit instrument for restoring
virtuous rule in a way that Ferneze was not. Queen Isabella per-
ceives the justice in the disclosure of her crimes:

I fear'd as much; murder cannot be hid.   [*Aside.*]   [V, vi, 46]

Although it is always an oversimplification to suppose that Marlowe is chiefly concerned with moral statement, that statement is still present in the inherited structure of the play.

The ending of *Edward II* thus appears to be morally unambiguous. Ultimately the virtuous are separated from the depraved, and each group receives merited justification or destruction. Ambiguity occurs only when we compare this traditional conclusion with the earlier scenes of political conflict, when Edward was the dissolute and prodigal King, Mortimer the forthright defender of English freedoms, and Isabella the deserted wife. Marlowe's use of the homiletic formula, especially in the concluding scenes of this play, engenders a dichotomy in the characters between moral absolutes and psychological complexities. Even in his most secular play, the homiletic tradition contributes an important part. This aspect of *Edward II* necessarily ignores much of what is new in Marlowe, and is critically significant only so long as it is seen as a residual force operating through the playwright's theatrical environment. The moral tradition, although much changed in its outward appearance, provides in *Edward II*, as in Marlowe's other works, a clue to the relationship between structural organization and moral statement. /**244**/

CLIFFORD LEECH

Marlowe's *EDWARD II:* Power and Suffering

The Marlowe Society production of *Edward II* at Cambridge, Stratford-upon-Avon, and London, in the summer of 1958, has been widely acclaimed, and I wish to take it as the starting-point for a discussion of the play. For indeed it was a production with several features worth noting. First, it was well spoken, both audibly and with a proper feeling for Elizabethan blank verse. It used a simple permanent setting, with entrances at the back and on either side, roughly in the manner of the Elizabethan stage. The acting-area was a fairly steep ramp, which had the effect of bringing the actors closer to the audience. But, above all, this production was characterised by something that we may call 'neutrality'. This is a quality generally absent from twentieth-century productions of Shakespeare and his contemporaries. The director, like the scholarly critic, will commonly try to find something that he can see as the 'meaning' of the play, and he will aim at emphasising the things in the writing that will bring that 'meaning' into sharper focus. If certain passages run counter to the alleged 'meaning', he will often not scruple to omit them. In recent years Shakespeare's histories and dark comedies have notably suffered in this way, and audiences have for some time expected to see not Shakespeare's *Hamlet* but the *Hamlet* that a particular director or actor has decided to give them. But the neutral acting-area of the Elizabethan theatre should give us a clue to the nature of most of its drama. The stage can at one moment represent Rome, at another Alexandria, it can be the open country or a king's palace, a ship at sea or a battlefield. In the same way the play itself

Reprinted from *Critical Quarterly*, I (1959).

is hospitable to all sorts of feelings and ideas that may find expression in the dramatist's words. Sometimes, indeed, the Elizabethans and Jacobeans did approach the 'drama of ideas', and in *Troilus and Cressida* and in Chapman's tragedies we may feel that the action and characters are subordinate to the working out of an intellectual theme. But these are extreme and uncharacteristic instances. At the opposite extreme, and still on a notable level of dramatic achievement, we find Beaumont and Fletcher choosing a particular dramatic action because they are interested in the way in which it will develop /**181**/ towards its point of conclusion: ideas and attitudes will emerge from time to time, but intellectual argument will remain a side-issue. Between these two extremes we have, I believe, the bulk of Elizabethan and Jacobean drama. Initially the playwright is attracted to a story because he sees it as representing, in a particularly striking way, a recurrent and significant pattern in human life. The fact that he sees certain patterns as significant depends on his having a total attitude to the world, a cosmology or *Weltanschauung*, and the stories he chooses will therefore be such as have a general congruence with that total attitude. But it will be the story, the dramatic action, that is in the forefront of his mind during the time of composition. He will not consistently be anxious for it to demonstrate the validity of his thinking, and in the course of the writing it will often happen that ideas and feelings will emerge that are altogether at odds with the initial intellectual impulse. In this respect he is far from the allegorist or the writer of a morality play, who is concerned throughout with the demonstration of a thesis. When he was writing *Edward II*, Marlowe was, I believe, much concerned with the ideas of power and suffering and the relation between the two, and it was this that led him to choose the subject. But during the actual process of composition what concerned him more directly was part of the spectacle of human life, the things that happened to Edward and Mortimer and Isabella and Gaveston. At times the impetus of their story led him indeed to ideas—like Fortune's wheel, the power of the Roman church, the 'unnaturalness' of rebellion, and the part played by Heaven in human affairs—that have little or no connection with the play's primary intellectual concern. Nevertheless, such ideas are there and clearly illustrate the multiplicity of statement that is typical of the drama of the time. In production, therefore, and in criticism, we should put our immediate stress on the thing that

was most fully and persistently alive to the dramatist as he was
writing, and that is the action and the human beings involved in it.
Each character must be allowed to make his bid for our attention
and our sympathetic response, despite the obvious fact that we shall
be more interested in some than in others. The Marlowe Society,
giving us a performance in which we felt the diffused vitality of the
human spectacle, seemed to make the play more available to us as a
whole than it had previously been. On the stage, through the persons
of the actors, we could become more deeply aware of the mental
pressures exerted on Edward and Isabella and the rest. The play was
their story, not a demonstration of the Tudor myth or of any private
scheme thought out by Christopher Marlowe. Nearly all the best
plays of the time have indeed this quality of objectivity, of belonging
ultimately to their characters rather than to the dramatist. And
contradictions, or at least dissonances, of idea are as much at home
in this drama as in our everyday conduct and thinking. When /**182**/
talking about the plays, we inevitably refer to the ideas that they
suggest to us; but we must never forget that a dramatist, when writing, is normally concerned with such things only in the second place.

   Though we are uncertain about the dating of Marlowe's plays, we
can be quite sure that *Tamburlaine* preceded *Edward II*. It is, therefore, worth looking back to *Tamburlaine* to see how even there we
have no simple demonstration of a unitary idea. Formerly this play
was seen as a highly subjective portrayal of Marlowe's own aspiring
mind, with the dramatist exulting in his hero's victories, sharing his
dreams of beauty and power, and experiencing something of Tamburlaine's own anguish in the recognition of time and death. Professor Roy W. Battenhouse, however, would have us take the play
as a critical presentation of a great disturber of men's peace, at
whose fall we should rejoice.[1] To say that both these views have an
element of truth is easy enough, but we should also see that they are
only two among the many ideas that jostle one another in the play.
Part I traces Tamburlaine's rise from obscurity to the point where
he can decide to make truce with all the world, content for a while
with his great power and his possession of Zenocrate. There is no
doubt that Marlowe can respond sympathetically to his hero: one
has only to read some of the verse to feel how close to self-identi-

---

[1] *Marlowe's Tamburlaine*, Nashville 1941.

fication Marlowe can at moments come. Yet it is in this same First Part that we have the spectacle of Bajazeth in his cage, his raging and suicide, and then the madness and death of his wife Zabena. When Zenocrate enters to find the dead bodies of the Turk and his empress, she and her maid Anippe cry out against Tamburlaine's cruelty, and Zenocrate prays that retribution will not fall upon him. And she begs the pardon of Jove and Mahomet for her own earlier indifference to their sufferings. Now we can take Zenocrate as a point of reference here, and we are not reassured when Anippe tells her that Tamburlaine, master of Fortune's wheel, is safe. Earlier, indeed, Marlowe's presentation of the slaughter of the Virgins of Damascus is such as to put a shadow on Tamburlaine's glory. When the first Virgin begs for pity for the town, we cannot banish from ourselves the need to listen. At the end of Part I, with Tamburlaine making peace and with Zenocrate as his bride, the dead bodies of Bajazeth, Zabena and the King of Arabia (who loved Zenocrate) are still lying on the stage, a sign of the price of military triumph. If Marlowe had stopped there, we should still feel an ambivalence in the play, an exaltation of the aspiring mind along with a realisation of its destructiveness, a delight in power and a sense of human suffering: we should need to associate the caged and despairing Bajazeth with Edward in the foul stench of his cell, in the barbarity of his murder. /**183**/

But Marlowe went on to write Part II of *Tamburlaine*, and there the shadows on the hero's face grow darker. He is not outside our sympathy: his love for Zenocrate, his very powerlessness to keep her, his almost pathetic attempt to re-create himself in the persons of his sons, all make him close to us, and at the same time he remains the great conqueror, triumphant in battle even when his last sickness is on him. Yet he falls into self-caricature in his attempts to find a satisfactory objectification of his power. Bajazeth's cage was a small device compared with the chariot drawn by kings that he uses in Part II. Here it is significant that 'Holla, ye pamper'd jades of Asia' became a comic catch-word in the years that immediately followed the first acting of the play. And Fortune's wheel, mentioned in Part I, is not now in Tamburlaine's control: the Prologue to Part II briefly tells us that the deaths of Zenocrate and Tamburlaine will be the principal matters of the play, so that from the beginning we are reminded of his power's limits. In this Part, moreover, he can be made ridiculous. Calyphas is no admirable young man, but we see his point of view when he comments on the tedium of his father's victories, on his own uselessness on the battlefield, and on the absurdity of encountering danger merely for glory's sake. When Calyphas has played cards instead of fighting, Tamburlaine comes back and kills him. The dramatist here is careful not to let Calyphas say a word in Tamburlaine's presence: if he had defended himself, he might have produced an argument that would, for the rest of the play, have made us feel the absurdity of Tamburlaine's course of action. As it is, the lonely, rather squalid, but not unsensible rebellion of Calyphas is made to take its place in the dramatic pattern without completely changing the character of that pattern. Moreover, the notion of divine retribution, hinted at in Zenocrate's speech in Part I, when she saw the dead bodies of Bajazeth and Zabena, becomes more evident in Part II. We have the story of Sigismund, the Christian who swore by Christ to keep the truce and then disregarded his oath for the sake of military advantage: in his defeat the Turks find evidence that God has taken His revenge. And at the end of the play, Tamburlaine has just burned the Koran, has denied the Prophet, and has come near to denying God, when he is stricken with his fatal sickness: 'I feel myself distemper'd suddenly,' he says, sixteen lines after his speech of blasphemy. It should perhaps be emphasised that there is nothing specifically Christian in these passages: Sigismund has sworn by Christ, by what he holds most sacred, and the non-Christian Turks understand that he is punished for that; Tamburlaine blasphemes against Islam, the faith that he would still hold were it not for his boundless aspiration. Along with all this, there continues from Part I the sense of what is entailed by suffering. Marlowe indeed is fascinated by the lengths a human being can go in the infliction of suffering, and also by the limits of human endurance. /**184**/ The kings who draw the chariot, and who are killed as soon as they can draw it no further, are very subordinate characters in the action, but what has happened to them is highly indicative of the playwright's trend of thinking. And Tamburlaine's mourning for Zenocrate and his attempts to compensate for her death, by threatening war against Heaven and by sacrificing men and cities to her memory, give formal expression to the idea of personal loss. What we find in Part II is, in fact, a more overt manifestation of strains that are dimly heard in Part I. Marlowe, we can be sure, was originally attracted to the theme of *Tamburlaine* because he was fascinated by, and sympathetic with, the aspiring mind: as he began to dramatise the story, he was gradually led to an awareness of suffering, in the hero and in his victims, and to a consideration of his inevitable fall. Fortune's wheel, divine retribution, the human inability to shore up the ruins of time—all these things came into his mind, all found their place in the two-part play. The different elements came together in such a way that the total work leaves no simple impression on us. And we should note, too, that the common judgment that Tamburlaine is a giant hero surrounded by pygmies is hardly justified: in Part II Marlowe has gone out of his way to put temporary stress on other figures—notably on Sigismund, Calyphas and Olympia—and the human touch which is given to each of them modifies our attitude towards the hero. The diffusion of interest among the characters of *Edward II* is thus not without foreshadowing in Marlowe's first major play.

But behind *Edward II* there stands not only *Tamburlaine* and doubtless other of Marlowe's work: there is also, it is generally believed, Shakespeare's Parts II and III of *Henry VI*. We need not consider Part I of *Henry VI*, for that is of more doubtful authorship and largely concerned with material of a different sort. But Parts II and III, which we might do well to think of as a two-part play on the 'Contention' between the two houses of York and Lancaster, have many points of similarity to *Edward II*. The fact that a number of fairly close verbal parallels have been noted reinforces the structural and thematic relationship which I am concerned with here. In both cases we have an action involving a king unfitted for rule, a rebellion which leads to the King's murder, and fluctuating fortunes in the civil strife, with characters on both sides gaining our sympathy in their moments of death. At the centre there is a man born to a position of power, but overshadowed by his father's renown, ready, indeed, if only it were possible, to find peace in obscurity. During the battle of Towton, Shakespeare's Henry is banished from the field by his warlike Queen and meditates on the destruction and on the quieter and more ordered life possible for the simple countryman. Marlowe's Edward, threatened with Gaveston's exile, offers rich bribes to his discontented nobles, and adds: /**185**/

> If this content you not,
> Make several kingdoms of this monarchy
> And share it equally amongst you all,
> So I may have some nook or corner left
> To frolic with my dearest Gaveston.   (I. iv. 69–73)

And, when he is a fugitive and takes his last refuge in the Abbey of Neath, he imagines the quiet joys of a life of contemplation:

> Father, this life contemplative is heaven.
> O that I might this life in quiet lead.   (IV. vi. 20–21)

And in both Shakespeare and Marlowe we find a series of characters who notably bid for our attention. Margaret the Queen, without scruple or evidence of human kindness, becomes an emblem of suffering when her son Edward is murdered after the last battle; Richard of York, wholly given over to the pursuit of kingship, has yet one of the most moving speeches in the play when he is taken prisoner and his enemies gather round him to mock before they kill; the Cliffords are strong and thoughtless warriors, yet Young Clifford's lament for his father at the end of Part II has so much authority that Professor F. P. Wilson has wondered if it is a later insertion in the play;[2] Edward of York, the lucky careless son of an ambitious father, is sketched with remarkable shrewdness, especially in the matter of his impolitic wooing of the Lady Grey; his brother Richard of Gloucester, more ruthless and cleverer than them all and increasingly dominant as the play comes to its end, ominously tells us in his last soliloquy of his dreams and his plans. The action, too, is spread widely through England, with a brief passage in France.

Marlowe, I have suggested, came in the writing of *Tamburlaine* to a fuller perception of the things that went along with the possession of power—its fragility, and the suffering that its free exercise involved. But in *Tamburlaine* he was telling the story of a man wholly successful in his conflicts with other men: the sufferings of the hero were merely the operations of time or of Fortune's wheel or of cosmic justice. Now we can assume that Parts II and III of *Henry VI* gave him a model for a play differently centred. His main figure could still be a man of power, but of power inherited not won, power insecurely held and ever limited by the opposition of other men. This entailed his giving greater prominence than in *Tamburlaine* to the subordinate figures in the drama, and thus in *Edward II* he came closer to Shakespeare's normal structural method than elsewhere in his writing. As in *Henry VI*, the action was spread widely through the country, from London to Tynemouth in the remote north and to Neath in South Wales, and, as in Part III of *Henry VI*, there was a

---

[2] *Marlowe and the Early Shakespeare*, 1953, pp. 117–18.

/**186**/ short excursion to France. The effect of this in Marlowe is, however, different from what we find in Shakespeare. In *Henry VI* it is justifiable to claim that the diffusion of the action brings more fully into mind the sense of the nation, and Henry's lament for his country's sufferings in Part III, II.v, constitutes a key-passage for the play. But in Marlowe the idea of the country and its war is very much in the background. *Edward II* is a more personal play than *Henry VI*, and the rapid movement of the action gives us the feeling of Edward being driven by the course of events haphazardly through his realm, until at the end he is confined to a small dark cell in which he is secretly murdered. It is as if all the time that cell were waiting for him, and his long journeyings were circuitous routes to that last place of suffering and humiliation. Marlowe, we shall see, makes strong use of the passage in Holinshed which says that he was continually taken, on Mortimer's orders, from 'one strong place to another, . . . still remoouing with him in the night season':[3] these shorter journeys are the last stages of his wanderings, until in the end even that motion stops and he is still at last. This difference is related to the fact that Edward is a more important figure in Marlowe's play than Henry is in Shakespeare's. For Shakespeare, beyond Henry lie England and the doom she must suffer through civil strife. For Marlowe, the concept of England means little—he was, after all, a servant in Elizabeth's secret police—and he cared only for what happened to the individual human being. He was interested in Edward, not as embodying a suffering England, but as a man, a man who had and lost power.

Yet it can be said that, at the beginning of the play, no one in *Edward II* makes a good impression on us. First we meet Gaveston, delighted to be recalled to England on Edward I's death. He makes it plain that he has no love for the London to which he has returned:

> Not that I love the city or the men,
> But that it harbors him I hold so dear,
> The king, upon whose bosom let me die,
> And with the world be still at enmity.   (I. i. 12–15)

Then he encounters three 'Poor Men' who wish to enter his service: he behaves churlishly until he reminds himself that they may have

---

[3] *The Historie of England* (vol. III), ed. 1585, p. 341.

their uses. Then in soliloquy he thinks of how he may 'draw the pliant king which way I please', and the devices he imagines show how he thinks to exploit Edward's homosexual leanings. When we meet the King and his nobles, we find Edward thinking only of Gaveston, whose worth we have already seen exposed, and the nobles pouring out their venom against him but with no indication that they have the country's good in mind. Then Edward and /**187**/ Gaveston meet, and we see Edward bestowing on him almost any office that comes into his mind:

> I here create thee Lord High Chamberlain,
> Chief Secretary to the state and me,
> Earl of Cornwall, King and Lord of Man.   (I. i. 154–6)

The King's brother, the Earl of Kent, though as yet wholly on Edward's side, protests:

> Brother, the least of these may well suffice
> For one of greater birth than Gaveston.   (I. i. 158–9)

Then we see Edward and Gaveston laying hands on the Bishop of Coventry, and the King sending him to prison and giving his see and revenues to Gaveston. Here we must recognise an ambivalence in Marlowe's attitude. The conduct of Edward and Gaveston is arbitrary and cruel, yet the references to the see of Rome and to the Bishop's wealth are in tune with the anti-Romish feeling which we find in *The Massacre at Paris* and which would awaken sympathetic echoes in many spectators of the time. As the first scene ended, the Elizabethan audience might well feel in two minds about the King and his favourite, being properly scandalised by their behaviour and yet taking in it a measure of delight.

In the second scene we meet Isabella, and her grief at Edward's desertion of her is likely to strengthen the audience's feeling against him. At once, however, we have a hint of a special relationship between the Queen and Mortimer. Her last words here are:

> Farewell, sweet Mortimer, and for my sake,
> Forbear to levy arms aginst the king.   (I. ii. 81–2)

We see her kindness for him ('sweet Mortimer') and her belief in having some power over him ('for my sake'), and also her wish for peace. But Mortimer's reply is brusque and has little love in it:

> Ay, if words will serve; if not, I must.   (I. ii. 83)

When we see the King and the nobles together again, Edward is confronted with a demand for Gaveston's exile. This king has no concern for his country:

> Ere my sweet Gaveston shall part from me,
> This Isle shall fleet upon the ocean,
> And wander to the unfrequented Inde.   (I. iv. 48–50)

He yields only because the Archbishop of Canterbury, as papal legate, threatens to release the nobles from their allegiance. And almost at once, as if this hint of Rome's power turns the scales, Marlowe gives Edward a line of verse that carries our sympathy to him. When Mortimer asks: /**188**/

> Why should you love him whom the world hates so? (I. iv. 76)

Edward's reply is simply:

> Because he loves me more than all the world.   (I. iv. 77)

We know what Gaveston's love is worth, yet this naïve utterance of Edward is enough to put us, for the moment, on his side: he becomes an emblem of the human need for love, the very human joy when love seems offered.

No sooner is Gaveston banished than the Queen persuades Mortimer, and through him the other lords, to consent to his recall. There is no hint yet of any infidelity on Isabella's part, yet she makes free use of her power over Mortimer, and Marlowe thus prepares us for a closer relationship between them. When the King learns that Gaveston may return, he entertains the kindest thoughts of the barons, and plans triumphs and revels. Then follows a significant conversation between Mortimer and his uncle. The older man counsels peace: 'The mightiest kings have had their minions,' he says, and quotes examples from history and mythology:

> Then let his grace, whose youth is flexible
> And promiseth as much as we can wish,
> Freely enjoy that vain, light-headed earl,
> For riper years will wean him from such toys.
>
> (I. iv. 397–400)

Mortimer replies that he has no objection to Edward's wantonness:

> Uncle, his wanton humor grieves not me.   (I. iv. 401)

Rather, he will not tolerate Gaveston's enjoyment of riches idly
bestowed on him and his mockery of those of more ancient lineage.
It is true that Mortimer refers to 'the treasure of the realm' and to
the fact that 'soldiers mutiny for want of pay', but in the speech as a
whole there is little sense of the kingdom's good. The objection to
Gaveston is the common objection to an upstart, and this comes out
clearly in Mortimer's final words in this scene:

> But whiles I have a sword, a hand, a heart,
> I will not yield to any such upstart.
> You know my mind; come, uncle, let's away. (I. iv. 421–3)

There is no act-division in the early copies of *Edward II*, but
modern editors usually end Act I at this point. It is therefore con-
venient to sum up here our initial responses to the four main characters: Gaveston we know for a rogue, though a lively one; Mortimer
is rough and self-centered, responsive, however, at moments to the
Queen; Isabella is anxious for Edward's love, yet we can see she
is playing dangerously with her power over Mortimer; Edward,
/**189**/ we should know without history's warrant, is doomed: he
can control neither his barons' unruliness nor his own blind passion.

We meet other associates of Gaveston at the beginning of the
next scene. The younger Spencer and Baldock are servants in the
household of the Earl of Gloucester, who has just died. The Earl's
daughter, Edward's niece, is betrothed to Gaveston: she is a rich
heiress, another prize that the King will give to his favourite, and she
has the misfortune to love Gaveston. Marlowe does not much develop this part of his story, possibly because to do so would over-
dangerously emphasise the homosexual element. Yet we have seen
enough of Edward's relations with Gaveston to find this marriage
painful. But Marlowe does exhibit more fully the characters of
Spencer and Baldock, and he lets us be under no illusion there.
Spencer gives his fellow servant advice:

> You must be proud, bold, pleasant, resolute,
> And now and then stab, as occasion serves.   (II. i. 42–3)

And Baldock replies that he is

> > inwardly licentious enough,
> And apt for any kind of villainy.   (II. i. 50–51)

To find equally frank avowals we must go to Marlowe's Jew of Malta or his Duke of Guise in *The Massacre at Paris* or to Shakespeare's Richard of Gloucester. These men are about to enter Gaveston's service and through him to serve the King, who welcomes them in the next scene. In that scene we have Gaveston's return and the immediate outbreak of fresh enmity: it ends with the barons' declaration of revolt and with Kent's abandoning his brother's cause. If we disregard act-division, for which, as we have seen, the early copies give us no warrant, we can regard this as the end of the play's first movement. From this point we have civil war, the barons fighting first for the removal of Gaveston and then for the removal of his successors in Edward's favour.

And at once there is a crucial moment in the presentation of Isabella. The King's forces are defeated, and Edward and Gaveston fly different ways in order to divide the barons' pursuing forces. Isabella is abandoned by her husband: she meets Mortimer and the rest, and tells them the route that Gaveston has taken. This is the first time she has acted against the King, and her final soliloquy in this scene shows how she hesitates between a new loyalty and an old hope to regain Edward's love:

> So well hast thou deserved, sweet Mortimer,
> As Isabel could live with thee for ever.
> In vain I look for love at Edward's hand,
> Whose eyes are fixed on none but Gaveston,
> Yet once more I'll importune him with prayers. /**190**/
> If he be strange and not regard my words,
> My son and I will over into France
> And to the king my brother there complain
> How Gaveston hath robbed me of his love.
> But yet I hope my sorrows will have end,
> And Gaveston this blessèd day be slain.   (II. iv. 59–69)

The change of Isabella from the wronged but loving wife to the woman acquiescent in her husband's murder has commonly been regarded as a blemish on the play. We should rather think of it, I suggest, as one of the most perceptive things in Marlowe's writing—at least in the planning, for one must admit that the words he gives her have not much life in them. Never before had he attempted the probing of a woman's character, for the presentation of Zenocrate, Olympia, Abigail, is for the most part emblematic. He knew a

woman's frustrated love could turn rancid, as Dostoievsky shows in
Katya's treachery to Mitya Karamazov, and Marlowe, like Dostoievsky, has not let the woman change without deep provocation.
We have seen how she has long been conscious of Mortimer's feeling
for her, how Mortimer for her is always 'gentle' or 'sweet' Mortimer,
how Edward has taunted her with his love for Gaveston and accused
her of infidelity. Now she finds herself deserted, with Edward's
reproach still in her ears. This is the turning-point for her, though
she does not know it yet. It is psychologically right that the moment
of crisis should come without her realising it.

In the scenes that follow we have Gaveston's capture, Edward's
attempt to see him before he dies, and Warwick's brutal despatching
of the favourite. There is an echo of Tamburlaine's blasphemy here.
Marlowe's early hero had urged his soldiers to worship only 'the God
that sits in heaven, if any god'. Now, when Gaveston asks 'Shall I
not see the king?', Warwick replies: 'The king of heaven perhaps, no
other king.' The scepticism of the 'perhaps' may be Marlowe's own,
but the conduct of Warwick is base. Gaveston is allowed no eloquent
last words, yet Marlowe suggests that he has a genuine desire to see
Edward once more. There is at least no final stress on his villainy,
and it is his killers who shock us and thus prepare us for their later
barbarity to Edward. When the King hears of Gaveston's death, he
vows revenge and in the same speech adopts Spencer as his new
favourite, making him Earl of Gloucester and Lord Chamberlain—
'Despite of times, despite of enemies'. There is *hubris* in this, and yet
almost at once Edward wins his first success in the play: he defeats
the barons and takes them captive. Warwick and Lancaster are
executed, going to their death with brief and obstinate words. Kent
is sent away in disgrace, Mortimer committed to the Tower. Here
Marlowe was in a difficulty: from Holinshed he knew that Mortimer
had taken no part in this battle, having submitted to the King before
/**191**/ it took place, but it would not do for him to follow his source
in this regard, for Mortimer must throughout be the dominant figure
among the barons. So we have the near-absurdity that Lancaster and
Warwick are executed, while Mortimer, the most outspoken of the
King's enemies and the suspected lover of the Queen, is given a
further chance of life. This could have been avoided if Mortimer had
been allowed to escape from the battlefield and to find his way at

once to France. Probably, however, Marlowe wanted to suggest that Edward was a man incapable of profiting from Fortune's momentary favour. This temporary victory of the King brings the second movement of the play to an end. That Mortimer is alive and Isabella's loyalty now doubtful makes evident the continuing precariousness of Edward's position, and it is clear too that in replacing Gaveston by Spencer he has learned nothing.

Kent and Mortimer are soon in France, Mortimer having escaped from the Tower, and they meet Isabella and Prince Edward, who have been sent on an embassy to the French King. Together they plan new wars, nominally on behalf of the young prince. Quickly the scene returns to England, and Edward is defeated and a fugitive. With Spencer and Baldock he attempts flight to Ireland but contrary winds drive him back to Wales. He takes refuge in the Abbey of Neath, but there he is quickly apprehended: Baldock and Spencer are taken to their deaths, the King to prison. Baldock, whom we first met as a villain in a puritan's disguise, is ready with rather hollow 'preachments', as his captor calls them, when he is led away to death. Marlowe has not much pity for these, though neither is he on their captors' side. In this scene, however, we have the beginning of the King's long journey to death. We have seen how he envies the monks their quiet life of contemplation, and when he hears the name of 'Mortimer' he shrinks and would hide his head:

> Mortimer! Who talks of Mortimer?
> Who wounds me with the name of Mortimer,
> That bloody man? Good father, on thy lap
> Lay I this head, laden with mickle care.
> O might I never open these eyes again,
> Never again lift up this drooping head,
> O never more lift up this dying heart!   (IV. vi. 37–43)

When he takes his farewell of Spencer, he cannot believe that Heaven is punishing him:

King Edward: Spencer, ah, sweet Spencer, thus then must we part.
Spencer Junior: We must, my Lord, so will the angry heavens.
King Edward: Nay, so will hell and cruel Mortimer;
                        The gentle heavens have not to do in this.   (IV. vi. 72–5)

Yet this denial of divine intervention is also in line with the general trend of the play's thought. There are few references to cosmic /**192**/ powers here: the conflict is on a purely human level, between a king who cannot control his lords or his passions and his unruly subjects who overreach themselves. By the end of the play Isabella has been sent to the Tower and all the rest of the prominent characters are dead, but it is their folly, their mismanagement of the situation, that has destroyed them. The heavens, whether 'angry' or 'gentle,' have it seems 'not to do in this'. But the scene of the King's capture is remarkable also for a piece of effective but unobtrusive symbolism. Before Mortimer's men arrive, Spencer has referred to a 'gloomy fellow in a mead below', who 'gave a long look after us', and it is this 'gloomy fellow' who betrays them. The stage-directions call him 'a Mower', and we must assume he comes carrying his scythe. At the end of the scene, when the King has been taken to prison and Baldock and Spencer are about to be put to death, the Mower asks for his reward. He has had only two lines to speak, but his presence on the stage makes it evident that the King is being cut down.

The abdication scene follows. There is no stress here on any sacredness in the idea of royalty, no suggestion of woe falling upon the land because of an act of deposition. But there is great poignancy in Edward's relinquishing of his crown. Like Faustus, shortly before or shortly after this play was written, he wishes time to stand still. 'Stay awhile, let be me king till night', he says, and then would have the day not cease:

> Stand still you watches of the element;
> All times and seasons, rest you at a stay,
> That Edward may be still fair England's king.   (V. i. 66–8)

An ironic touch of legality is given to the affair in that it is the Bishop of Winchester who comes to demand the crown, and, when Edward proves obstinate, he is told that his son will 'lose his right'. He prays to be able to 'despise this transitory pomp And sit for aye enthronizèd in heaven'. For a moment he admits his guilt, but at once retracts the admission:

> Commend me to my son, and bid him rule
> Better than I. Yet how have I transgressed,
> Unless it be with too much clemency?   (V. i. 121–3)

Marlowe could enter fully into the mind of a man whose power was

slipping away from him. He had shown Tamburlaine in his attempt
to build his power on surer foundations than life allows and in his
final vain persuasion of himself that his sons would reign and con-
quer in his behalf. Now he shows us a king bereft of his crown, the
symbol of the power already lost. Yet even that symbol was some
kind of protection. As soon as it is gone, Edward is told of a change
in his jailor and his place of imprisonment. Further changes are to
come, and each for the worse. From the Earl of Leicester he is given
/**193**/ to Sir Thomas Berkeley, and then to Gurney and Matrevis,
and finally to Marlowe's fictitious executioner, Lightborn.

The remaining scenes alternate between the court, where Mortimer, now Lord Protector and the Queen's lover, is all-powerful but
intent, for safety's sake, on the King's death, and the places where
Edward and his jailors are. The barbarity of these latter scenes
makes them painful to read or to see or to speak of. No other tragic
figure in Elizabethan or Jacobean times is treated in the degrading
way that Mortimer permits for Edward. Henry VI is suddenly
stabbed, Richard II dies fighting and eloquent, Richard III and
Macbeth are killed in battle, the Duchess of Malfi makes a brave and
pious speech before she is strangled, Marlowe's own Faustus dominates the scene in his hour of despair.[4] The Jacobean playwrights
could think of strange ways of torment and murder, but they never
tear at our nerves as Marlowe does in this play. First we have the
brief scene in which the King, on his journeying with Matrevis and
Gurney, begs for water to drink and to clean his body. Their response
is to take water from a ditch, pour it over the King's face and shave
off his beard. In the last scene in which he appeared, Edward had
been robbed of his crown: now he is further stripped, is nearer the
ultimate humiliation. This incident of the shaving is not in Holinshed. Marlowe found it·in Stow's *Annals*,[5] and it is significant that he
decided here to supplement his primary source. The scene of the
murder is dominated by the figure of Lightborn, who comes with
Mortimer's commission. This is the professional murderer, devoid of

---

[4] Especially in the A-text (1604), which W. W. Greg has seen as a corrupt
version of Marlowe's final handling: cf. *Marlowe's Doctor Faustus* 1604–1616:
Parallel Texts, Oxford 1950, esp. pp. 129–32.

[5] Cf. *The Annales of England*, ed. 1592, p. 343, where the incident is recorded
with the marginal gloss 'King Edward shauen with colde water'. Cf. *Edward II*,
ed. H. B. Charlton and R. D. Waller (revised ed. 1955), pp. 50, 191–2.

pity but curiously intimate with his victim. He pretends to sorrow for the King's wretched state, and urges him to rest. Edward is half-ready to trust him, yet can sleep only for a moment, his fears returning strongly upon him:

> Something still buzzeth in mine ears
> And tells me if I sleep I never wake.
> This fear is that which makes me tremble thus;
> And therefore tell me, wherefore art thou come? (V. v. 102–5)

Then he has only two brief speeches more:

> I am too weak and feeble to resist.
> Assist me, sweet God, and receive my soul!   (V. v. 107–8)

and:

> O spare me, or despatch me a in trice.   /**194**/   (V. v. 110)

And then the murder is done. The manner of its doing has been softened by most editors, who have inserted a form of stage-direction not in the early copies. There can, I think, be no doubt that Marlowe intended the mode of killing to be that narrated in Holinshed and clearly indicated by Lightborn in his talk with the jailors at the beginning of the scene. That indeed is how it was staged in the recent Marlowe Society production, and I think rightly. The mode of killing may have been one of the reasons why Marlowe chose this story for dramatisation. We have seen how in *Tamburlaine* he could hint at something near the ultimate in human suffering in referring to the fate of the kings who drew their conqueror's chariot. In *Faustus* he imagined damnation. Here in *Edward II* he stages the ultimate physical cruelty. He was a man who speculated on, and brought alive to his mind, the furthest reaches of human power and of human suffering and humiliation. These things, he saw, men could do and had done, could suffer and had suffered, and his wondering mind gave them dramatic shape. And 'the gentle heavens have not to do in this'. There is no justice which works in this way.

Not so long ago it was possible for readers of Marlowe, and of the dramatists who followed him, to look on such scenes as relics of a barbarous though brilliant age. We have not to-day that way out, for evidence is plentiful that in this twentieth century there are Lightborns enough. I do not think that, when he wrote the play, Marlowe had a moral purpose: he was intent only on the imagining of an ultimate in suffering. Such imaginings are dangerous, for a cruelty grown familiar is the greatest corrupter. Nevertheless, Marlowe has brought before us part of the truth about men, and we must learn to recognise and to control it.

In the last scene of the play Fortune's wheel turns for Mortimer and Isabella, and the young King mourns for his father. This is briefly and almost casually done. It was necessary that the story of Edward's reign should be rounded off, and that Mortimer's stratagems should entrap him. But Marlowe's interest in this was not profound. He had traced with some care the working of power's corruption in Mortimer and the slow hardening of Isabella's heart, but he could part with them as perfunctorily as with Gaveston or Spencer. There is indeed a rather empty rhetoric in Mortimer's acceptance of the turning wheel and his readiness for what may come:

> Farewell, fair queen; weep not for Mortimer,
> That scorns the world, and, as a traveler,
> Goes to discover countries yet unknown.   (V. vi. 64–6)

Certainly it would be difficult to find two other lovers in Elizabethan drama who parted with words so chill.

In this play the final impression is of Edward's suffering. It is bound up with power, the power that Edward loses, the power that /**195**/ Mortimer wins, the power he delegates to Lightborn. If a man had no power over other men, there could be no suffering such as Edward knew. There could be other forms of anguish, but not this. And Marlowe, in a story where there was much to interest him, comes into full command of his imagination when he considers the last stages of Edward's journey. The association of the King and Gaveston, the process of Isabella's inconstancy, the barons' resentment of the favourite of humble origin, the slow transformation of Mortimer from a quarrelsome noble to a ruthless autocrat, the changing loyalties of Kent, the lightly sketched relations of the royal and the papal power—all these are part of the play, and they help to give to it the solidity of the world we know. Nevertheless, these things form the setting for the individual Edward's solitary journey to his end. And for Edward Marlowe does not ask our liking: he is foolish, he is at his best pathetic in the belief that Gaveston loves him more than all the world, he is cruel to his wife and drives her to

Mortimer, he knows himself so little that he thinks he erred only in too much clemency. There is barely a redeeming moment in the long presentation of his conduct. Yet what Marlowe has done is to make us deeply conscious of a humanity that we share with this man who happened to be also a king. If there were a touch of greatness or even much kindness in him, as there is in Shakespeare's Richard II, we could remember that along with his suffering and find some comfort in it. As it is, we know only that he has human folly and in his suffering makes contact with an ultimate.

There is no theory here which Marlowe illustrates, no warning or programme for reform, no affirmation even of a faith in man. The playwright merely focuses attention on certain aspects of the human scene. In *Tamburlaine* he had already contemplated power, and saw that the spectacle inevitably included suffering. Here the suffering, still consequential on the exercise and the dream of power, is the major fact. /**196**/

EUGENE M. WAITH

EDWARD II:
The Shadow of Action

> But what are kings, when regiment is gone,
> But perfect shadows in a sunshine day?

The weakness of Edward II, the speaker of these lines, not only deprives him of the fascination exerted by other Marlovian heroes but affects the character of the entire play. None of the dialogue can match the glitter of the greatest speeches in *Tamburlaine* or *Doctor Faustus* or even of the remarkable opening speech of *The Jew of Malta*. The story of such a king inevitably lacks the magnificence radiated by one who seeks to rule the world or command the legions of hell. Yet it is a mistake to underestimate Marlowe's achievement in this play. Only *Tamburlaine* is more completely an artistic success. There the dramatic possibilities of what we have come to consider the typical Marlovian hero are given their logical fulfillment in a design which is both grand and neat. *Doctor Faustus*, justly famous for the extraordinary scenes at the beginning and the end, is seriously impaired by the discordant tone of most of the material in the middle scenes (the third and fourth acts of recent editions). The high jinks with the Pope, and the Emperor, and the Duke of Anholt, though an inevitable part of the story, thoroughly relevant to the characterization of the hero, and quite possibly from the pen of Marlowe, destroy the impression of unity in a way that other comic scenes, such as those with Wagner, do not. There is an artistic miscalculation here which no solution to the textual problems can remedy. In *The Jew of Malta* there is a notorious change of tone

Reprinted from *Tulane Drama Review*, VIII (1964).

after the opening scenes, transforming the play, it would seem, from tragedy into some other genre, though whether this is farce, melodrama, or something else is hard /59/ to say. No other play of Marlowe's can seriously compete for inclusion among his best.

With respect to coherence, then, *Tamburlaine* and *Edward II* stand alone, and it is remarkable that they should stand together in any category, for in almost every way they are completely, and very interestingly, different. Even the coherence which I attribute to both of them is achieved in the two cases by almost opposite means. In *Tamburlaine* the technique, not quite so simple as it looks, is to depict the hero's triumph over increasingly powerful enemies up to the moment of his death. The sheer force of this personality as realized in Marlowe's verse and demonstrated in action dominates the play. Every other character serves as a foil or a reflector; each victory is greater than the last and leads the hero one step further. The uncomplicated singleness of this line of development is obvious. It seems doubtful that even the "fond and frivolous gestures" which the printer omitted as tedious digressions would have destroyed the almost primitive coherence of this structure, though they might have blunted its effect. On a graph one might represent it as a single line rising steadily to the last scene of the second part, where it finally plunges down.

A graphic representation of the structure of *Edward II* would show the interesections of at least five lines, each corresponding to the rising and falling fortunes of a major character. The diffusion of interest, due to Marlowe's choice of a weak and usually inactive protagonist, has been noted by every critic. Edward, more often than not, is the victim of the series of schemes which form the episodes of the play, and the importance thus robbed from him attaches to the perpetrators of the schemes. Yet the play is less episodic than *Tamburlaine*. An effect of interlocking is achieved, partly by the simple device of preparing in one episode for the episode to follow, but even more by revealing (and in some cases creating) an intricate net of relationships between the King's chief friends and enemies: Gaveston, the Spencers, the barons, Queen Isabella, and Mortimer. Furthermore, the effect of this structural coherence is strongly reinforced by the repeated expression of a very limited number of emotions. Not only is the play consistently serious in tone, but it is dominated by grief and the desire for revenge, only two of the emotions traditionally considered proper /60/ for tragedy. The firm control of this pattern of emotional response is one of the chief artistic merits of the play.

The reign of Edward II was not merely "troublesome," as the title page of Marlowe's play calls it; it was a disastrous failure. Its events lent themselves readily to two kinds of treatment, both familiar in the sixteenth century: to *De Casibus* tragedy as seen in *The Mirror for Magistrates* (where in fact the story of Mortimer appeared), and to preachment against the effects of evil counsellors. The two were not incompatible, of course, and both were moral in intent, but where the moral of one was broadly philosophical, stressing the fickleness of fortune and the vanity of human wishes, the moral of the other was practical and political. It was this second kind of moral which Holinshed, Marlowe's principal source, found in the story of Edward II as a whole:

> . . . he wanted judgement and prudent discretion to make choise of sage and discreet councellors, receiving those into his favour, that abused the same to their private gaine and advantage, not respecting the advancement of the common-wealth.[1]

In the play there are vestiges of both sorts of interpretation of the events. For example, when the King is captured, he says:

> Whilom I was powerful and full of pomp;
> But what is he whom rule and empery
> Have not in life or death made miserable? (IV. vi. 13–15)

—a pure nugget of *De Casibus* moralizing, to which Baldock shortly adds: ". . . all live to die, and rise to fall" (IV, vi, 111). The Queen is given a lucid statement of the moral Holinshed saw:

> Misgoverned kings are cause of all this wrack:
> And, Edward, thou art one among them all
> Whose looseness hath betrayed thy land to spoil. (IV, iv, 9–11)

Yet neither of these conventional interpretations of the historical events is so placed as to control the meaning of the play. Edward's reflections seem to grow out of a mood which finds several other equally striking manifestations in a highly emotional scene to /61/ which I shall return. The Queen's solemn speech, accompanied,

[1] *Chronicles* (London, 1587), III, 342.

one might guess, by emphatic finger-shaking, is ironically cut short by Mortimer, who tells her that if she is going to be a warrior she must not talk so much. If Marlowe does not deny these implications of his hero's story, neither does he seem to be primarily concerned with them. They appear incidentally, as if part of some other design.

Harry Levin and two more recent critics of the play, Clifford Leech and Douglas Cole, have argued persuasively that Marlowe was less interested here in politics or morals than in the personal tragedy of suffering man.[2] Their judgment seems to me fully supported by the placing of the morals just quoted and also by the relation of the story of Mortimer to the play as a whole. When he is ordered to execution by the young Edward III, Mortimer bursts out in reproof of fortune and scorn of the world, forcibly recalling to any reader of *The Mirror for Magistrates* the moral drawn from his story there: that fortune hurls down those "whom she heaves," and that men should avoid "High clymyng, brybyng, murdring, lust, and pryde.[3] In Marlowe's play the emphasis on fortune is equally explicit and a warning against "high clymyng" is at least implied. Furthermore, this speech of Mortimer's, his last in the play, serves as a summing up of his career, and though it does not exhaust the meaning of Marlowe's portrayal of the character, it comes nearer to doing so than do Edward's passing references to his fall from high place. Mortimer's tragedy, unlike Edward's, may fairly be assigned to the *De Casibus* tradition, and this is precisely the classification suggested by the title-page: "The troublesome raigne and lamentable death of Edward *the second, King of* England: with the tragicall *fall of proud* Mortimer . . ." Thus a *De Casibus* tragedy concerning Mortimer is included within the framework of a play about the troubles of Edward. In an analogous fashion, the conventional moral patterns to be seen in the /**62**/ fall of Edward are present in the play without dominating the design.

The figure of intersecting lines already used to suggest one aspect of the design of the play (the pattern made by the rising and falling

[2] Harry Levin, *The Overreacher* (Cambridge: Harvard University Press, 1952), p. 88; Clifford Leech, "Marlowe's 'Edward II': Power and Suffering," *Critical Quarterly*, I (1959), 181–196; Douglas Cole, *Suffering and Evil in the Plays of Christopher Marlowe* (Princeton University Press, 1962), pp. 161–187.

[3] *The Mirror for Magistrates*, ed. L. B. Campbell (New York: Barnes and Noble, 1960), p. 84.

fortunes of the major characters) is also an appropriate indication of the emotional pattern, for this is a play of blocking—of characters crossing each other and reacting to the frustration of being crossed. They are as desirous of having their wills and acting in total freedom as Tamburlaine himself, but desire here seldom leads to fruition; and fruition never lasts. "I'll have my will," King Edward says (I, i, 78), and "It is our pleasure; we will have it so"(I, iv, 9); Mortimer in this same scene says to the barons:

> My lords, now let us all be resolute,
> And either have our wills or lose our lives.   (I, iv, 45–46)

The contest is engaged and soon Edward is saying, "Nay, all of them conspire to cross me thus" (II, ii, 95). The intersecting lines may represent not only the fortunes but the wills of the chief characters, and as they thus seek to trammel one another, we are made aware not merely of the ensuing political chaos but of the profound emotional disturbance resulting from frustration. King Edward: "My swelling heart for very anger breaks . . . The headstrong barons shall not limit me" (II, ii, 198, 260). As instances of this sort of emotional response multiply, it becomes clear that the most powerful feelings in *Edward II* are aroused by the desire to break out of some constriction—a desire which increasingly seems doomed to disappointment. The repeated expression of feelings such as these gives the play its distinctive tone, contributes importantly to its meaning, and thus provides the structural coherence which the sporadic introduction of a moral interpretation of history fails to do.

Since the emotions of the major characters so rarely find release in action which brings them what they desire, it is not surprising that very few of the speeches have the triumphal ring of the memorable lines in *Tamburlaine*. Except in such infrequent scenes as those of the King's short-lived victory over his barons, the intensity of feeling seems almost to be produced by the impossibility of success, and the characteristic tone of the play is therefore /**63**/ muted. Compared to the sound of Tamburlaine's "high astounding terms," most of the threats and rages of this king give the impression of a whisper, just as he himself, compared to such a prototypical king, is but a shadow. Though the entire play is a protracted conflict of wills, there is no part to tear a cat in.[4] As momentary triumph turns

[4] See Levin, pp. 86–87.

to defeat and envisaged action fails to take place, the resounding shout of achievement gives way to the stifled cry.

.   .   .

Up to this point the structure of the play has been described generally and in terms of the effect it produces. Before examining in some detail the way in which the emotional pattern is related to the structure it is necessary to refer to a few structural facts. In the Oxford edition,[5] which preserves the format of the earliest surviving edition, it is a play of 2670 lines, undivided into acts or scenes. The act divisions of standard modern editions do not correspond to structural breaks with the possible exceptions of those following "Act I" and "Act IV." The first of these, following the decision to recall Gaveston, does indeed end one cycle of Edward's relations with his barons; for their reversal of the banishment upon which they have insisted brings the situation back to what it was at the opening of the play. The break after "Act IV" follows the capture of the King, and thus sets off a final block in which the imprisonment and death of the hero are presented. There is nothing meaningful, however, about the division between acts "II" and "III" (falling between the dispatch of Gaveston with Pembroke's men and his capture by Warwick) or between acts "III" and "IV" (falling between Edward's victory and Mortimer's escape to France with Kent). In the last instance there is indeed a lapse of time and a new development in the plot, but the same could be said about the break that occurs some fifteen lines later before the action shifts to France, or the next break when it returns again to England. Throughout this entire middle section of the play there is a strong sense of continuity and hardly more reason to make an act division in one place than in another. /**64**/

One might think of a tripartite division, then, consisting of the first 720 lines (the modern "Act I") the next 1286 lines ("Acts II–IV"), and the final 684 lines ("Act V"). Even these blocks are not very substantial, however, and the important subdivisions of the action correspond rather to the relationships between King Edward and the other major characters. David Bevington has shown what such a structure owes to the moraltiy-play tradition, where one or sometimes two principal characters successively encounter groups

[5] *The Works of Christopher Marlowe,* ed. C. F. Tucker Brooke, 1910.

of others,[6] though Marlowe has complicated this arrangement considerably by overlapping the stories of these relationships. Gaveston's story opens the play and extends through about half of it to line 1306, but his chief successor as favorite, Spencer, appears at line 724 and plays an important part for the next 1100 lines. About 100 lines after his introduction another important movement is begun—the break between the King and his brother, the Earl of Kent—continuing for some 900 lines. Still later, but about 150 lines before the action involving Gaveston has ended, we get the first hint that the Queen, hitherto pathetically loyal to her husband, may leave him for Mortimer, and about 250 lines after Gaveston's death we are given the first expression of the aspiration which will transform Mortimer from an apparently public-spirited baron, critical only of the King's misdeeds, into the Machiavellian schemer who will murder for power. Finally, some 50 lines after the beginning of this development, comes a hint that the young prince may remain loyal to his father. The movements involving the Queen, Mortimer, and the young prince continue to the end of the play. Gaveston's rise and fall in the first half of the play is approximately balanced by Mortimer's in the second, but overlapping both are the rise and fall of Spencer, the shifting relationship with Kent, and the change in the attitude of the Queen.

More details could be added, but these may be sufficient to show that the component parts of this structure may better be thought of as movements than as separate blocks or sections. The main action, the story of Edward II, advances from beginning to end with no well-defined stopping places, and consists in fact of a series of subsidiary stories of his relationships with certain important figures. Two or three of these are often running concurrently, /65/ interwoven with each other. Each of them has the effect of altering slightly or a great deal the viewpoint from which the King is seen, so that, as several critics have remarked, the sympathies of the audience are apt to be markedly changed from one part of the play to another. At one end Gaveston brings out most clearly the King's licentiousness and irresponsibility; at the other, Mortimer's treason and cruelty bring out the pathos of the King's plight. When the long-suffering Kent finally loses patience with his brother, the

[6] *From Mankind to Marlowe* (Cambridge: Harvard University Press, 1962), pp. 234–244.

audience may be expected to share his feelings, and when he repents of his revolt, the audience too may feel that opposition has gone too far.

The arrangement of the component movements, then, has a great deal to do with the subtle balancing of sympathies which both Clifford Leech and Douglas Cole have commented on. It has also to do with an emotional progression—a gradual though not steady intensification of feeling which is immediately obvious if one compares the early scenes, in which Edward uncertainly exercises such power as he has, with the last ones, in which, stripped of all power, he endures the agony of his imprisonment and death. There is no doubt that these scenes at the end are the most emotional as well as the most moving in the play. In view of what has been said about the characteristic emphasis in *Edward II* on frustration, it may not be surprising that the utmost confinement produces the maximal emotional response. The progressive intensification of feeling is also a movement toward a final snare.

.   .   .

The subsidiary movements of the play not only contribute to the ultimate ensnaring of Edward, but also display somewhat comparable patterns, interesting in themselves. Marlowe's handling of Gaveston, for instance, brings out first his selfish and opportunistic nature as he plans how he will exploit the King's homosexual infatuation. He is ecstatic at his good fortune but emotionally unengaged with his royal friend, and even the day-dreams of his bright future show little depth of feeling. His appraisal of the exceptional favor he can expect is expressed in a couplet where the traditional sun-king image is given an unusual turn to emphasize serviceability rather than power: /66/

> What need the arctic people love starlight,
> To whom the sun shines both by day and night? (I, i, 16–17)

It is only in the scenes where he is being forced from the King or where he is being pursued and captured that we find eloquent hints of something more: "Sweet sovereign, yet I come / To see thee ere I die" and "Treacherous earl, shall I not see the king?" (II, v, 94–95; III, i, 15). As these suggestions of emotional commitment are wrung from him by despair of success and even of life, so the most powerful statement of his aspiration comes when the barons are forcefully planting themselves in his path. Ambition is thoroughly blended with spite, the desire for revenge on those who would hem him in:

> Base, leaden earls, that glory in your birth,
> Go sit at home and eat your tenants' beef,
> And come not here to scoff at Gaveston,
> Whose mounting thoughts did never creep so low
> As to bestow a look on such as you.   (II, ii, 74–78)

It is abundantly clear that his defiance of the barons greatly strengthens the coalition of forces opposed to him and therefore leads almost directly to the frustration of his hopes. Though finally a victim of treachery as well as superior force, he helps to create the movement toward his confinement and death, and in so doing foreshadows what the King will do. The story of Gaveston, occupying the first half of the play, gives the pattern of this movement and of the increasing display of feeling which accompanies it.

The story of Spencer (of Spencer Junior, that is, who is more important than his father) is a variation on that of Gaveston. Shown first as a clever young man, confident that Gaveston will recommend him to the king, and full of cynical advice for his friend Baldock about how to make good at court, Spencer soon comes into conflict with the barons. There are fewer exchanges of threats and insults than in the story of Gaveston. Instead, we hear Spencer encouraging the fighting spirit of the King and expressing his own emotional reaction to the power of the barons in terms of the feelings which he thinks the King should have: "Were I King Edward . . . would I bear / These braves, this rage . . . ? (III, ii, 10, 12–13). Even more clearly than in the case of Gaveston, /67/ the favorite's emotions are in part surrogates for those of the protagonist. When Spencer and Baldock are captured with the King and are sure of their own fate, they surprise us as Gaveston does, by the intensity of their feeling for Edward. Moreover, their words on this occasion express not only personal grief such as Gaveston seemed to feel, but a sense of the tragic significance of the destruction of a king:

> Rent, sphere of heaven, and, fire, forsake thy orb!
> Earth, melt to air! Gone is my sovereign,

.   .   .

We are deprived the sunshine of our life.(IV, vi, 101–102, 105)

The image used in Gaveston's first speech to express his cocksure self-confidence is charged now with despair. Perpetual arctic night has replaced perpetual arctic sunshine.

The Queen's story is highly ironical. Like every major character, she contributes to her own undoing, but unlike Gaveston or Spencer, she does not start with high hopes. Instead, she moves, like the King himself, from unhappiness to disaster by way of a period of hope and even success. In the process she is transformed into the very thing her worst enemy falsely accuses her of being, so that a slander is made into a truth. When she first appears she is already caught cruelly by her love for Edward, who is neglecting her for Gaveston. Her first words describe an extravagant gesture of despair. When Mortimer asks where she is walking, she replies, "unto the forest . . . To live in grief and baleful discontent" (I, ii, 47–48). Nevertheless, her loyalty to the King obliges her to beg the barons not to revolt, and as Edward becomes more unreasonable in his obsession with his minion, provoking the barons still further, her dilemma becomes more acute. A moving sequence in the fourth scene of the first act shows Edward's heartlessness to her, her tormented state of mind when left alone, and then her intercession with the barons on behalf of Gaveston, in the hope of winning her husband's approval. Her success in bringing about the revocation of Gaveston's banishment is due to her power over Mortimer, of which she seems to be aware, since she singles him out, though there is no indication that she is interested in him the way that Gaveston has insinuated. Mortimer is a means to reinstating herself /**68**/ with Edward. Though these emotional entanglements are lightly sketched by Marlowe, to the dismay of many of his critics, they rest upon subtle and sound psychological observation. This entire process by which she moves into an adulterous attachment is not dramatized, but it is made understandable. When a momentary display of affection by the King is succeeded by further evidence of his passion for Gaveston, the Queen mentions to Mortimer the King's suspicions of them—in itself a step toward greater involvement. Then in a soliloquy she admits to herself that she could happily live with Mortimer.

Thus the Queen moves from one kind of trap into another. At first her affair with Mortimer, coinciding with her departure for her native France, appears to be an emancipation, and indeed, for a time, she gains not only freedom of action but the capacity for imposing her wishes upon Edward and England. In history it was in fact she whose power brought the King to his knees, but Marlowe arranges matters differently. It soon becomes apparent that Mortimer is the real power. At first his ambitions do not conflict with hers, and she is willing to play the role of collaborator, but when her son, the young prince, begins to oppose Mortimer and rally support for the cause of legitimacy, the Queen is caught even more fatally than before. She is driven to pleading with her son for the life of her lover as once she pled with Mortimer for the return of her husband's lover. This time she is not successful, and failure is followed by commitment to prison. As Marlowe shows her to us, there are only three scenes in which she is not gripped by the agony of conflicting loyalties.

It has already been suggested that the story of Mortimer follows a more conventional pattern—that of *De Casibus* tragedy. Until the last moment, when he is condemned to death, he suffers less from frustration than the characters discussed so far. Though he shares with the barons in the first part of the play the problem of dealing with a capricious and irresponsible king, he is normally confident of ultimate success and resourceful in suggesting practical means of achieving it. With the Queen he is courteous, attentive, but not passionate. It is typical of him, when the Queen addresses a moral speech to the rebellious lords fighting for her against the King, that he cuts her off with: "Nay, madam, if you /**69**/ be a warrior, / You must not grow so passionate in speeches" (IV, iv, 15–16). Throughout his transformation from a reformer to a self-seeking tyrant, he remains primarily a fighting man with some of the ambitions but none of the enthusiasm of a Tamburlaine. The relatively unemotional tone of most of his speeches gives a negative confirmation of the thesis that in this play strong feeling is normally the result of denial and constriction. The prospect of imprisonment elicits even from Mortimer a brief but stirring speech which is the first indication of his ambitions:

> What, Mortimer, can raggèd stony walls
> Immure thy virtue that aspires to heaven?
> No, Edward, England's scourge, it may not be;
> Mortimer's hope surmounts his fortune far.   (III, iii, 72–75)

And at the end he is clearly moved by the stroke of fortune which has cast him down from the heights. Scorn for fortune and the world prompts his most eloquent speech.

. . .

The general outlines of Edward's story have been sufficiently recalled. Examination of a few scenes in which he appears will reveal the pattern of his emotional responses, to which all the other elements in the design of the play are subordinated. In Act I, Scene iv, for example, occur some of the willful speeches, quoted earlier, which show the King and the barons locked in conflict. Unable to frighten the barons from their determination to banish Gaveston, he tries to appease them with the offer of important posts, ending with the plea:

> Make several kingdoms of this monarchy
> And share it equally amongst you all,
> So I may have some nook or corner left
> To frolic with my dearest Gaveston. (70–73)

This is as irresponsible as heaping honors on Gaveston in the first scene, and it constitutes a more extravagant display of feeling. The more he is opposed, the more wildly Edward talks. A soliloquy follows, in which he conjures up a scene of fantastic revenge with /70/ falling towers, fires, and flooded streams. Then comes the parting from Gaveston with protests of eternal love, followed by a meeting with the Queen in which Edward treats her with the utmost cruelty. The original frustration provokes a series of violent emotions, shadows, as it were, of the action Edward cannot take.

His treatment of the Queen leads in turn to her agonized intercession with the barons and to Gaveston's recall. The end of this sequence is one of the few places in the entire drama where the emotional tension is eased by a reconciliation. The let-up does not last, however. By the second scene of Act II the King is being "crossed" again, and is swearing that he shall not be limited by his barons, though already it is clear that few of his threats will be followed by action. The trap seems to have opened slightly only to close again more firmly than before.

These two scenes are characteristic of the presentation of the King in the first half of the play and of the movement of his story from one frustration to another. Rage gives way to submission, which provokes more rage in a cycle which is not broken until after the death of Gaveston. When news of the death is brought, Edward's first reaction· is a perfect expression of his emotional range up to this time: "O shall I speak, or shall I sigh and die!" (III, ii, 122). The alternatives, "speak" or "sigh" are no more than a choice of volume for the expression of feeling, and the corollary of death attached to the second alternative is the ultimate restraint, to which all the others are prelusory. Immediately after this speech, however, comes the brief period (covering only 200 lines) in which Edward's feelings, aroused by the murder of his favorite and worked upon by Spencer, are channeled into effective action. For once a threatening speech is followed by battle, in which the courage of the King turns defeat into victory. A note of excitement and pleasurable anticipation is introduced, and the tone of the play modulates into a major key. There is even an occasional echo of the characteristic tone of *Tamburlaine*. At the end of Edward's moment of power comes one fine speech in which this unusual tone is clearly heard:

> Gallop apace, bright Phoebus, through the sky,
> And dusky night, in rusty iron car,
> Between you both shorten the time, I pray, /**71**/
> That I may see that most desirèd day
> When we may meet these traitors in the field. (IV, iii, 43–47)

For us these lines inevitably carry also the overtone of another speech which they inspired, and which Shakespeare assigned to Juliet, waiting for the night and Romeo. Incongrouous as this association may be, it serves perhaps to highlight an irony present in Marlowe's lines, that Edward is looking forward to meeting his rebellious queen on the field of battle among the other traitors: "Welcome, a God's name, Madame . . ." (41). It is the one time in the play when the King is capable of greeting opposition with something like a lover's desire, or expressing desire with the expectation of fulfillment.

The pattern of disappointed expectation is rapidly reestablished. The next brief glimpse of the King shows him compelled to flee despite brave, defiant words. After this comes the important scene of his capture. Wolfgang Clemen has commented on the comparative brevity of the speeches in the first half of the play and the increased use of set speeches, notably the formal lament, in the second half.[7]

[7] *English Tragedy before Shakespeare* (London: Methuen, 1961), pp. 156–158.

Whether or not the first part of the play is expressively deficient, as Clemen believes, there can be no doubt that the fuller expressiveness of the second part creates an impression of intensified emotion which is entirely suitable to the total design, for in this part of the play failure, the chief cause of powerful emotion, is deepening. Act IV, Scene vi, where Edward is captured in an abbey, provides excellent examples of his renewed and intensified response to frustration. First it takes the form of longing for inactivity and death, recalling "O shall I speak, or shall I sigh and die!" He comments in the *De Casibus* tradition on the misery that power and pomp brought him, and praises the contemplative life. Going a step further, he lays his head on the abbot's lap and says:

> O might I never open these eyes again,
> Never again lift up this drooping head,
> O never more lift up this dying heart!   (41–43)

Both gesture and words are extraordinarily revealing. They seem /72/ almost emblematic of the King's powerlessness and prophetic of his imminent death. The mower who has detected the King's presence, and now enters with the barons, may well be, as Clifford Leech suggests, another symbol of death.

Roused from his contemplative lethargy, King Edward loses his Stoic composure and speaks with an extravagance reminiscent of earlier scenes:

> Here, man, rip up this panting breast of mine
>
>   .   .   .
>
>   . . . Lay me in a hearse,
> And to the gates of hell convey me hence.
> Let Pluto's bells ring out my fatal knell
> And hags howl for my death at Charon's shore   (66, 86–89)

The last lines express an intensification of feeling not only in their desperate imperatives, but through the vast extension of significance which Edward sees in his coming death, making it sufficient to fill the underworld with lamentation.

In the first scenes the King has been little better than a captive, unable to act without his barons' consent or to free himself from his infatuation. After temporary emancipation, physical capture is followed logically by imprisonment. In the first scene of the fifth act

Edward is visited by Leicester and the Bishop of Winchester and forced to abdicate. Here occur the King's longest and most passionate speeches, as he wavers between compliance and futile resistance. In the middle of one speech, where he is begging for time, are five lines which perfectly balance and oppose those earlier lines beginning, "Gallop apace, bright Phoebus":

> Continue ever thou celestial sun;
> Let never silent night possess this clime.
> Stand still you watches of the element;
> All times and seasons, rest you at a stay,
> That Edward may be still fair England's king.   (64–68)

Stasis replaces action as the object of desire because action, difficult enough at the beginning of the play, cannot even be contemplated now that the moment of power has passed. Or, more precisely, can be contemplated only in fantasy, for before the King finally surrenders his crown he indulges in a few furious threats. The stage /73/ direction here, "*The King rageth*," makes, for the reader, an interesting association with Herod, the archetypal rager, whose greatest fury was also provoked by the frustration of his plans. In the Coventry Shearmen and Tailors' play is the direction, "*Here Erode ragis in the pagond and in the strete also.*"[8] Edward, constrained to give up even the sign of his power, is to "rage" in a tradition well established in the popular theatre, possibly sawing the air with his hand in a manner Hamlet would have disapproved of, but in any case giving unmistakable signs of intense feeling carried almost to the point of madness. The scene ends with another effective piece of business. After the crown has been carried away Edward seizes and tears a piece of paper on which Mortimer's name is signed. "This poor revenge hath something eased my mind," he says, underscoring the significance of his barely-subsided rage. Inability to perform any effective action has brought the King to a higher peak of emotional response than he has previously reached, and he shows his awareness not only at the end of the scene, that unpacking his heart with words is a poor substitute. The king who can only rage and tear the name of his enemy is nothing:

> But what are kings when regiment is gone,
> But perfect shadows in a sunshine day?   (26–27)

---

[8] *Chief Pre-Shakespearean Dramas*, ed. J. Q. Adams (Boston: Houghton Mifflin, 1924), p. 163.

For Marlowe, one might answer, such a king may be a potent asset if the shadow of political action is made manifest as eloquent emotion.

In the murder scene Edward is given only a few speeches, and those of only moderate length. It is the situation which must speak—torture added to confinement, and finally the brute force of the murderers. First Matrevis and Gurney describe the King's heroic endurance of indignity and pain. Then Lightborn[9] arrives and orders a red-hot spit, a table, and a feather-bed to be in /74/ readiness. Then, apparently, he opens the foul "vault" where the King has been kept and brings him out to lie on a bed. The pathos of the King's state of mind and body, vividly described in the dialogue, is heightened by his immediate suspicion that Lightborn has come to murder him. Lightborn's attempts to allay this suspicion and persuade the King to sleep suspend the inevitable action and heighten the tension of the scene. A good deal has been written recently on the gruesome appropriateness of the actual murder,[10] but one detail which has not been emphasized is particularly appropriate to the design of the play, and that is the way in which the King is presumably held down at the last. There are no stage-directions here, and we can only infer from Holinshed how Lightborn's equipment is used.

> . . . they came suddenlie one night into the chamber where he laie in bed fast asleepe, and with heavie featherbeds or a table (as some write) being cast upon him, they kept him down . . .   (III, 341)

Lightborn orders the table to be laid down and stamped on, "But not too hard, lest that you bruise the body" (no signs of his Machiavellian enterprise are to be left), and whether the featherbed is also used we cannot tell. What seems certain is that Edward is subjected to the final pain of the red-hot spit while pinned down on his bed by the table, and that in this most rigid confinement a cry is wrung from him which Matrevis fears "will raise the town" (V, v, 113). When action is psychologically or physically impossible, speech remains to express Edward's increasing torment; when speech is

---

[9] In his edition of the play, W. D. Briggs notes that the name "Lightborn," a translation of "Lucifer," is given to a devil in the Chester Creation play (*Marlowe's Edward II* [London: David Nutt, 1914], p. 193).

[10] See William Empson, "Two Proper Crimes," *Nation*, 163 (1946), 444–445; Levin, p. 101; Cole, pp. 180–181.

denied only this partially stifled cry is possible. Appalling as the entire scene is (no Elizabethan stage-horror exceeds this), it is the perfect culmination of the main movement of the play.

"The tragical fall of proud Mortimer" and the sentencing of the Queen occupy most of the last scene, but at the end we are presented with a tableau dominated by the corpse of Edward II. Here Edward III offers up to the body of his father, the inactive protagonist, the head of Mortimer, the active antagonist, and though the young king has taken vigorous action, he too has been caught /75/ by events he was unable to stop in time, and is therefore reduced to tears:

> Sweet father, here unto thy murdered ghost
> I offer up this wicked traitor's head.
> And let these tears, distilling from mine eyes,
> Be witness of my grief and innocency.   (99–102)

The design of the play differs from that of *Tamburlaine* not only in being more complex but in the total impression it gives. Where *Tamburlaine* seems to open up ever wider prospects up to the moment of the hero's death, *Edward II* closes down until the focus is upon a prison, a death-bed, a bier. *Tamburlaine's* chief emotions are related to vast human potentiality, with only a final moment of regret that all is not possible, while in *Edward II*, all the emphasis falls on the pathos and horror of predicaments in which man is inextricably caught. /76/

WOLFGANG CLEMEN

Dramatic Speech in
EDWARD II

In *Edward II* we encounter the same artistic problem as faced us in
The Jew of Malta. For here is a play which on the one hand shows
close structural affinities with the chronicle plays, in that it has a
stirring plot with a rapid flow of incident and plenty of variety,
while on the other hand it has points of contact with tragedy in its
attempts to bring on to the stage heart-rending scenes filled with
passionate utterances, deep pathos, and high tragic dignity.[1]
Another striking thing about the play is that the kinds of situation
which, at an earlier stage in the evolution of English drama, would
have been turned into entirely static episodes or declamatory show-
/**154**/ pieces by a series of long and exaggeratedly rhetorical set
speeches, here take the form of swiftly unfolding scenes of action
containing a good deal of well-developed dialogue. Examples of this
are the baiting of the King by the Barons (I. i. 74–133, I. iv. 8–93),
the King's parting from Gaveston (I. iv. 106–69), his grief and
mourning at Gaveston's departure (I. iv. 304 ff.), and his triumph
at the defeat of the rebellious Barons (IV.iii.1ff.). The new dramatic
technique employed in these and certain other episodes brings into
prominence a whole variety of changing motive forces in the play;
it enables us to apprehend all these episodes with great vividness as
real actions carried out by the characters with and against one an-

Reprinted from *English Tragedy before Shakespeare*, translated by T. S. Dorsch
(London: Methuen & Co., 1961).
    [1] Much has been written about the novel features of this play as a tragedy
of character and a tragic history, and about its structure, its characterization,
and its content. See, e.g., Ellis-Fermor, Levin, Poirier, Boas, Wilson, Briggs.

other. Moreover, we no longer find odd moments singled out from the course of events and raised to an artificial intensity by means of set declamations—mere pictures, so to speak, though given the illusion of life; instead, we seem ourselves to be participating in what is taking place.

In *Edward II* it is made quite clear that the characters not only carry the emotional burden of the play, but also sustain its plot; on the other hand, it is equally clear that the plot is not solely dependent on what they do. Marlowe has struck a balance between a plot whose events are directed by its hero and one which develops independently of him and reacts upon him. It is true that the King sets certain events in motion, but he has also to maintain a passive role in the plot. This plot is broken up into a great many separate episodes, most of them quite short, but we can follow it as a close-knit, coherent and logical chain of cause and effect, for in all the episodes the person and character of the King are in some way involved. Thus Marlowe made an appreciable advance towards what is commonly described as 'character-drama', but he was not equally successful all along the line. He was so intent on creating a fast-moving plot, especially in the earlier part of the play, that he did not leave himself enough room to develop the emotional significance of particular moments and to work out his situations in an unhurried way. The scenes follow one another much too quickly, and there are too many of them; they do not take root in our memory, as do the scenes in Shakespeare's histories from *Richard III* onwards, which by themselves form pictures with a symbolic impact and /**155**/ remain unforgettably in our minds as miniature plays in their own right. For all his skill in complicating the plot, the composition, especially in the first two-thirds of the play, is hurried and breathless, and nothing is carried through to its proper conclusion. For long stretches the language is entirely factual and its choice is determined by the practical consideration of keeping the plot moving; it supplies information, instruction, explanation, question and answer, and is all the time concerned solely with externalities. There are moments, indeed, when the emotional atmosphere begins to grow more intense, but the poetic power which is necessary to translate it into words almost at once fades away. We get no further than isolated outbursts of feeling, which are too abruptly handled and do not impart their tone to the accompanying dialogue in the scene. Thus

Marlowe's new dramatic technique conveyed too little of what the set speech had earlier given us too much of. He had not yet found for himself a language which, like that of Shakespearian tragedy, was capable of representing every kind of incident concretely, and which was at one and the same time succinct, emotionally satisfying, and forceful in expression. Even in *Edward II* he was still hovering uncertainly between two different levels of style; he could not reconcile his poet's command of language with his capabilities as a dramatist.[2]

This discrepancy is particularly noticeable in scenes in which some approach is made towards the expression of emotion but is not sufficiently followed up. An example of this occurs in Act I, Scene iv, where Edward falls into a monologue as he is grieving over Gaveston's departure, and will not pay any attention to the Queen and the other persons on the stage:

> [*Re-enter the King, mourning*]
>
> *King Edward:* He's gone, and for his absence thus I mourn.
> Did never sorrow go so near my heart
> As doth the want of my sweet Gaveston;
> And could my crown's revenue bring him back,
> I would freely give it to his enemies
> And think I gained, having bought so dear a friend. /156/
>
> *Queen Isabella:* Hark, how he harps upon his minion.
> *King Edward:* My heart is as an anvil unto sorrow,
> Which beats upon it like the Cyclops' hammers,
> And with the noise turns up my giddy brain
> And makes me frantic for my Gaveston.
> Ah, had some bloodless Fury rose from hell
> And with my kingly sceptre struck me dead,
> When I was forced to leave my Gaveston.
>
> *Lancaster:* *Diablo!* What passions call you these.
> *Queen Isabella:* My gracious lord, I come to bring you news.
> *King Edward:* That you have parlèd with your Mortimer.
> *Queen Isabella:* That Gaveston, my lord, shall be repealed.
>
> (I. iv. 304 ff.)

Here is a formal lament of the familiar type, but it is cut short, and we are immediately plunged into matter-of-fact dialogue. The earlier lament of the Queen when Edward repulses her is even more abruptly cut short (I. iv. 163 ff.), as is that of the younger Spencer when Edward is led away (IV. vi. 99 ff.).

[2] Cf. Tucker Brooke, *The Works*, p. 309.

Just the same kind of discrepancy may be observed in the soliloquies, especially those in the early part of the play. In these soliloquies the mythological imagery and classical parallels and the rhetorical exaggeration of the curses and protestations seem to be based on the stylistic pattern of the earlier classical tragedies, and they are curiously at variance with the very different language of their context.[3]

On one occasion, in the second half of the play, the Queen embarks on a speech of welcome to her friends on their return to England; this quickly gives place to mournful reflections on the state of affairs then prevailing, and then she goes on to appeal to the absent Edward. At this point the younger Mortimer interrupts her:

> Nay, madam, if you be a warrior,
> You must not grow so passionate in speeches./**157**/
>
> (IV. iv. 15–16)

This interruption of Mortimer's seems to be symptomatic of what Marlowe himself did on more than one occasion when 'passionate speeches' showed signs of breaking into his play. He was sensible that long-drawn set speeches in the manner of Tamburlaine would act as clogs on his new technique of rapid movements.[4] But apart from this consideration, he must have felt that for King Edward, whom he put into the play more as a passive than an active character, an entirely different style of speech must be adopted from Tamburlaine's passionate, highly eloquent declarations of his purposes, which stand as substitutes for action. The speech-technique especially of the later scenes enables us to see that active emotion has resolved itself into a tragic passivity, to correspond with which new forms of expression have had to be created.

It is not until the second half of the play that the set speech once more comes into its own as a legitimate feature of the dramatic architecture. Marlowe now deliberately employs this medium in order to make it clear that Edward's role is that of a martyr, and in order to awaken our sympathies for him in his suffering and to ininvest his figure with pathos, dignity and a measure of splendour. In the first half Edward's role is to a larger extent that of an active participant in the action; in this second part he comes to the fore

---

[3] Cf. Gaveston, I. i. 50–72; Queen, I. iv. 170–86; also the dialogue between the two Mortimers, I. iv. 384–418.

[4] See Briggs's note on IV. iv. 41, in his edn. of *Edward II.*

much more as a sensitive and suffering soul, and not the least effective means of creating this impression is the entirely different language, much more intense than that of the first part, by which he is made to reveal himself. In about the middle of the play Edward's awakening to the necessity of resisting the Barons and the change in him from apathy to activity are indicated by means of a set speech containing the great vow of vengeance that he utters on his knees (III. i. 128 ff.); so now, after the reversal of his fortunes, his new role as a passive sufferer is also inaugurated by means of speeches that are given special prominence. However, it is noteworthy that what would earlier have been a speech of self-revelation in the form of outright monologue is now addressed to another person and is accompanied by stage-business. As far as subject-matter is concerned, the words that Edward addresses to the Abbot are the same as those which princes who had fallen from prosperity /**158**/ into misfortune had been in the habit of repeating in English tragedy from the time of *Gorboduc* onwards. This time, however, it is not the sympathy of the audience that is indirectly being invited, as in earlier examples, but that of the Abbot; and since various of the other persons present are addressed in turn, the whole speech gives an effect of dramatic compression, and of belonging naturally to the dialogue-sequence of which it forms a part:

> Father, thy face should harbor no deceit.
> O, hadst thou ever been a king, thy heart,
> Piercèd deeply with sense of my distress,
> Could not but take compassion of my state.
> Stately and proud, in riches and in train,
> Whilom I was powerful and full of pomp;
> But what is he whom rule and empery
> Have not in life or death made miserable?
> Come, Spencer; come, Baldock, come, sit down by me;
> Make trial now of that philosophy
> That in our famous nurseries of arts
> Thou sucked'st from Plato and from Aristotle.
> Father, this life contemplative is heaven.
> O that I might this life in quiet lead.
> But we, alas, are chased, and you, my friends,
> Your lives and my dishonor they pursue.
> Yet, gentle monks, for treasure, gold nor fee,
> Do you betray us and our company.

(IV. vi. 8–25)

Whereas in this scene there are only comparatively short self-revelatory speeches of this kind (cf. 37 ff., 61 ff.), the central interest of the next scene, the scene which represents the abdication of the King, lies in two long set speeches, the longest in the whole play. The way in which Marlowe uses these two speeches brings out once more his powerful sense of drama; they add depth to the symbolic procedure of handing over the crown, and in them the figure of the King is endued with a genuine pathos very different from the impression he gave at the beginning of the play. Here Marlowe has contrived one of those great situations, packed with /**159**/ significance, which would be sure to call out the deepest sympathy and interest in the audience of his day. And at this moment he deliberately slows down the tempo, and makes of this episode a profoundly moving spectacle which, like the penultimate scene in the dungeon, is thrown into relief, by means of its concentration and the detail with which it is developed, against the rapidity of movement that marks the other scenes.

These abdication-speeches, which have often been compared with the great abdication-speech in Shakespeare's *Richard II* (IV. i),[5] show how Marlowe set about the task of creating a form of self-revelation which should reflect both past and present circumstances, and thereby make this episode the focal point of the plot; and also of bringing out the vehemence with which the King's passions are torn between conflicting impulses—an effect which is much more vividly produced here than in Shakespeare's play. Once again, as in *Doctor Faustus*, we see the attempt to portray a spiritual conflict through the medium of the set speech. Moreover, the various elements that form the subject-matter, the review of the situation, the self-contemplation, the inner conflict, and the epigrammatic summing-up of the moral, all these things, together with the stage-business and the way in which the speaker interrupts his own reflections to address the bystanders, combine to produce a new form of set speech; and it is one which, even if some of its motifs remind us of the declamation and emotionalism of past days, is much more successful than the earlier type as dramatic self-expression, and is at the same time more closely in tune with the situation presented on the stage. Even now we have not completely got away from sententious maxims, such as

[5] Cf. Briggs, op. cit., 182–3.

> But what are kings when regiment is gone,
> But perfect shadows in a sunshine day?   (V. i. 26–7)

However, passages of this nature, in their very versification empha-
sizing the independence of the single line, are very much in the mi-
nority. The speeches now display a greater homogeneity of structure
and a subordination of the individual parts to the total /**160**/
effect, and this is reflected even in the verse-structure, in contradis-
tinction to that of *Tamburlaine*.[6] Just as he does in *Faustus*, Marlowe
succeeds here in making the speeches express what is at that very
moment going on in the speaker's mind, but this time he adds external action as well in the gestures of the King and the reactions of
the other characters (e.g., V. i. 96–111). Thus we are now well on
the way towards the dramatized and fully dramatic set speech which
Shakespeare was to handle with such consummate mastery, and
which he was to endow with new profundities of thought and
feeling. /**161**/

---

[6] Cf. Tucker Brooke, 'Marlowe's Versification and Style,' *SP*, XIX, pp. 186–
205.

GLYNNE WICKHAM

Shakespeare's King Richard II and Marlowe's King Edward II

'The reluctant pangs of abdicating Royalty in Edward furnished hints which Shakespeare scarcely improved in his *Richard II*; and the death-scene of Marlowe's King moves pity and terror beyond any scene, ancient or modern, with which I am acquainted.'—Charles Lamb.

The title page of the First Quarto of *Richard II* (1597) describes the play as 'The Tragedie of King Richard the Second'. The First Quarto of *Edward II* describes that play on its title page as 'The troublesome raigne and lamentable death of Edward the second, King of England: with the tragicall fall of proud Mortimer'. These titles suggest that Shakespeare's play is a true tragedy while Marlowe's is really a Chronicle play with tragic undertones. Certainly the stage-history of the two plays appears to confirm this assumption, if only because *Richard II* has remained in the vanguard of the professional repertory while Marlowe's play, if frequently discussed in books of criticism, is rarely produced and then normally by adventurous amateurs. I want in this essay to question this assumption and to suggest that of the two plays *Edward II*, despite its shortcomings, is the true tragedy in the classical sense of the word /**165**/ and that *Richard II* is really the Chronicle play with tragic consequences.

That Shakespeare was in debt to Marlowe for the dramatic treatment of the deposition and downfall of a king is not in doubt: nor is there much question that a simple repetition of Edward's fate in terms of Richard's reign would have held little appeal either to the Lord Chamberlain's company of actors or to their patrons. Thus if

Reprinted from *Shakespeare's Dramatic Heritage* (London: Routledge & Kegan Paul, 1969).

Richard II does represent a borrowing there is good reason to suppose that the difference of treatment is as notable as the original borrowing.

Any sensitive director will notice this, I think, immediately he comes to consider casting the two plays: for where the King and Bolingbroke of *Richard II* are matched in *Edward II* by the King and Young Mortimer, Marlowe's play demands actors to play Gaveston and Young Spencer and an actress to play Queen Isabella whose artistry transcends talent in a way that the supporting cast of Shakespeare's play does not. I am not saying that the gardener in *Richard II*, Gaunt, York, the Bishop of Carlisle, Northumberland and the Queen can be played by anybody: only that with these parts in the hands of competent actors the director can still hope to provide his audiences with a presentable production of the play. He could not have the same confidence however (or should not) when tackling *Edward II* in these circumstances. The reason for this is that Gaveston, Spencer and the Queen in one way or another collectively bring both Edward and Mortimer to their ruin where Richard is the victim of circumstance and his own folly. Some directors might well argue that the part of Lightborn in *Edward II* also requires exceptional care in casting.

The casting problem, once it has been remarked, points the way to differences in the narrative line of the two plays which are no less significant from the standpoint of stage-production. The first of these is the contrast in the fate of the respective antagonists: Mortimer is led off to execution and his severed head is added to the funeral furniture on Edward's hearse in the closing scene, while Bolingbroke, anxious and disillusioned as he may be, wears Richard's crown as King Henry IV at the play's close. This difference in the fate of the antagonist could /**166**/ be said to be simply one of the facts of history to which the dramatists were tied by their sources, the Chronicles; but it may also indicate a difference of moral and artistic purpose since both dramatists felt free to alter the ordering of historical event if it suited them and their actors to do so. The second difference in narrative line relates to the initial cause of conflict. Richard, by banishing Bolingbroke, makes him into his antagonist and, by depriving him of his titles and estates, provokes in Bolingbroke a degree of personal animosity that serves as a rallying point for general discontent. Edward's troubles start for the opposite reason, the revocation of the banishment served on Gaveston in the previous reign, an action which in creating general discontent serves to create a need for a leader in the ranks of the opposition. The question of consequence to the dramatic development of *Edward II* is 'who will fill this role?' and the answer is Young Mortimer. This is never a question of consequence in *Richard II* since it is obvious from the outset that Bolingbroke is the offended adversary: the question there is whether he can find sufficient support to claim compensation or revenge. The one point that both plays have in common is the personal contribution made by Edward and Richard respectively towards answering these questions in a manner that invites their own destruction. Thus these differences in the narrative line of the two plays reinforce the difference which the casting problem exposes: taken together they suggest strongly that Marlowe and Shakespeare were working to very different ends.

Alerted to such a possibility, we can escape from the usual critical preoccupation with parallelism grounded in Charles Lamb's famous aphorism quoted at the head of this Essay and examine the plot structure of both plays more objectively.

In *Richard II* Shakespeare allows us to see two kings fulfilling the same primary function of their calling and thereby allows us to judge them as men in terms of their actions. Each is given one scene, a test case, the circumstances of which are very similar. The subject is a charge of sedition. In Act I, scene i, Mowbray is accused by Bolingbroke of plotting against Richard. The King suspects a private vendetta and questions Gaunt to /**167**/ this effect; but Gaunt confirms to the King that the quarrel springs from

> . . . some apparent danger seen in him [Mowbray]
> Aim'd at your highness, no inveterate malice.

Richard, however, having accepted this and having allowed the formal Trial by Combat to take place vacillates at the last minute and in Act I, scene iii—'The Lists at Coventry'—when the full heraldic ritual of the law has reached its climax, forbids the Combat to go further and pronounces banishment on both the contestants. A more inappropriate moment to reach such a decision and a more inappropriate solution to the problem could scarcely be imagined. The sentence of banishment (I, iii, 118–53) delivered, according to Richard, to avoid 'the dire aspect/Of civil wounds plough'd up with

neighbours' swords', invites this very sequel, since two wrongs
cannot make a right. To this injustice, as foolish as it is arbitrary,
Richard immediately adds another by cutting the ten-year sentence
on Bolingbroke to six for no better reason than that he is moved by
Gaunt's 'sad aspect', even though he has just silenced a far more
eloquent Mowbray with

> It boots thee not to be compassionate:
> After our sentence plaining comes too late.

Richard is thus presented to us as a weak-minded, self-indulgent
man whose personal failings preclude him from discharging two of
the most important functions of kingship efficiently: the administra-
tion of justice between individuals and the preservation of civil order.
In Act V, scene iii, Bolingbroke is presented to us as King confronted
with a situation similar to that of Act I, scene i, the Oxford plot
against the King's life. With Aumerle in his hands, his father York
speaking as his accuser and his mother pleading for his pardon, what
is the King to do? He listens carefully to both sides (Shakespeare
lavishes a hundred lines on plea and counter-plea) and then as the
Lord's Annointed should, mingles mercy with his justice. He par-
dons the sinner who has confessed and repented, but orders the /168/
immediate arrest and execution of those who have not. His conduct
is exemplary. Where Richard was impetuous, arbitrary and self-
contradictory, Bolingbroke is patient, self-possessed and consistent.
Where Richard acted on whim, Bolingbroke acts on principle.
Similarly, where in other scenes Richard encourages extravagance
and effeminacy in Court circles, Bolingbroke in this scene condemns
his own son's conduct as 'unthrifty', 'wanton' and 'dissolute'. Judged
as men, therefore, there can be no question but that Bolingbroke is
much better fitted to wear the crown that Richard; and Shakespeare
plans both the structure of his play and his dialogue to ensure that
we should recognize this important fact. Yet where an opportunist
might regard this verdict as the end of the matter and sufficient to
account for Richard being dead by the end of the play while Bolingbroke is alive and King, Shakespeare regards it as only the beginning. Bad King Richard may be, but for all that he is God's choice,
he is the Lord's Annointed. And who are mortal men to judge an
issue of this magnitude?

This question is put to the audience simply and straightforwardly

in the second scene of the play (a scene, alas, more often cut in production than left in place). The Duke of Gloucester's widow asks
John of Gaunt to revenge his brother's murder. Gaunt's reply is
categoric.

> God's is the quarrel; for God's substitute [i.e. King Richard],
> His deputy annointed in His sight,
> Hath caused his death: the which if wrongfully,
> Let heaven revenge; for I may never lift
> An angry arm against His minister.

True to this principle, Gaunt never takes arms against Richard nor
incites others to do so even on his son's behalf. On his death-bed he
upbraids the King to his face and prophesies both personal and
national disaster as the price to be paid for his abuse of his vocation
and privilege. Gaunt's son however, like Lucifer and Adam before
him, is tempted to take the law into his own hands. In the Parliament
scene of Act IV, scene i, Bolingbroke is first warned by the Bishop of
Carlisle of the consequences of plucking this forbidden fruit. /169/

> . . . let me prophesy;
> The blood of English shall manure the ground,
> And future ages groan for this foul act;

Gaunt's famous vision of 'this blessed plot, this earth, this realm,
this England' will be translated into,

> The field of Golgotha and dead men's skulls.
> O, if you raise this house against this house,
> It will the woefullest division prove
> That ever fell upon this cursed earth.
> Prevent it, resist it, let it not be so,
> Lest child, child's children, cry against you 'woe'!

Thirty lines later it is Richard himself who plays the role of Eden's
serpent.

> Here, cousin, seize the crown;
> Here cousin;
> On this side my hand, and on that side yours.

Emotionally, for protagonist and antagonist on the stage and for
every spectator in the audience, this is the climactic moment of the
play. Richard's metaphor of the well with its two buckets is ironically

apt: for as Richard abdicates so Bolingbroke falls. Divine providence deserts Richard the moment Bolingbroke yields to temptation and takes the crown. The blasphemy implicit in Bolingbroke's

'In God's name, I'll ascend the regal throne'.

is now confirmed and the 'many years of sunshine days' wished him by Richard are swiftly transformed into the threats, anxieties and storms that are to deprive him of any pleasure in the sceptre he wields and to deny him the repose and comfort of sleep.[1] Nor does God's wrath end there. Rebellions breed like boils; battle follows battle; Cain kills his brother Abel; Sodom and Gomorrah are exterminated, and a second Flood overwhelms England in the Wars of the Roses.

Thus *Richard II*, when its structure is examined, is seen to be not so much a tragedy in the classical sense as a political /170/ morality in the mediaeval sense. Expulsion from the Garden of Eden will follow disobedience to the Coronation oath as surely as it followed Adam's disobedience in respect of the Tree of Knowledge. King Richard is a tragic figure who moves us more by pathos than by horror in his fall; but he is merely the first victim of Bolingbroke's crime against the nation, contributor though he may be to his own downfall. As anyone who saw the complete Cycle of these history plays presented by the Royal Shakespeare Company in 1964 and 1965 will know, *Richard II* is a prelude to a catastrophe and not a self-contained tragedy despite its title; for it is the English nation that is to be crucified and England itself that is to become 'the field of Golgotha and dead men's skulls' in the seven plays that follow and together span the course of English history in the fifteenth century.

Marlowe's *Edward II*, by contrast, is not a prelude; it is not an historical morality; it is an entity; it is a tragedy. Like Richard, Edward is young, impetuous and extravagant: both of them are self-indulgent, but there is a marked difference in the form this self-indulgence takes. Likewise with Young Mortimer who, in his grasp of political reality and his firmness of purpose resembles Bolingbroke and thus provides an antagonist for Edward as sharply contrasted as Bolingbroke appears when measured against Richard. Yet again there is a difference. These differences reside in the emphasis which

[1] See *Henry IV*, Pt. 2, III, i, 4–31.

Marlowe and Shakespeare place respectively upon psychology of characterization and political morality when compressing their source material into dramatic form. Edward is presented as a thorough-going homosexual and masochist: this aspect of Richard's character, if present, is quite peripheral to the main action: he is certainly narcissistic, but that is not nceessarily the same thing. Mortimer is presented as a heterosexual adventurer with marked sadistic tendencies; Bolingbroke is not a sadist but does labour under a sense of personal injustice. Once this is recognized it will be seen why Gaveston, Young Spencer and the Queen (as I remarked earlier) present such difficulties in the casting of *Edward II*: they are lynchpins within the structure of this play, where Mowbray, Aumerle /171/ and Queen Anne are only useful types in *Richard II*. Divine providence figures in both plays, but again this is used very differently.

If *Edward II* is exposed to an examination of the narrative line of the kind we have just applied to *Richard II*, it will quickly become apparent how the two plots diverge. The seeming resemblance which the subject of banishment gives to the opening scenes is superficial: for where Richard uses banishment to inflict an injury on two families, Edward by revoking it repairs one to a friend. Richard's conduct is reprehensible by any standards: the worst that can be said of Edward's is that it is unwise. Gaveston's role however is crucial; for not only does he alienate Edward's spiritual and temporal advisers by his flamboyant behaviour, but he drives a wedge of distrust between Edward and the Queen. If active homosexuality in a young King can be excused by the nobility (and Marlowe gives Old Mortimer ten lines in Act I, scene iv, to plead for tolerance on this score) the Queen cannot brook it in her husband. A lonely young Frenchwoman in an alien country, she first becomes subject to depression.

Mortimer Junior: Madam, whither walks your Majesty so fast?
Queen Isabella: Unto the forest, gentle Mortimer,
                      To live in grief and baleful discontent,
                      For now my lord the King regards me not,
                      But dotes upon the love of Gaveston.   (I, ii, 46–50)

This is not a general complaint but one based on detailed observation.

> He claps his cheeks and hangs about his neck,
> Smiles in his face, and whispers in his ears,
> And when I come, he frowns, as who should say,
> 'Go whither thou wilt, seeing I have Gaveston.'

It is the mixture of 'grief and baleful discontent' in the Queen that is to undo Edward: for the more Gaveston provokes Edward to slight her womanhood, the easier victim does she become to any young man who is prompted by lust or self-interest or both to flatter her femininity. Such a man is Young Mortimer—/**172**/ 'gentle Mortimer', 'sweet Mortimer'. These physical relationships—Gaveston's with Edward and Mortimer's with the Queen—develop visually and verbally as the play proceeds. At first they are tentative and subtle; but, as commitment increases, they become less discreet. The point of no return is reached in Act I, scene iv, where the Queen surprises her husband in Gaveston's company. Edward is screwing himself up to part with Gaveston following the second banishment which he has signed. It is an intensely sado-masochistic parting, with Edward enjoying an ecstasy of grief as he is verbally flayed by Gaveston for his treachery. The climax comes at line 137.

Edward:	The time is little that thou hast to stay,
	And therefore give me leave (*note the order of those words:*
	Gaveston is to give Edward leave) to look my fill.
	But come, sweet friend, I'll bear thee on thy way.
Gaveston:	The peers will frown.
Edward:	I pass not for their anger—
	(*at this point the line is broken; there is a pause; something*
	happens; then it continues)
	Come let us go
	O that we might as well return as go.
	Enter Queen Isabella.

This curt stage direction marks the final breach between Edward and Isabella. In production Isabella must be seen to enter one and a half lines earlier following Edward's 'I pass not for their anger—' that is, at the point where the line is broken and Edward embraces Gaveston. This is what occupies the pause. Caught thus in the act, Edward, who has already thrown discretion to the winds in dismissing the anger of his nobles, dismisses her's as rashly.

> 'Fawn not on me, French strumpet; get thee gone!"

From this point forward the scene gets steadily more intemperate and hysterical and reaches its climax at lines 165–70.

Queen Isabella: Witness this heart, that sighing for thee breaks,
How dear my lord is to poor Isabel. /173/
King Edward: And witness heaven how dear thou art to me.
There weep; for till my Gaveston be repealed,
Assure thyself thou com'st not in my sight.
Exeunt [King] Edward and Gaveston.

The Queen then breaks down completely in the following soliloquy. The structure, pace and emotion of the scene demands that what Edward calls Heaven (and Isabella) to witness in line 167 is his physical relationship with Gaveston. What he should do at this point therefore is to walk slowly and deliberately to Gaveston and kiss him on the mouth, leaving the Queen to recoil in horror at the truth now wholly revealed. For the next fifteen lines Isabella has the stage to herself. The next person to enter, in company with other lords, is Mortimer. Edward has sealed his own doom.

Queen Isabella: Ah Mortimer! Now breaks the king's hate forth,
And he confesseth that he loves me not.

The divorce, in nature at least, is complete, and Mortimer wastes no time in seizing his opportunity.

Mortimer Junior: Cry quittance, madam, then, and love not him.

Inflection, eye and gesture suffice to suggest the next step: and once Young Mortimer's ambition has been supplied with this double objective of possessing both Isabella and the crown, the wheel of Fortune starts to raise him up and to carry Edward down. The repeal of Gaveston's banishment transpires to be only the prelude to his death: the flight of Mortimer from England only the prelude to his return under Isabella's banner and as custodian of the heir-apparent. Edward withstands these blows to his pride and confidence with remarkable resilience and fortitude. There is no talk from him of sitting on the ground and telling sad stories of the death of kings while battles rage round him: only a high courage in the field, a self-righteous blaze of indignation and an obstinate adherence to his own nature. Young Spencer (who where stage make-up is concerned should clearly bear a strong physical resemblance to Gaveston) simply refills the gap in his life left by the departed Gaveston, a second pirate succeeding to the duties of the first. Edward /**174**/ cannot control or escape his own nature and this leads him to the act of political folly that is destined to cost him his life. With all his enemies captured and· in his power, he singles out Young Mortimer for imprisonment instead of execution with the other rebels. Thus given a second chance Mortimer escapes and returns with Isabella to subject Edward to a crushing military defeat. Neither Edward's courage nor his generosity can save him now. Betrayed at Neath Abbey, stripped of his regalia and friends at Kenilworth and crucified in the cesspits of Berkeley Castle, Edward's fall arouses pity and terror in the spectator of truly tragic proportions. Meantime we see Mortimer possessed of Isabella and aspiring, under the guise of Lord Protector to Prince Edward, to rule as a dictator in the land.

> The prince I rule, the queen I do command,
> And with a lowly congé to the ground,
> The proudest lords salute me as I pass;
> I seal, I cancel, I do what I will.   (V, iv, 48–51)

This is another Faustus, another Tamburlaine, another Hitler or a Stalin. Yet beyond position lies the opportunity that such power provides to indulge the nature that craved it. Mortimer wants power in order to be feared.

> Feared am I more than loved; let me be feared,
> And when I frown, make all the court look pale.[2]

The young puritan of Act I, scene iv, who condones Edward's 'wanton humour' but cannot abide gaudy apparel and luxury, reveals himself to be a sadist devoid of compassion and seeking to inflict pain on his victims. It is in this spirit that he commissions Gurney, Matravis and Lightborn to undertake their heartless and despicable errands, having first won round Isabella to connive at Edward's murder. Both Isabella and Mortimer are betrayed by the circumstancial evidence of the return of Mortimer's letter to Gurney into the hands of the young Prince Edward and are executed for their crimes. /**175**/

Thus both Edward and Mortimer, protagonist and antagonist of this drama, die violently as victims of their own natures; but Ed-

---

[2] Dramatic precedent for these sentiments is provided by the bombastic tyrant Herod of the Towneley Cycle following the massacre of the Innocents.

ward, the masochist homosexual playboy, and Mortimer, the sadistic heterosexual puritan, are deliberately contrasted as rulers in the course of the play's action and both found wanting. Marlowe achieves this with an 'alienation effect' worthy of Brecht. The most interesting feature of it, at least in rehearsal and production, is the impact which it has upon the emotions of the audience. For most people, Edward's conduct in respect of Gaveston and more particularly in respect of the Queen, evokes a kind of horrified fascination together with a rapid withdrawal of respect: the beneficiary is Mortimer whose solid virtues and championship of the Queen win the sympathy and admiration that is draining away from Edward. In the central section of the play Mortimer acquires an ascendancy over Edward in the esteem of the audience by presenting himself as the fearless champion of the oppressed and the rooter-out of corruption in high places. This ascendancy is maintained so long as it is on the Queen's, Prince Edward's and the country's behalf that his courageous and at times desperate actions are undertaken. Immediately it becomes clear however that this seeming generosity is merely a cloak for his own ambitions, Mortimer, like King Edward before him, begins to lose the audience's respect. The character whom Marlowe uses to effect this *volte-face* is Edmund, Earl of Kent, who first deserts Edward in Act III, scene iii (banished for speaking his mind), only to regret in Act IV, scene v, the folly of his decision to join Mortimer. On the battlefield near Bristol a dim realization of Mortimer's real intentions dawns upon him which leads him to speak his mind in soliloquy.

> Edward, this Mortimer aims at thy life.
> O fly him, then! But, Edmund, calm this rage;
> Dissemble, or thou diest; for Mortimer
> And Isabel do kiss while they conspire;
> And yet she bears a face of love forsooth.
> Fie on that love that hatcheth death and hate.
>
> (IV. v. 19–24)

Kent's suspicions are immediately confirmed in the latter part of the scene by Mortimer's ambivalent attitude to Prince /**176**/ Edward and by his brutal treatment of his elderly prisoner, Old Spencer. As this happens so King Edward begins to rise again in the esteem of the audience. Dignified in defeat, loyal to his friends, generous to his enemies, he grows in stature as suffering, first spiritual, then physical, descends upon him.

> O Gaveston, it is for thee that I am wronged;
> For me both thou and both the Spencers died!
> And for your sakes a thousand wrongs I'll take.
> The Spencers' ghosts, wherever they remain,
> Wish well to mine; then tush, for them I'll die. (V, iii, 41–5)

His resignation to grotesque indignities and his fortitude under torture release a nobility of spirit which serve in the auditorium to engender an anger against the perpetrator of this cruelty and which the strict, poetic justice of the manner of Edward's murder only serves to increase. Better an Edward with all his faults (they are at least hot-blooded and warm-hearted) than a Mortimer with his, reared as they are on envy, pride and the pleasure derived from inflicting pain. It is these astonishing reversals of sympathy which create the remarkable alienating effect. Our emotions may well be engaged subjectively with the fortunes of the principal characters, indeed Marlowe takes great pains to ensure that they are: but at the play's close we cannot escape viewing both protagonist and antagonist objectively. The cathartic draining of pity and fear leaves the mind free to distinguish tints of virtue from shades of vice and to assess Princes in terms of the effect of power upon their characters. We may apply our conclusions to English Princes, but the historical source material of the play itself is strictly subordinate to moral and psychological issues of universal application which this historical source material serves to illustrate.

Thus, if I am anywhere near correct in this analysis of the narrative line of Edward II, it would seem that Marlowe was here attempting to write a tragedy in the full classical sense of the word. English history of the fourteenth century is used in the true Aristotelian sense of 'myths', the hero is a Prince and 'harmartia', 'peripeteia' and 'discovery' are all used schematically to effect a catharsis. Edward is the hero and his 'harmartia' /**177**/ is his inability to observe that discretion in his relations with Gaveston urged upon him by his peers. As a willing accomplice to Gaveston's outrage upon the Bishop of Coventry in Act I scene i (lines 175–207) he brings down a curse upon his head.

Gaveston: He shall to prison and there die in bolts.
King Edward: Ay, to the Tower, the Fleet, or where thou wilt.
Coventry: For this offence, be thou accursed of God!   (I. i. 197–9)

This folly reaches its climax in Act I scene iv when Edward's treatment of the Queen translates her love to hate and provides Mortimer with his opportunity to focus opposition to Gaveston on his own leadership. The 'peripety' or reversal follows Edward's military victory over his opponents and is contained in his decision to order their immediate execution but to reserve Mortimer for judgement and punishment at a later date (III, iii). The following scene (IV, i) contains Mortimer's escape and thus the start of Edward's overthrow. The discovery begins at the end of Act IV when Edward becomes Mortimer's prisoner, and extends through Act V to reveal both the other half of Edward's nature and the true colours of both Mortimer and Isabella. These revelations are so juxtaposed as to produce a cathartic effect in terms of both pity and terror.

The case therefore for regarding Marlowe's *Edward II* as a successful attempt at tragedy in the Aristotelian manner is a strong one. If accepted it certainly provides the producer in the theatre with a much stronger directive for casting and rehearsal than Marlowe's own cumbersome title. The latter invites episodic treatment of historical narrative for its own sake which, if followed, dilutes the concentrated attention upon character which makes this play the remarkably close-knit entity that it really is. By the same token, a literal interpretation of Shakespeare's title for *Richard II* invites the cutting of all material that is not strictly relevant to Richard's fall, a treatment which, if followed, inevitably destroys the wide-ranging political morality invested in the fortunes of Henry Bolingbroke for which Richard's tragic fall is only the launching platform.

It is my contention therefore that Marlowe's play may fairly be described as neo-classical in intention and execution, /**178**/ the sort of product, in short, that might be expected from a Cambridge graduate in 1590. Shakespeare's play, just as self-evidently, is not: rather does the relationship of its form to its content spring naturally from the native, English dramatic tradition, grounded on biblical narrative treated typologically. The key to the interpretation of the parable lies in Act III scene iv, which appropriately enough is set in a garden. It is there that Queen Anne hears the rumour that her husband is to be deposed.

Gardener: Depress'd he is already, and deposed
              'Tis doubt he will be: . . .
Queen: Thou, old Adam's likeness, set to dress this garden,
              How dares thy harsh rude tongue sound this unpleasing news?
              What Eve, what serpent, hath suggested thee
              To make a second fall of cursed man?
              Why dost thou say King Richard is deposed?
              Darest thou, thou little better thing than earth,
              Divine his downfall?

This is not just a casual, rhetorical response to shock and distress: it is a deliberate forecasting of the events of the next scene couched in prefigurative language designed to equip the audience to interpret the parable that the play represents as it approaches its points of crisis, Bolingbroke's 'disobedience' and the consequences that this will have for everyone in England for generations. This is indeed tragedy, but Christian in spirit and cast in a form not dreamed of by Aristotle or the ancient Greeks. /**179**/

Selected Bibliography

BERDAN, JOHN M. "Marlowe's *Edward II.*" *Philological Quarterly*, III (1924), 197–207.

BOAS, F. S. *Christopher Marlowe: A Biographical and Critical Study.* Revised edition. Oxford, 1953.

BRADBROOK, M. C. *Themes and Conventions of Elizabethan Tragedy.* Cambridge, 1935.

BRODWIN, LEONORA L. "*Edward II:* Marlowe's Culminating Treatment of Love." *ELH*, XXXI (1964), 139–155.

COLE, DOUGLAS. *Suffering and Evil in the Plays of Christopher Marlowe.* Princeton, 1962.

ELLIS-FERMOR, UNA M. *Christopher Marlowe.* London, 1927.

KNOLL, ROBERT E. *Christopher Marlowe.* New York, 1969.

KOCHER, PAUL H. *Christopher Marlowe: A Study of his Thought, Learning, and Character.* Chapel Hill, N. C., 1946.

LEVIN, HARRY. *The Overreacher: A Study of Christopher Marlowe.* Cambridge, Mass., 1952.

MAHOOD, M. M. *Poetry and Humanism.* London, 1950.

MILLS, L. J. "The Meaning of *Edward II.*" *Modern Philology*, XXXII (1934), 11–32.

MORRIS, BRIAN, ed. *Christopher Marlowe* (Mermaid Critical Commentaries). London, 1968.

MORRIS, HARRY. "Marlowe's Poetry," *Tulane Drama Review*, VIII (1964), 134–54.

REESE, M. M. *The Cease of Majesty: A Study of Shakespeare's History Plays.* London, 1961.

RIBNER, IRVING, "Marlowe's 'Tragicke Glasse.' " In *Essays on Shakespeare and Elizabethan Drama in Honor of Hardin Craig.* Ed. R. M. Hosley. Columbia, Mo., 1962. Pp. 91–114.

ROBERTSON, TOBY. "Directing *Edward II.*" *Tulane Drama Review*, VIII (1964), 174–183.

STEANE, J. B. *Marlowe: A Critical Study.* Cambridge, 1964.

WILSON, F. P. *Marlowe and the Early Shakespeare.* Oxford, 1953.